Social work with older people

Social work with older people

Approaches to person-centred practice

Edited by Barbara Hall and Terry Scragg

 Open University Press

Open University Press
McGraw-Hill Education
McGraw-Hill House
Shoppenhangers Road
Maidenhead
Berkshire
England
SL6 2QL

email: enquiries@openup.co.uk
world wide web: www.openup.co.uk

and Two Penn Plaza, New York, NY 10121-2289, USA

First published 2012

A catalogue record of this book is available from the British Library

ISBN-13: 978-0-33 524420-1 (pb)
ISBN-10: 0-33-524420-3 (pb)
eISBN: 978-0-33-524421-8

Library of Congress Cataloging-in-Publication Data
CIP data applied for

Typesetting and e-book compilations by
RefineCatch Limited, Bungay, Suffolk
Printed and bound in the UK by Bell & Bain Ltd, Glasgow

Fictitious names of companies, products, people, characters and/or data that may be used herein (in case studies or in examples) are not intended to represent any real individual, company, product or event.

Contents

List of boxes, tables, figures

Boxes

Tables

Figures

Editors and contributors

Barbara Hall (editor) was Head of Training and Development for West Sussex County Council and is an Associate Lecturer, Department of Social Work and Social Care, University of Chichester.

Terry Scragg (editor) is a social work Practice Assessor, working with the University of Chichester.

Gill Butler is Deputy Dean, Department of Social Work and Social Care, University of Chichester.

Rick Fisher is Senior Lecturer in Adult Nursing, School of Health and Social Care, Bournemouth University.

Chris Gaine is Professor of Applied Social Policy, Department of Social Work and Social Care, University of Chichester.

David Gaylard is Senior Lecturer in Social Work, Department of Social Work and Social Care, University of Chichester.

John Gisby is Business Development Officer, Care Training Consortium, West Sussex County Council.

Vivienne Kilner is a Social Worker, West Sussex County Council Adult Services.

Andrea Linell was a Training and Development Officer for West Sussex County Council.

Andy Mantell is Senior Lecturer in Social Work, Department of Social Work and Social Care, University of Chichester.

Debbie Smallbones is a Social Worker, West Sussex County Council Adult Services.

Chris Smethurst is Senior Lecturer in Social Work, Department of Social Work and Social Care, University of Chichester.

Sally Stapleton is Locum Consultant and Lead Clinical Psychologist, West Sussex, Sussex Partnership NHS Foundation Trust, Older People's Services.

Graham Tooth was a Training and Development Officer and Practice Teacher for West Sussex County Council.

Christine Wright is a Social Worker, West Sussex County Council Adult Services.

Acknowledgements

In editing this book we would like to thank a number of people who have helped at various stages of the production process. They have variously provided suggestions and ideas for chapters and case studies or have commented on earlier drafts. They include Gill Constable, Janet McCray, Marie Price, Rosemary Pavoni and Sue Craig.

Throughout the writing stage we have been supported by Katherine Hartle whose editorial guidance, encouragement and support has been invaluable. We would also like to thank Abigail Jones from the editorial team.

Introduction

Barbara Hall and Terry Scragg

This book challenges the perception that social work with older people is professionally unfulfilling and lacks the challenges and demands practitioners seek in other areas of practice. Social work with older people has traditionally been seen as a lower status activity compared with work with other service user groups, and is often regarded as work that can be undertaken by unqualified staff. This view is reinforced by comments from regulators and some managers who question the need for qualified social workers to work with older people, seeing it as an unnecessary and expensive overuse of qualified professionals.

The view that social work with older people has a lower priority than other groups has become more prevalent since the community care reforms of the 1990s with their emphasis on rationing resources and providing routine responses to need. However, this contradicts the views of service users, whose expectation of social work is for a more personalized service with practitioners demonstrating greater expertise and understanding of older people's needs.

A tendency to ignore the needs of older people is further increased by the current financial pressures on local authorities as they ration access to services through ever-tightening eligibility criteria. This is happening at a time when there is growing demand for services from a rising population of older people. This situation only serves to further stigmatize older people who need support, and reinforces the structural oppression evidenced in many service settings. Underlying much of this is a deep seated ageism, where discrimination against older people is tolerated and witnessed almost weekly in revelations of abuse, neglect and poor quality care experienced by users of health and social care services.

This book, by adopting a person-centred approach, argues that older people need a high quality social work service that recognizes their wider needs, with an awareness of, and sensitivity to, the often difficult, complex and distressing issues they face. This in turn demands the support of experienced and skilled practitioners.

Structure of the book

The book is divided into three parts. Part 1, 'Setting the context and the importance of values', provides a broad overview of a number of key themes. Chapter 1 explores a range of issues that inform social work with older people, including the importance of reflective practice, the nature of social work and its value base, different approaches to understanding older people, and the organizational context within which social work practice takes place. Chapter 2 discusses the development of social care policies and practices, constructs of ageing that have influenced these policies, and the impact of debates on health and social care policy for older people, including current economic policies which will further damage services for older people.

Part 2, 'Equality and diversity in working with older people', focuses on a diverse range of themes and approaches to ageing and social work practice with older people. Chapter 3 describes the diversity of the minority ethnic population, cultural backgrounds and life histories of older minorities, and the way that access to effective care can be influenced by attitudes within communities and those providing services. Chapter 4 focuses on mental health and the factors that support or hinder good mental health, including indicators of risk in depression and suicide. Chapter 5 explores work with people with dementia, emphasizing the concept of 'personhood' and its influence on dementia care. This chapter also explores the crucial issue of communication and the value of life story work. Chapter 6 charts the changes in services for people with learning disabilities and the common health problems faced by individuals whose life expectancy now mirrors that of the wider population. The needs of families and carers are considered, and the chapter concludes with an exploration of person-centred practice and personalization following recent policy developments. Chapter 7 describes some of the long-term conditions that impact on older people, and policies and practices that are intended to support individuals and their carers to assume greater control of their situation and manage their conditions more effectively. Chapter 8 explores loss and bereavement, describing models of grief and approaches to work with older people utilizing skills from counselling, including work with people who are terminally ill. Chapter 9 examines assumptions and expectations about older people's sexuality and the range of professional responses, including recognizing those with different sexual orientations. The chapter concludes with guidance for practitioners. Finally in this part, Chapter 10 explores spirituality in the lives of older people, the relationship between spirituality and religion and how spirituality is expressed in a diverse society. It discusses approaches practitioners can use when working with older people.

Part 3, 'Enhancing the well-being of older people and safeguarding issues', concludes the book with two chapters that are of critical importance in work with older people. Chapter 11 is concerned with an exploration of the concept of risk and how it is constructed and understood by practitioners, and how different interpretations and assessment of risk can undermine the independence of the older person. It concludes with an exploration of the emotional impact of working with risk for practitioners. Finally Chapter 12 focuses on the importance of safeguarding in the lives of older people, including a review of current legislation and policy guidance, and discussions of the prevalence of abuse of older people, and of how empowering individuals can help reduce the likelihood of abuse, with guidance that can enhance the practitioner's approach to safeguarding the older person.

How to use the book

This book has been written primarily for the undergraduate social work student and those qualified social workers undertaking post qualifying courses. The book is intended to be accessible, enabling you to explore the wide range of themes and approaches in social work with older people. You will find a variety of written styles across the different chapters, which reflect the writers' professional interests, experience and specialist knowledge. How you use the book will very much depend on your particular needs. First and foremost it is intended to be a practical resource to support you in your practice when working with older people. You could read each succeeding chapter, or alternatively dip into different chapters depending on your professional interests. However you use the book we hope you will find the learning activities prompt you to reflect on experiences, situations and events commonly found in practice, with case studies designed to help you to explore different approaches in greater depth, and which are intended to further your understanding of particular topics. Each chapter has suggestions for further reading, including books and websites, with which you can extend your understanding of particular themes or areas of practice. Above all we hope that the book will encourage you to consider the challenges and rewards of working with older people, by providing evidence that helps counteract the negative beliefs about older people and their lives, and in turn helps you work in partnership with the older person in a way that meets their expectations and more fully meets their needs.

PART 1
Setting the context and the importance of values

1 Reflective social work practice with older people: the professional and the organization

Barbara Hall

After reading this chapter you should be able to:

- discuss the nature of reflective social work practice and the place of values in social work with older people;
- describe some key sociological and psychological concepts relating to ageing and their impact on practice;
- express some ongoing debates surrounding the nature of social work with older people;
- understand the impact of legislation and policy on organizations and professional practice;
- consider the implications of a systemic perspective on social work practice with older people.

Introduction

This chapter introduces the reader to reflective practice and the impact of personal and professional values and stereotypes on social work practice with older people. The chapter argues that reflective social work practice is one part of the jigsaw of effective service provision and that organizations have responsibilities to create environments where social workers can practise effectively. Consideration is given to some key sociological and psychological perspectives which impact professional practice, policy development and implementation. The chapter charts some of the historical development of social work practice with older people and some key theoretical perspectives that impact both policy and practice development. In looking at earlier 'watershed' reports we question why so many policy initiatives have failed to be implemented adequately. Finally the chapter offers a brief consideration of the impact of understanding organizations as systems and what that might mean for social work practice with older people. The final part of the chapter offers opportunities for further exploration of systemic approaches in social work and social care.

Learners and learning

Entwistle (1984) suggests there are two key types of learner. First there are 'information seekers', who focus on the accumulation of facts and learn through creating patterns. Then there are the 'understanding seekers', who search for personal meaning, relating what they learn to their past experience, and exploring potential connections and potential discrepancies. In other words, they are reflecting. Marton and Säljö (1984) show that deep learning is more likely when a reflective approach is used. They differentiate between a deep approach and a surface approach to learning. The first is characterized by an intention to understand material for oneself, a vigorous and critical personal interaction with knowledge content, relating ideas to one's previous knowledge and experience, relating evidence to conclusions, and examining the logic of arguments. This approach to learning they considered to be 'knowledge transforming'. A surface approach, however, they describe as being 'information reproducing', where ideas and information are accepted passively, where there is no reflecting on purpose or strategy and the memorizing of facts and procedures becomes routine.

What is reflection?

Reflection is about deep learning. It is a thought process which involves looking back at events and asking questions retrospectively or looking forward (crystal ball gazing) and asking questions prospectively. It also involves a self-assessment of practice and a search for learning points and the identification of learning and development needs. Boud et al. (1985: 19) define reflection as 'an activity in which people recapture their experience, think about it, mull over it and evaluate it'.

This way of understanding the process of reflection has the advantage of connecting with the ways social workers work, particularly through the process of supervision, and, as a student, the keeping of reflective journals and logs.

What is reflective practice?

Reflective practice is the application of the skill of reflection with the intention to improve our professional practice. Schön (1983) suggested that the capacity to reflect on action in order to engage in a process of continuous learning was one of the defining characteristics of professional practice. The cultivation of the capacity to reflect **in** action (while doing something) and **on** action (after you have done it) has become an important feature of professional development programmes and professional practice.

Reflection **on** action is where the practitioner analyses their reactions to the situation after the event and explores the reasons for their behaviour at the time, and the consequences of their action. This is usually a process undertaken in case reviews and in supervision. Reflection **in** action can be described as a practitioner's ability to 'think on their feet'. It revolves around the notion that within any given moment, when faced with a professional issue, a practitioner usually connects with their feelings, emotions, prior experiences and knowledge and brings these to bear on the situation they are facing.

Some argue that 'real' reflective practice needs another person as mentor or supervisor who can ask appropriate questions and challenge thinking and also challenge practitioners' underlying beliefs and values, as these impact decision making where risk is a central feature. Reflective practice capability when working with older people is a critical skill. Older people who become the focus of social work practitioners are usually the most vulnerable of the age group, and as such, issues concerned with risk, capacity for informed decisions and safeguarding can often be central to decisions about an older person's future safety and welfare. Alongside those considerations practitioners will also be trying to balance the rights that older people have to expect the least intrusive intervention to ensure their maximum independence. Moon (2004) suggests:

- Emotion is central to the reflective process.
- Reflection is always about 'my own' process (i.e. always in the first person).
- Some people cannot reflect.

Yip (2006) crucially argues however that self-reflection can only be constructive under the right circumstances. In hostile circumstances where you are unsupported or oppressed, then self-reflection needs to be approached with caution. A safe and supportive learning environment where mistakes are perceived as opportunities for learning needs to be in place for constructive reflection to take place. Argyris (1982) supports this view and encourages organizations to create learning environments where what he calls 'double loop learning' encourages the questioning of processes, procedures and policies which do not work well, particularly from the perspective of the service user. An example of this might be a referral process that requires the service user to have to frequently repeat their story to different practitioners.

Mental maps, single and double loop learning

Argyris and Schön (1974: 30) argue that people have mental maps with regard to how to act in situations. They suggest it is these maps that guide people's actions rather than the theories they espouse. Argyris (1982) was of the view that people are generally unaware of the maps or theories they use. He described these two aspects as 'theories in use' and 'espoused theory'. Argyris argued that effectiveness results from congruence between the two theoretical approaches.

Argyris also identified what he called 'single loop' and 'double loop' learning. Single loop learning can be described in terms of exploring improvements to existing rules or processes and procedures for working in an organization, known as 'thinking inside the box'. Single loop learning poses the question 'how'; how could things be done better, how could processes and procedures be improved?

'Double loop' learning is potentially uncomfortable for the individual and the organization as it can mean challenging the organization's underlying principles and assumptions. It is about 'thinking outside the box'. Double loop learning fosters questions about 'why' things are done in the way they are. Most organizations do not foster this kind of fundamental challenge to their thinking and their ways of doing things. The 'why' questions were the focus of much of Argyris's work which has been about exploring how organizations can increase their capacity for double loop learning as part of the reflective process.

The personal experience of reflection

Cottrell (2003: 170) talks about the value for individuals of being able to stand back occasionally and reflect about such things as our aims, responses, feelings and perform- ance. In considering the question 'What is reflection?' she argues that 'reflection is a type of thinking. It is associated with deep thought aimed at better understanding.' She helpfully explores eight headings, which unpack the personal experience of reflection and help identify the reflective process in some of its constituent elements, amongst which are: the process of making sense of the experience through its analysis; weighing up the experience; going over the experience looking at it from different perspectives; achieving a deeper honesty. She suggests that it is through reflection that we can come to acknowledge things we find difficult to admit to ourselves. 'In other words, we review what was said or done, weighing up the consequences and considering what the alter- natives might have been. We evaluate whether we would do things differently if given the chance again or whether we were right first time' (Cottrell 2003: 173).

Scragg (2009: 143) highlights the view that reflective practice is an essential skill that all social work practitioners should develop alongside other health and education professionals: 'This questioning approach, which looks critically at your thoughts and experiences, is an essential element in thinking about your practice and deciding how you can make changes in your approach that could improve your practice in the future.'

The responsibility of the organization

These approaches to reflection centre mainly on the capacity of individual practi- tioners to consider and explore their work in depth and detail, as a personal learning journey. Reflection is a very helpful process but it also needs to be considered in the light of the impact of the system within which the practitioner works. As in social work practice, where psychopathology and systemic perspectives offer balance to under- standing complex situations, a similar balance needs to be struck between the impact of an individual's professional practice (values, beliefs, capacity for reflection, etc.) and an understanding of the constraints imposed by the system and how they affect the practitioner's capacity to practise effectively.

Some organizational conditions for person-centred planning

Person-centred approaches require practitioners to engage in ongoing critical self- reflection and to be supported by their employing organizations to do so. It is an emotionally and intellectually demanding approach, which as well as needing appropriate and sufficient resources, also requires good supervision and support for the practitioner to enable them to reflect, question and develop a different approach to practice, particularly with regard to the use of their professional power. Such person-centred approaches need to be supported fully by organizational processes that are person centred, and developed and designed around the needs of service users. In some circumstances, person-centred practice requires a reframing of one's beliefs and approaches to the work and a questioning and appraisal of one's underpinning values. For practitioners working with older people, it can mean questioning one's personal value base about growing older and older age. Some social workers would argue strongly that person-centred practice offers real opportunities to revive and to practise skills that have been shelved for some time because of the impact of care management.

The implementation of effective person-centred social work approaches in non-person-centred organizations, where practitioners are not encouraged or given time to reflect, to question, to explore mistakes, or to explore 'double loop' learning, would be very difficult indeed.

Values and practice

A dictionary definition is that values are 'a principle, standard, or quality considered worthwhile or desirable. One's principles or standards, one's judgment of what is valuable or important in life' (www.dictionary.com).

Knowing the nature of our values is actually quite difficult and understanding their impact even more so. They (values) come in the first instance from our families, from school, and from what we learn as we are educated; then professional values impinge, and values at work join the mix. What is the impact of this values 'stew' on how we perceive older people, and how does it impact our practice?

Egan (1998) suggests that we need to develop empathy, which requires the social worker to be able to put themselves in the clients' shoes, or to enter their epistemological and ontological worlds. This can be quite difficult to do, particularly when one's personal values are transgressed or challenged as in the case of abuse of older people, or child abuse, for example. It seems in these challenging circumstances that our professional values do have the capacity to change within acceptable professional and social parameters, especially where those transgressions and challenges are rooted in what feels like 'social justice'.

Banks (2001: 6) suggests social work values are 'a set of fundamental moral/ethical principles to which social workers should be committed'. Pattison (1998: 344) however contests that the concept of values derives its popularity and legitimacy from the fact that it is an apparently simple, universally acceptable concept 'delighting all and offending none because most people do not take the trouble to think about what it actually means in their own lives and that of others'.

Person-centred practice

Person-centred practice is a values-based perspective about what each of us would wish to experience with regard to choice, independence and dignified treatment if we were cast in the role of the service user. Person-centred planning is designed specifically to 'empower' people, to directly support their social inclusion, and to directly challenge their devaluation. As a social worker, we may well hold person-centred values, but might work in an organization where services still define need and thus compromise our values and capacity to remain person centred. As professionals we may also find ourselves challenged by older people who have a different view about their needs and how they might be met. It may be that the latter is a scenario likely to be met more frequently as the so-called 'baby boomers' become the older people requiring services.

Dominelli, quoted in Adams et al. (2002: 18) suggests that social workers have to become skilled mental acrobats who can juggle contradictory positions with ease when it comes to putting their values into practice.

Activity 1.1

What aspects of person-centred planning do you find most challenging?

Are there any work processes that make person-centred approaches more difficult for you as a practitioner, or for service users?

The perspective of 'selfhood'

The following discussion provides an opportunity for practitioners to reflect on the concept of selfhood as a useful approach to understanding aspects of ageing that impact us all and the importance and significance of affirmation as an empowering intervention, regardless of the presenting problem.

In trying to grasp more personal aspects of growing older the notion of selfhood has been studied extensively across disciplines. In gerontology the notion of 'loss of self' has been prevalent in discussions about ageing; this is particularly so with regard to dementia, but also with regard to the notion that ageing itself diminishes an individual's self value. Bastings (2003: 96) found that 'the cultural value of the self is deeply connected to one's usefulness to society'.

Moore (1980: 159) suggests that 'It is not a cynical observation that society is only interested in 'successful' agers who do not stress the community or make demands on its resources' and also descriptively contends that:

> Frequently a transition to senior years or into retirement exposes an individual to social attitudes which make a capable person feel unintelligent, unemployable, asexual and socially inadequate. Modern research indicates that many of the mental and human changes seen in senior people are not biological effects of ageing but are due to their fateful existence of a part imposed on them by an unfeeling society. It has been said that society's prejudices against the elderly indoctrinate us while we are young, but affect us

when we are old . . . by ignoring the needs of a vulnerable minority which we are inevitably going to join, we are burying ourselves.

(Moore 1980: 159)

The notion of 'selfhood' is based on the seminal works of William James (1918) and G.H. Mead (1934) who define the notion of self within social contexts. Mead (1956: 212) defined the self as 'a character, which is different from that of the physiological organism proper . . . it comes into being through social processes'.

Aquilina and Hughes (2006: 150) present a distinction between 'inner' and 'outer' selves, the former denoting 'the private and subjective experience of being self aware' and the latter signifying 'public observable aspects of self, which depend on psychosocial structures including social relations'. Discussions concerning ageing benefit from these perspectives and provide a conceptual framework for working with older people which sees communication skills at its core, and life experience and ageing as a mechanism for learning, development and wisdom, both for the older person and the practitioner.

Sabat and Harré's influential work (1992) on selfhood and dementia suggests that we work throughout our lives on constructing our self-identity. Their social constructionist approach argued against the dominant assumption of loss of self in the ageing process and as dementia progresses. They used two in-depth case studies to show how self remains intact despite severe cognitive decline. 'The threatened disappearance of selves is not directly linked to the disease process, but to the behaviours and reactions of others' (1992: 249).

Sabat (2002: 109) went on to develop 'a social constructionist tripartite approach to personhood', known as the Selfs 1–3 framework.

Self-1 comprises one's personal identity (the I, me, mine, myself and my selves).

Self-2 comprises one's mental, emotional and physical attributes (for example, my past achievements in terms of what I can do and my beliefs and desires about them).

Self-3 is the socially presented self/selves or personae, the roles we take on and the appropriateness with which we behave in social situations.

We have lots of Selves-3 related to our different roles and social circumstances (parent, friend, colleague, student, lover, partner, professional, carer, cared for). Self-3 is constructed and nurtured through interaction with others and is thus more vulnerable than Self-1 and Self-2.

Self-3 very much depends on the affirmation and reciprocity of others to nurture it; without that from others we become vulnerable. It is thus easy to see how Self-3 can become fragile without affirmation, and can be destroyed through lack of nurturing. For many older people social isolation will deny opportunities for such affirmation.

> **Activity 1.2**
>
> Consider how you would apply the Selfs 1–3 framework to yourself.
> Consider how you could apply the Selfs 1–3 framework to service users.

Some sociological perspectives

Three commonly expressed sociological perspectives for consideration now follow. Each perspective is underpinned by a set of values and implications for practice. With regard to Argyris's (1982) work, they could be regarded as 'theories in use or espoused theory': it will depend on the practitioner. Nonetheless there are likely to be elements of each of these perspectives that underpin our practice with older people.

Disengagement theory

Sociological literature presents a range of competing theories of ageing: disengagement theory at one end of the spectrum and successful ageing theory (sometimes described as activity theory) at the other. The genesis of the disengagement viewpoint is that older people themselves initiate the disengagement process. It does not take into consideration any societal processes and structures that curtail older people's opportunities for engagement.

Disengagement theory (Cumming and Henry 1961) though extremely controversial then and now and offering a bleak portrayal of old age, nonetheless has had a profound effect on views about ageing. Disengagement theory sees the older person's withdrawal from society as part of the natural ageing process, and as part of the normal pattern of life. This theoretical perspective essentially sees old age as the time when people are preparing themselves for death. This includes the severing of relationships and ties. Ageing from this theoretical perspective naturally brings with it a growing sense of powerlessness, loneliness, loss of role, loss of sense of purpose and with it increased dependency. From this theoretical perspective the position of older people as a non-productive and costly burden on society is easily assimilated as the cultural norm and becomes implicit in political and economic arguments (this is explored further in Chapter 2).

Olsen (1982) criticizes the disengagement approach for ignoring the impact of social class on ageing experiences and how class structure and its social relationships prevent the majority of older people from enjoying a variety of opportunities or advantages. The disengagement perspective, it could be argued, feeds the negative stereotypes of ageing as the part of life to be feared, which in turn creates the circumstances driving disengagement and the negative stereotyping of older people, impacting their quality of care.

Activity theory

At the opposite end of the spectrum, activity theory is about successful ageing and contends that people develop ideas about themselves and their identity from two major sources: the things that they do, and the roles they fulfil in life. This theory identifies the many roles that people give up as they age, and the impact this has on people's identity. Hence this theoretical perspective argues that new and meaningful activities need to be substituted for those that have been lost. The view from this theoretical perspective is that activities in later life are essential to restore one's sense of well-being and value. To be worthwhile, activities need to have personal meaning; they can be solitary, with people, formal and informal – anything that gives meaning and value to the individual. Successful ageing begins then to equate with active ageing, denying the limitations of old age as long as possible.

This theoretical perspective needs to be tempered with the reality that some older people cannot maintain an active lifestyle, and some may not have the resources to maintain active roles. The danger of this theoretical perspective is that in an increasingly judgemental society, strapped for cash to support health and well-being, older people who do not remain active are perceived as responsible for their own decline and are therefore blameworthy. Activity theory has also been criticized for being overly idealistic and for forcing 'middle-class moral and family-oriented' activities onto older people (Katz 2000: 143).

Continuity theory

The last of the sociological theories we will consider in this chapter is the continuity theory of ageing. This theoretical perspective contends (Atchley 1989) that our values, preferences and patterns of behaviour remain consistent over our life span regardless of the life changes we experience. Continuity theory argues that the latter part of life is simply a continuation of the earlier part of life: how we are as younger people will be how we are as older people, and the patterns we have developed over a lifetime will determine our behaviours and beliefs and values in older age. This does not deny the capacity for change over a lifetime but values the developments made and their impact on us as older people.

Andrews (1999) challenges the ageist culture that pervades and argues that old age should not be wished or theorized away, and that doing so is in itself an ageist activity. She suggests that the challenge is not to conquer old age but to challenge the ageist culture to which we belong. Without a lifetime behind us she argues that we have no history, no story and no self.

Stereotyping older people

Some writers have argued that the growing use of the term 'elderly' is indicative of society's, professionals' and policy makers' tendency to lump older people together as though they have homogenous needs which warrant only the need for homogenous political and policy responses. This is compared to the less frequently used term in Britain of 'elders' which signifies and dignifies older age as bringing with it wisdom, and a value to society that could only be offered through the individual process of ageing and maturity.

Stereotypes are essentially sets of beliefs which shape the way we think and behave in everyday life. They affect the way we see ourselves and the way in which we see and understand others. It is clear that negative stereotypes about ageing begin to influence people's perceptions a long time before the ageing process sets in and can leave people feeling pessimistic about their future as well as stifled when they eventually reach old age (see Moore's quotes earlier). So a rather miserable summary of stereotypical views of ageing and older people is that older people are negatively stereotyped both as individuals and as a group/strata of society. They are stereotyped as being dependent and thus a drain on resources, unhappy and tired with life, senile, disengaging from relationships and consequently waiting for death.

Negative stereotypes unsurprisingly can interfere with older peoples' enjoyment and flourishing in the latter part of life and they can also have a detrimental impact on people's health and well-being as they age. Stereotypes about ageing are subtly internalized years before people become old and can become deeply embedded and taken for granted. This is so for social workers as well as for the general population.

There are studies that support the idea that stereotyping older people has a direct link to the health and well-being of older people. Levy et al. (2000) found that older people who hold negative stereotypes about themselves (e.g. viewing themselves as senile as opposed to wise) display a more negative response to stress, have lower self-efficacy and impaired cognitive function, and are more likely to have a negative view of other older people.

Levy et al. (2000) also reported that negative stereotypes affected older people's performance and attitudes, and that these negative beliefs contributed to serious illness and even death (because of the impact on people's will to live, and the meaning and value they placed on their life). Holding negative perceptions of the ageing process is thus not a minor problem for older people as it impacts upon many areas of life such as their motivation, mental health, physical health and even mortality. It is imperative that social workers are mindful of the impact of these stereotypes on individuals' self value, worth and health.

There is some good news though, and it is that holding positive views about ageing has a beneficial impact on older people. Levy et al. (2000) also found that by holding positive views about ageing, life expectancy increased by about 7.6 years. This added more years to life than low blood pressure, low cholesterol, not smoking and taking regular exercise – these only add one or two years of life expectancy.

So what does all of this mean for the role of social workers and social work with older people? What we have explored so far are the perspectives that influence the individual practitioner's personal approach to practice. To understand social work with older people more fully we need to explore the conceptual frameworks that influence practice, and also the contextual factors that shape social work practice with older people.

Differing perspectives on the nature of social work with older people

Healy (2005) cited in McDonald (2010: 42) explores a range of perspectives identified through discourse analysis that offer a framework within which social work with older people can be understood. McDonald's outlines (pp. 42–4) have been slightly adapted below:

Biomedicine Power lies in the expertise of the knowledgeable physician in this medical model of disease detection and management. Evidence suggests however that health inequality is largely governed by social and economic factors.

Economics This perspective is about rationing and allocating scarce resources to those at greatest risk of admission to hospital or residential services. This was and continues to be a key cornerstone of community care policy. Individuals' capacity to pay for care services determines how much service will be provided, and the increase of eligibility criteria levels is a regular response to decreasing local authority budgets.

Law This is presented as objectively setting out rules, however critics see it as a system based on class, gender and status inequalities. Older people may be perceived as being subject to excessive surveillance/intervention on the basis of assumed legal 'duties of care'.

Psychology Psychological theories explain human motivation and functioning. Psychology considers sources of continuing disadvantage over the life course which become manifest in old age and this insight may be used for therapeutic intervention. Critical practice requires an ability to analyse the impact of personal biases on profes- sional practice (as we have noted above with regard to 'espoused theory', 'theory in use' and stereotypical bias).

Social science An example of this perspective is the 'social construction' of dementia, which acts as an alternative explanation of dementia as a cognitive deficit or as an organic disorder of the brain. The 'problem' is thus located outside the individual as an outcome of social structures or socially created rules (or at least exacerbated by them).

Consumer rights Older people are seen as consumers of social goods, which are quality assured through the operation of 'quasi' market systems, the notion being that only the effective and efficient suppliers of care services will survive. The role of the social worker as care manager becomes aligned as the purchaser of services, and the state becomes the quality assuring regulatory authority. Within this perspective also lie organizational approaches that are consumer based rights movements trying to secure a better deal for their members.

Spirituality Social work has evolved from philanthropic and religious organizations and this is particularly so with regard to welfare services for older people. At an indi- vidual level the valuing of non-material things may have a particular congruence with older people's lives and priorities.

McDonald (2010: 44) surmises that these different perspectives underpinning interventions in social work 'lead to different and sometimes conflicting understanding of the issues that affect older people'. She suggests that choice 'will depend partly upon the orientation of the practitioner, and to a large measure on the orientation of the organization or team within which they work'.

Alongside this mélange of theoretical approaches to practice, and the impact of organizations on practice, lies the indisputable impact of changing demographics.

The impact of demographic change

The 2010 Dartington review on the future of adult social care highlights that population change is the most frequently cited factor that affects demand and expenditure on adult social care and that most policy documents refer to the challenge of an ageing population. The review notes that:

> This is not a new notion. The expression 'demographic time bomb' is now over thirty years old and predictions that in its wake the welfare state would become unaffordable or unsustainable have not been borne out by actual experience. We persist in seeing ageing as a burden rather than a benefit, and that increased longevity is a problem not a success. Nevertheless current and future projections are sobering.
>
> (Humphries 2010: 25)

The UK 2001 Census of population (ONS 2003) showed that there were more than 11 million people aged 65 and over in the UK, and that 18.6 per cent of the population was over pensionable age. The increase in the proportion of older people is sadly not applauded as the result of significant social and medical progress giving people the opportunity to live longer and more productive lives; rather, the demographic changes are being heralded politically (implicitly, if not explicitly) as the next 'scourge' on society, with the next generation of older people (the 1945–1965 post war baby boomers) being increasingly demonized as the thieves of their children's futures and their children's future burden because of their cultural, demographic, economic and political dominance (Willets 2010).

McDonald (2010: 6) more positively suggests:

> older people occupy a strategic civil, economic and political position, the ramifications of which will pose major issues for policy makers and service providers. It also means that debates about the 'meaning' of old age in terms of citizenship, rights and individual well being are ripe for debate.

Thus the context of social work with older people is challenged by an unprecedented change in demography, and will be challenged by the impact of the life experiences and expectations of the next up and coming generation of older people. This challenge to social work is also set in the context of the critical economic downturn of 2008, with significant cuts in public sector funding impacting access to social care. Additionally the complexity of funding and the costs of care make concerns about dependence in old age even more worrying.

As far as local authority social work practice is concerned Glendinning (2007: 453) points out:

> England is relatively unusual in international terms, in that access to publicly funded social care and support is restricted to those who have both high levels of need, as measured by Fair Access to Care Services (FACS) criteria, and who also have very low levels of assets and incomes. People with resources (including housing) over £23,000 cannot access publicly funded social care, however great their needs for support. Despite the national assessment framework provided by FACS, its application varies between local authorities depending on the resources available locally. Access to other social care services and resources (including the Independent Living Fund, NHS-funded continuing care and housing-based support) depends on a complex range of eligibility criteria that variously take into account medical and nursing care needs; capacity for self-care; risks of harm; financial circumstances; and the availability of informal care.

Social work practice that has essentially had its focus on this small minority of older people and their access to publicly funded care has inevitably had its impact, scope and transforming potential narrowed. Some would argue that that has been the intended consequence of the introduction of care management.

The international definition of social work

Having looked at some theoretical models of ageing, and some context, we turn our attention now to definitions and conceptual frameworks for social work practice with older people.

The International Association of Schools of Social Work and the International Federation of Social Work agreed a definition of social work in 2001 which espouses a systemic definition of social work:

> The social work profession promotes social change, problem solving in human relationships, and the empowerment and liberation of people to enhance well-being. Utilising theories of human behaviour and social systems, social work intervenes at points where people interact with their environments. Principles of human rights and social justice are fundamental to social work.
>
> (IASSW 2001)

Theoretical frameworks for social work practice

Payne (2006) presents a helpful account, both from an historical perspective and a position informed by current debate about the nature of social work today. He presents social work as a territory bounded by three main roles. Such roles are of course not linear; there may be elements of all three roles in any work with one service user or family:

1   **Individualism-reformism:** this refers to social work as an activity that aims to meet social welfare needs on an individualized basis. Social work performs a social order role helping to maintain social cohesion by providing welfare services effectively.
2   **Socialist collectives:** this approach focuses on promoting cooperation within society in order that the most oppressed and disadvantaged can gain power and take control of their own lives. Social work is seen as having a transformational role, helping to change societies to be more inclusive and supportive.
3   **Reflexive-therapeutic:** this approach is focused on promoting and facilitating personal growth so that people are enabled to deal with the suffering and disadvantage they experience. It is a therapeutic role, helping individuals develop their capacities in social relationships.

It is clear from the literature that social work can be conceptualized in a range of different ways. Thompson (2005) argues that what constitutes social work is 'up for grabs'. He emphasizes the extent to which powerful groups and institutions not only define what constitutes social work but also define the limits of policy and practice. He seeks to identify key themes related to existentialism ('a philosophical theory emphasizing the existence of the individual person as a free and responsible agent determining his own development' – OED). In doing so he argues that social work premised on the principle of existentialism should be:

* **ontological:** sensitive to the personal and social dimensions and the interactions between the two;
* **problem focused:** sensitive and responsive to the existential challenges we all face, but particularly those that are related to social location and social divisions;
* **systematic:** with a clear focus on what we are doing and why (our goals and our plans for achieving them);
* **reflective:** open minded, carefully thought through and a source of constant learning rather than a rigid, routinized approach to practice;
* **emancipatory:** attuned to issues of inequality, discrimination and oppression, and geared towards countering them where possible.

(Thompson 2005: 24)

None of these approaches to understanding social work is static, and none focus on the significant 'control and safeguarding' and statutory powers of the social work role. The nature of social work is clearly shaped by the society within which the practitioner exists, and the prevailing value base/s and beliefs about 'what works'. The notion of 'what works' for service users, however meaningfully described in the language of person centredness, will inevitably (in our current way of seeing things) have at its heart the following vexing questions: What does the intervention cost? Is it cost effective? Can it be delivered more cheaply? It is an 'organizational cost' rather than a 'service user value' driven form of social work practice, and thus not necessarily practice which is guided by evidence of what works for service users, rather what the organization considers it can afford to offer?

Thompson (2005: 8–9) also suggests that social work can be seen as distinctive in terms of:

- the central role of statutory duties;
- the challenge of managing the tensions between care and control;
- the dilemmas of being 'caught in the middle' (between the needs of the individual and society's needs, where sometimes societal ills are the underlying issues, for example, poverty, inequalities and discrimination, social exclusion);
- the need to do society's 'dirty work' (by this Thompson (p. 6) refers to social work as a 'sweeping up' operation, clearing up the problems caused by the failure or gaps in other social policies or systems); and
- the primacy of a commitment to social justice.

These care and control tensions – and the balancing of individual and societal need and this idea of doing society's dirty work and 'sweeping up' issues – sharply highlights the need for practitioners to have opportunities to reflect on the complexity of social work with older people, and indeed the potential tensions that practitioners may experience with each of the key players (the service user, the family, the GP, the employing organization).

Key roles in social work

Asquith et al. (2005) have identified the following as key roles in contemporary social work practice:

- counsellor
- advocate
- assessor of risk and need
- care manager
- agent of social control.

These differing complex roles can create tensions for both social workers and the older people with whom they work, particularly in the context of the employment of social workers in statutory services. McDonald (2010: 41) cites the research of Manthorpe et al. (2008) noting that that this is one of the few sources of information derived from interviews with older people themselves about their perceptions of the social work role. For ease of reference and to give weight to their importance, their perceptions are given here:

- Social workers' roles are seen as unclear and variable.
- Older people look for an approach that is knowledgeable about their needs.
- They look for an approach from the social worker that is 'on their side'.
- Criticism is directed at social workers who appear not to understand the needs of older people.
- Criticism is directed at those social workers who are obviously driven by agency agendas.
- Of critical importance to acceptable social work practice is the knowledge of physical, social, psychological and economic issues that older people experience.

Additionally, and compellingly, McDonald (2010: 41) notes: 'Social workers who are driven solely by an organizational mandate are easily "rumbled" by older people, and may deliver services that are not wanted and not needed'.

The administrative focus of social work with older people

Lymbery (2005: 2) drawing on the work of Payne (1996) discusses the three different strands of social work theory and action (noted above) labelling Payne's welfare orientated approach (individualism-reformism) as an 'administrative' approach. Lymbery argues there have been eras when these models have had more agency, but the administrative model has generally typified social work with older people and this is particularly so post-'community care'.

Lymbery argues that the 'administrative' focus has had the following effect: 'This has created a climate of practice which can often be experienced as arid and unfulfilling by practitioners, bearing relatively little relation to the genuine needs or desires of older people' (2005: 2).

What can we learn from the recent history of social work?

There is agreement that it is critical for social workers to have an understanding of the social and political contexts of their work and a clear understanding of how political ideologies influence social work practice and shape its direction. Key reports in the relatively recent history of social work (Seebohm 1968; Barclay 1982; Griffiths 1988) have surprisingly articulated similar criticisms of, and aspirations for, the 'social services' system, including the practice of social work, the importance of focusing on preventative work, the centrality of the development of collaborative partnerships across health and social care and the importance of community development.

It is worth recounting some of the aspirations of the Seebohm Report (1968) and Barclay (1982) as they provide some insight into the frustrations of recent governments, concerning the lack of speed of implementation of more recent reforms enshrined in *Modernising Social Services* (DH 1998), *Our Health, Our Care, Our Say* (DH 2006), *Putting People First* (DH 2007) which lays the ground for the personalization of services and self-directed support, and the most recent Health and Social Care Bill (2011) which aims to change the landscape of health and social care commissioning.

The implementation of Seebohm (1968) had significant expectations of the development of the then new Personal Social Services Departments, based within local authorities (and thus responsible and accountable to elected members). 'This new department will, we believe, reach far beyond the discovery and rescue of casualties, it will enable the greatest possible number of individuals to act reciprocally, giving and receiving service for the well being of the whole community' (Seebohm 1968: 15).

The Barclay Report (1982: 35–61) saw the functions of social workers to:

- 'see people and their needs as a whole and take account of their views about what services, if any are to be provided';
- 'acknowledge the value of individuals and recognise their right to self determination':
- promote community networks and engage in 'social care planning' (that is, work to alleviate existing and future social problems through responding to individual need, planning responses for a local population, working with other agencies and strengthening voluntary organizations);
- act as a 'broker and negotiator' with a knowledge of local community resources, balancing casework with wider patch based community work;
- work with other services, negotiating and advocating on their clients' behalf.
- act as 'rationers and gatekeepers' of scarce resources.

Reading these excerpts from influential past reports demonstrates the clear foci that have recurrently emerged, and still emerge to the present day. Different administrations have attempted to shift the focus of social care and social work and to curtail costs, but none more profoundly than the implementation of care management and the new public management ethos of the 1990s. Prior to the introduction of care management the post war emphasis had been on residential, nursing and hospital provision. However, as early as the 1950s there was reaction against these institutional forms of care; some of the reasons were to do with cost, some to do with the inhumane nature of some of the care provided. A particular prompt was a change in Social Security regulations in the early 1980s, which made it easier for people with low incomes entering independent homes to claim what is now known as Income Support towards the cost of their care. With access to this source of funding based on financial entitlement rather than any objective assessment of people's needs, the number of independent residential and nursing homes rocketed (12,000 in 1979, 46,900 in 1982 and 161,200 in 1991). Of the calls for reform, the most significant was that of the Audit Commission (1986) which provided a scathing critique of the failure of government policy to achieve care in the community (Glasby and Littlechild 2004).

The impact of care management

Care management was introduced following the NHS and Community Care Act 1990. Lymbery (2005: 180) suggests that it was quite different to its origins in the USA where:

Particular emphasis had been placed on the role and skills of the social worker not just in coordinating packages of care but in building and sustaining high quality interpersonal relationships with service users. This element of the care management role has been actively discouraged in the British context.

Preston-Shoot (1996: 26) also articulates these concerns:

Social workers have been drawn into routines rather than professional servicing; into implementing agency procedures, such as case management, contracting and purchasing and budgeting, rather than engaging, investing emotionally in and being with clients. Social work is at risk of ceasing to be a vision, a system of values and principles, imbued with and concerned with the implementation of a critical value frame and knowledge base . . . and of losing human contact as its core purpose.

Because of the administrative and procedurally driven focus of care management, many argued there was no longer a need for skilled or qualified social workers. Appointing care managers who were not qualified social workers became commonplace, and this contributed bilaterally to the devaluing of social work with older people, and it could be argued to older service users themselves. The impact of closer collaboration with health has also generated the view that social workers were in danger of losing their professional identity.

It is certainly true that care management for older people has become highly bureaucratic, and this is linked to the model of care management that was adopted: that of 'social care entrepreneurship' (Payne 2000: 82–91) where a range of care services from different providers are coordinated by the social worker. The notion that care management would assist the social worker to put the service user's needs first has been challenged by the continuation of service driven decisions, partly because of the lack of creative service provision in an underdeveloped market, the speed with which social workers are required to operate (delayed discharges and associated financial penalties are an example here), burgeoning case loads which work against creative relationship based practice, and the overemphasis on assessment to the detriment of the monitoring and review aspects of care management.

Command and control management and its impact on practice

Although the International Association of Schools of Social Work and the International Federation of Social Work agreed definition of social work (IFSW 2001) above espouses a systemic definition of social work and echoes Payne's (2006) three social work and social action categories, it does not include any hint of the implications on social work practice of 'command and control' (hierarchical) management with its emphasis on performance management. Nor is there very much literature concerning systemic approaches, or understanding the impact of command and control organizational approaches on the delivery of social work with older people. Systemic approaches to therapeutic interventions in social work contexts are well documented with regard to psychodynamic vs. systemic family therapies but organizational/management paradigms and their influence on social work practice is little researched. However, Parsloe writing in 1996 (p. 112) highlights the impact of managerial control versus professional control on the practice of social work arguing that:

> Control stifles ideas and routinises practice, as is all too clearly illustrated by some of the social work which is now carried out by overworked and over managed front line staff in social services departments. Professionals must feel that their first and paramount responsibility is to those they serve, their students, clients or patients, to themselves and to their professional peers. This responsibility must take precedence over their accountability to the organisation for which they work. I am not arguing for individual professional anarchy but for recognition of the dual role of many people, especially those who work in the service industries. They are essentially bureau professionals and the challenge for them, and for those who are managers in service organisations, is to recognise the two aspects of the job, and frame the appropriate structures and organisations to support both.

Parsloe's quote emphasizes the impact of 'managerialism' which has been central to ideas about the effective provision of public services, and underpins 'New Public Management' thinking which has been at the core of the 'development' of the public sector since the 1980s. If reforms outlined in 1968 (Seebohm) and emphasized in different decades through influential reports up to the present day have not been successfully implemented, and where countless restructurings of organizations still result in the same issues being problematic (child and adult protection issues, poor quality care and support, spiralling costs) it begs the question whether a radical and fundamental rethink is required of the way that service sector 'command and control' hierarchical organizations work. Einstein is attributed as having defined insanity as 'doing the same thing over and over again, and expecting different results'.

Thompson (2005: 176) comments that 'there is an emphasis on the manager's right to manage, a focus on managerial power (that) has been part of a broader process of deprofessionalisation, attempts to reduce the autonomy and professional standing of social workers'. Critics would argue that this has also been the case for the majority of public sector professionals, as a result of the performance-managed target-driven tick box culture.

Case study

Mary has recently joined an older people's social work team from a neighbouring local authority. She has been in post for three months and can see that the way things are done in her new team are not efficient and have a detrimental affect on older people. Many of the systems in place create delay, add work, and require the passing of the case from practitioner to practitioner before any decisions are made. Sometimes the delay in decision making has a marked impact on the older person's quality of life.

- What would you advise Mary to do?
- How easy or difficult is it for practitioners who can see new or different ways of doing things to implement new approaches in the work place?
- Are there working practices in your service which could be changed to improve outcomes for service users?

Comment

These are the types of questions which will help you to understand which parts of the system are adding value to the service user experience, and which are processes that serve the organization (in systems terms, what is value work, and what is waste?). The evaluation of internal processes is likely to raise 'double loop learning' questions, and will need an environment where reflection is safe.

Understanding organizations as systems

It is encouraging that approaches to understanding social work and social care organizations as systems are becoming more mainstream; this is particularly noticeable in the field of child protection (Munro 2011) but also increasingly so in social care with adults, including older people (see access links to the May 2011 Care Conference Report below). Thinking about organizations as systems means a different way of thinking and a different way of managing and doing the work. For service users and social workers it has the potential for transforming the work and the design of the service, and more importantly, improving outcomes for service users.

The manifestation of command and control thinking sees organizations as:

> Top down hierarchies, work is designed in functions, managers make decisions and workers do the work. Managers make decisions using budgets, targets, standards; they seek to control the workers with a variety of management practices – procedures, rules, specifications and the like. The management ethic is to manage budgets and manage people.
>
> (Seddon 2003: 47)

Seddon's diagram (see Table 1.1) shows the key differences between 'command and control' driven organizations, and those underpinned by systems thinking. Think of the middle column as the factors that underpin the functioning of the organization, the way in which it gets the work done, its focus.

You can see from the table that taking a systems view is to think about the organization from the 'outside in'. That means having a very clear understanding of customer (service user) demand and designing the organization (the system) around those needs.

Table 1.1 Command and control versus systems thinking

Command and control thinking		Systems thinking
Top-down, hierarchy	**Perspective**	Outside-in, system
Functional	**Design**	Demand, value, flow
Separated from work	**Decision making**	Integrated with work
Output, targets, standards: related to budget	**Measurement**	Capability, variation: related to purpose
Contractual	**Attitude to customers**	What matters?
Contractual	**Attitude to suppliers**	Cooperative
Manage people and budgets	**Role of management**	Act on the system
Control	**Ethos**	Learning
Reactive, projects	**Change**	Adaptive, integral

Source: Reproduced with kind permission of John Seddon (2008: 70).

If the customers' (service users') demands change, the organization of the system needs to change to accommodate it. The organization works and adapts to become as responsive as possible to service user needs.

> To enable control in this high variety environment it is necessary to integrate decision making with work (so workers control the work) and use measures derived from the work. These 'real' measures are of much more use than arbitrary measures like targets and standards. The role of management shifts from an adversarial, hierarchical one to a complementary one: working on the system.
>
> (Seddon 2008: 71)

One senior adult services manager presenter at the 11 May Care Conference put it like this: 'Our staff are customer focused, our current system of work is not.' An organizational system aligned to the needs of service users and the aspirations of social workers would be very powerful.

Summary

The chapter commenced with a discussion about the importance of reflective practice and also outlined some common sociological and stereotypical perspectives about older people which can and do impact practice. After considering the impact of demographic trends the chapter considered some theoretical perspectives concerning social work practice with older people. The chapter argues that social work practice, as well as being a personal activity bound by professional perspectives and values, is also bounded by organizational requirements and procedures, which reflect political, economic and policy considerations. The management paradigm delivering this was noted as the command and control paradigm. After a review of some of the landmark reports and a critique of care management the question was asked, why does so much change ideologically and yet so little change when it comes to outcomes for service users? Finally the chapter briefly introduces the notion of organizations as systems, linking to the opening view of the chapter that organizations need to be aligned to customer need to allow social workers to practise effectively, and reflect meaningfully and holistically on their practice.

Further reading

Middleton, P. (ed.) (2010) *Delivering Public Services that Work, Vol. 1:. Systems Thinking in the Public Sector: Case Studies*. Axminster: Triarchy Press.

Seddon, J. (2008) *Systems Thinking in the Public Sector*. Axminster: Triarchy Press.

Conference notes from 'The Vanguard Care Conference May 2011 – What really matters?', available at: http://www.systemsthinking.co.uk/home.asp.

References

Adams, R., Dominelli, L. and Payne, M. (eds) (2002) *Critical Practice in Social Work*. Basingstoke: Palgrave.

Andrews, M. (1999) The seductiveness of agelessness, *Ageing and Society* 19: 301–18.

Aquilina, C. and Hughes, J. (2006) The return of the living dead: agency lost and found? In J.C. Hughes, S.J. Louw and S.R. Sabat (eds) *Dementia, Mind, Meaning and the Person*. Oxford: Oxford University Press.

Argyris, C. (1982) *Reasoning, Learning and Action: Individual and Organizational*. San Francisco, CA: Jossey Bass.

Argyris, C. and Schön, D. (1974) *Theory in Practice: Increasing Professional Effectiveness*. San Francisco, CA: Jossey Bass.

Asquith, S., Clark, C. and Waterhouse, L. (2005) *The Role of the Social Worker in the 21st Century*. Edinburgh: Scottish Executive Education Department.

Atchley, R.C. (1989) A continuity theory of normal ageing, *The Gerontologist* 29(2): 183–90.

Audit Commission (1986) *Making a Reality of Community Care*. London: HMSO.

Banks, S. (2001) *Ethics and Values in Social Work*, 2nd edn. Basingstoke: Palgrave.

Barclay, P. (1982) *Social Workers: Their Role and Tasks* (the Barclay Report). London: Bedford Square Press.

Bastings, A.D. (2003) Looking back from loss: views of the self in Alzheimer's disease, *Journal of Aging Studies* 17: 97–9.

Boud, D., Keogh, R. and Walker, D. (eds) (1985) *Turning Experience into Learning*. London: Kogan Page.

Cottrell, S. (2003) *Skills for Success*. Basingstoke: Palgrave Macmillan.

Cumming, E. and Henry, W.E. (1961) *Growing Old*. New York: Basic.

DH (Department of Health) (1998) *Modernising Social Services*. London: HMSO.

DH (Department of Health) (2006) *Our Health, Our Care, Our Say*. London: HMSO.

2 Contextualizing the experience of older people

Chris Smethurst

After reading this chapter you should be able to:

- discuss the key themes in the evolution of contemporary social care policy and practice;
- identify how changing constructs of age and ageing have influenced policy;
- critically evaluate the impact of economic and ideological debates on health and social care policy for older people;
- discuss the implications for older people of contemporary agendas in health and social care.

Introduction

This chapter will explore some of the political, ideological and policy issues that have shaped the experiences of older people since the early 1980s. The rationale for exploring these themes is that person-centred practice does not exist in a vacuum: practitioners are influenced, if sometimes unconsciously, by societal attitudes to ageing and older people. These attitudes are reflected in the social policy that defines health and social care practice. Policy is also driven by political ideology, economic choices and imperatives. It is convenient, for policy makers and governments in particular, to present their political and ideological choices in the language of universal values: those concepts and beliefs that are assumed to be shared by the majority of the population (Ferguson and Lavalette 2005; Carey 2009; Vojak 2009).

The language of 'values' arguably makes potentially contentious policy and practice less easy to challenge. The claim to universalism and morality makes it possible to dismiss critics as being self interested, old fashioned and resistant to change (Ferguson and Lavalette 2005). Therefore policies are frequently presented as self evidently the 'right thing to do'. Economic determinants of social policy are similarly presented as rational, pragmatic responses to the real world of financial necessity. The interrelationship of ideology and economics is not always transparent: to encourage their acceptance by the public, ideological and political choices are frequently portrayed by governments as being born of economic necessity (Scharpf 1997; Schmidt 2002). This chapter will explore how these themes have become interwoven with social constructs of ageing, to provide the policy context in which person-centred practice occurs.

Dependence, independence, interdependence: why language matters

Contemporary debates concerning health and social care for older people have been largely dominated by funding issues. Considerations of short term financial cost frequently triumph over those of longer term social benefit, to the extent that policy is dominated by questions of affordability (Wilding 2000). Consequently, since the early 1980s, social welfare has been portrayed by UK governments as something of a residual luxury, subservient or oppositional to the national imperatives of wealth creation and economic competitiveness (Beresford 2005).

Within this context, citizens are divided into those who receive welfare and those who pay for it. The latter occupy the moral high ground of 'taxpayer', on whose good grace the recipients of welfare are 'dependent' or a 'burden' (Fineman 1998). Ottenheimer (2008) illustrates how the use of language influences attitudes and provides the psychological frame through which issues are conceptualized and understood. She illustrates how the term 'tax burden' has negative connotations which undermine the legitimacy of taxation as a vehicle for social cohesion. Similarly the term 'dependency' is frequently characterized as an avoidable predicament, to be contrasted with the morally superior condition of 'independence' (Fineman 1998).

Avoiding dependency through making prudent choices and saving for old age has become an important moral discourse in the United Kingdom: older people who have received state-funded social care have recently been unfavourably contrasted with those who have 'had to sell their homes to pay for care'. Wider structural considerations of the economic marginalization of older people, and 'pensioner poverty' are rather lost in an argument that sets older people against one another in an individualized discourse of fairness and prudentialism: 'those who have worked hard and saved hard are being penalised for their good behaviour' (*Daily Express*, 28 March 2011). Similarly, the superior material and social benefits accrued by the older, 'baby boomer' generation are compared with those of the austerity generation, whose taxes will have to pay for them (Inman 2010).

Both prime ministers Blair and Cameron placed entitlement to state welfare assistance within a moral discourse of 'playing by the rules'. Those who play by the rules win a grudging entitlement to state benefits, although these are given with the suspicion that this entitlement may not, in fact, be genuine (Beresford 2001; Spicker 2002). Consequently, dependency is discouraged through a combination of moralizing and bureaucratic deterrence. Although aimed primarily at the young, the unemployed and disabled people, the stigmatizing messages of deterrence appear to contribute to the low take up of benefit entitlements by older people (Audit Commission 2004; Currie 2004; Price 2006). In addition, there is some evidence that many older people internalize negative messages about dependency. These may contribute to a sense of shame at not being self-reliant, or to critical attitudes towards others perceived as not contributing to society (Townsend et al. 2006; Clarke and Warren 2007; Tanner and Harris 2008).

Concepts of dependency and independence have been dominant themes in health and social care policy for older people. However they are often understood as having contrasting meanings, to the extent that dependency is seen as the direct opposite of independence (Lister 1997). Consequently, dependency and independence are often addressed in policy as binary opposites (Lymbery 2010). Similarly, self-reliance and personal autonomy are seen as prerequisites of full 'citizenship', which can only be achieved by moving people from a state of dependency to one of independence (Pateman 2000; Williams 2001).

This oversimplifies the complex pattern of interdependence and mutual obligation that are characteristic of modern society (Cordingley and Webb 1997; Lymbery 2010). Research indicates that older people are well aware of these distinctions, even if policy makers are not: interdependence, being both a giver and receiver of emotional and practical support, is a feature of many older people's lives and is a key determinant of well-being and sense of worth (Godfrey et al. 2004: 213).

Older people as a 'social problem'?

Older people are frequently assumed to have needs, aspirations and characteristics that are uniform (Tanner and Harris 2008). Consequently, debates concerning dependency and independence have more than an abstract significance. Older people are typically perceived as wealth consumers, rather than wealth creators, and as a threat to national economic growth (Walker 1999). Similarly, older people are presented as a real, or potential, economic and emotional burden on the younger population (Stevenson 2008). Within this context, the needs of older people are frequently considered within a narrow paradigm of care and dependency, placing them in a subordinate position which objectifies and devalues them (Calnan et al. 2006; Llewellyn et al. 2008).

Activity 2.1

Consider the following labels:

The elderly

Mentally infirm

High dependency

Vulnerable

When these labels are applied to older people, to what extent do you think this influences how they are perceived and treated by others?

How do you think these labels, and the perception and behaviour of others, may affect how older people may see themselves?

Thornton (2002) asserts that the labels attached to older people have been instru-
mental in the construction of ageing as a social problem. According to Estes (1979: 13):

> Aging becomes a social problem only when some social group successfully
> labels it as such. Further, the more influential the group doing the labelling
> the more widespread the acceptance of the label. A form of power accrues to
> those politicians, policy makers, administrators, practitioners and researchers
> who construct the versions of reality that then determine social policies and
> intervention strategies.

Older people may internalize the negative stereotypes of ageing. These can shape their
expectations and behaviour to the extent that the stereotypes become self-fulfilling
prophecies (Kite and Wagner 2004). This can take the form of lower expectations of
material well-being and quality of life compared to those of the younger population
(Dominy and Kempson 2006; Scharf et al. 2006). Similarly, older people may accommodate ageism: by accepting restricted life opportunities, by passively accepting
medical and social care interventions, or by being reluctant to access services or
'trouble' others (Abbott et al. 2000; Minichiello et al. 2000; Foster et al. 2001; Hughes
and Goldie 2009). In addition, the deference exhibited by many older people may
manifest itself in 'decisional dependency': an apparent reluctance to take decisions
independently of relatives or professionals (Gibson 1998). The lesson for practitioners
is that the apparent passivity of many older people is not an inevitable consequence of
age, but a tacit recognition of the reduced status afforded to them.

A more positive view of ageing?

Kumar asserts that, in the latter part of the twentieth century, 'collective identities' of
age and class, gave way to more 'pluralised and privatised forms of identity' (1995:
122). These subjective identities are not static but are continually subject to revision
and redefinition (Giddens 1991). Although this process can give rise to a sense of alienation and insecurity, an opportunity arises for individuals to break free of the constraints
of collective identities and choose: 'designer lifestyles – chosen by the wearer rather
than imposed by the sociologist or policy planner' (Carter 1998: 8). This presents
ageing as an opportunity for personal fulfilment and redefinition, beyond the
restraining influence of categories, labels and stereotypes.

First, the definitions of 'older', 'old age' and 'ageing' should be evaluated. The
terms imply fluidity; age is not static and ageing is an incremental process. The term
'older' implies a definition in relation to something else; this 'other' may itself be a
fluid and evolving concept. Sheehy (1995: 62) summarizes the mood of the times:

> Most baby boomers don't feel fully 'grown up' until they are into their 40s.
> When our parents turned 50, we thought they were old! But today, women
> and men I've interviewed routinely feel they are five to 10 years younger than
> the age on their birth certificates. Fifty is what 40 used to be; 60 is what 50

used to be. Middle age has already been pushed far into the 50s – in fact, if you listen to boomers, there is no middle age. So what's next?

The determinism of chronology may be denied or affirmed by the individual's experience or, perhaps as importantly, aspiration. Tinker (1997) points out that at 60 years an individual is at an equidistant point between the ages of 30 and 90. However, societal expectation and social policy frequently assumes all individuals, post 60, have shared needs and aspirations. Consequently, an evolving argument asserts that traditional constructs of ageing have been too deterministic, assuming uniformity in the experience and aspirations of older people (Thompson 1992; Tinker 1997; Tanner and Harris 2008). This approach gives equal, or superior, value to biographical narratives and humanistic, as opposed to biological and economic, constructs of old age (Birren et al. 1996; Edmonson and Von Kondratowitz 2009).

This analysis has developed to suggest that the experience of ageing is influenced by the norms and imperatives of consumer societies. The individual's sense of identity may increasingly be defined by the aspirations of consumer culture, and in this respect older people do not differ markedly from the rest of the population (Rees Jones et al. 2008). However, Carrigan and Szmigin (2000) assert that the advertising and marketing industries do not reflect this reality. Older people are either ignored or caricatured: they are presented in stereotypical terms *against* which aspiration is defined. Similarly, Davidson (2005) illustrates the extent to which media coverage of older people is dominated by portrayals of victims, dependency and decay.

However, older people are valued if they can convince us that they are 'young at heart' or 'good for his/her age'. Bytheway (2000) notes a trend to deny the significance of ageing; this emphasizes that older people 'haven't changed'; they are still youthful and 'ageless'. This is not an empowering rejection of ageist labels, but a celebration of youth and a tacit acceptance of the stereotypes of old age (Andrews 1999; Bytheway 2000). Andrews (2000) offers a challenge to this cult of youthfulness; she recalls the black civil rights slogan and urges us all to be 'Ageful and Proud'.

Activity 2.2

Consider the idea of being 'Ageful and Proud' (Andrews 2000).

To what extent does this reflect your own aspirations for old age?

Although the notions of agelessness and a 'youthful' old age do not really challenge the subordinate position of older people in society, there is increasing attention being given to the 'dignity' of older people (Woolhead et al. 2004). However, government initiatives such as Dignity in Care (SCIE 2010) can perhaps be seen, less as a celebration of positive ageing than as a need to assert basic rights in the face of dehumanizing treatment in care settings. Greenberg et al. (2004) suggest that the younger population's fear of growing older results in a variety of distancing strategies. This can manifest itself in ageist language and dehumanizing behaviour towards older people. Similarly, the reality for many older people *is* an experience of physical decline. Paradoxically, exhortations to embrace the dignity of the older person occur in a societal context where the ageing body is viewed with distaste.

Ageing, ageism and economics

Ageist assumptions and beliefs are woven into the fabric of British society to the extent that they assume the status of received wisdom and 'common sense' (Biggs et al. 2006). These assumptions are evident in the uncritical use of the term 'Old Age Dependency Ratio', a key measure in government planning. This ratio is defined as the number of people of pensionable age divided by number of people of working age. The assumption here is that people are automatically dependent and economically unproductive once they reach retirement age.

These notions have been challenged by the emergence of debates and initiatives which emphasize 'Active Ageing'. The transition to old age is reframed as the 'Third Age', with an emphasis on forging a positive identity for older people as active contributors to society. Recent social policy has embraced this notion of active ageing (PIU 2000; Angus 2006). These initiatives have combined quality of life issues with pragmatic, economic considerations. The latter have particularly focused on measures to retain older workers in employment to counteract the 'pensions crisis'. Governments have become increasingly concerned about the trend for people to live longer and retire earlier, leaving a potential shortfall in pension provision (Pensions Commission 2006). Consequently, within recent years, practical steps have been taken to increase the retirement age and to combat age discrimination in the workplace (Equality Act 2010).

Arguably, these measures represent a tacit acknowledgement of the 'political economy' perspective, which asserts that the requirements of capitalist economies reinforce structural divisions and inequality (Estes 2001). Consequently, older people may share a common experience: of exclusion from the workforce, economic marginalization and 'structured dependency' upon welfare and family support (Walker 1981, 1987). Parallels can be drawn between the political economy perspective on ageing and the Independent Living Movement's analysis of disability. Disability is socially constructed: society disables individuals by denying them access to employment and life opportunities. Any ensuing marginalization and dependency is then seen by society as being *caused* by the impairment rather than by social construction and exclusion (Oliver 1990, 1996; Priestley 1999).

Exclusion, marginalization and older people

The notion that certain groups are marginalized and excluded from participation in society has been highly influential in policy formation. 'Social Exclusion' has been defined as:

a complex and multi-dimensional process. It involves the lack or denial of resources, rights, goods and services, and the inability to participate in the normal relationships and activities, available to the majority of people in a society, whether in economic, social, cultural or political arenas. It affects both the quality of life of individuals and the equity and cohesion of society as a whole.

(Levitas et al. 2007: 25)

Activity 2.3

Using the definition by Levitas et al. (2007) above consider the extent to which ageism could contribute to the social exclusion of older people.

Tackling social exclusion was a major policy theme of the Blair-era Labour government. However, older people were not really prioritized in an agenda that primarily focused on young people and the unemployed. Typically the New Labour administrations viewed employment as the pathway to social inclusion and were criticized for minimizing the effects of structural disadvantage in reducing the life opportunities for marginalized groups (Jordan 2001). Government initiatives for older people have been accused of adopting similarly narrow, psychological explanations for exclusion (Biggs et al. 2006). These embrace a 'you're as old as you feel' narrative by assuming that a positive outlook, and staying healthy and active, are the paths to inclusion (DWP 2005). Arguably these do not effectively challenge the effects of poverty and age discrimination on the marginalization of older people.

Research by the Centre for Social Justice (2010) suggests that government policy has largely failed to address the exclusion of older people. Poverty is a particular problem with 2.3 million (20 per cent of the older population) living below the poverty line (CSJ 2010). It would appear that poverty is the most important causal factor in the social exclusion of older people (Scharf 2007). It is a sad indictment, that sixty years after the foundation of the modern welfare state, so many older people live with insecurity caused by poverty.

A future free from fear: origins of the welfare state

The post-war British welfare state emerged from a coalescence of the values and economic methods that had underpinned Britain's war effort. The Beveridge Report was published in 1942, when victory in the Second World War was, for the first time, beginning to look a possibility. It used suitably combative language in its reference to the slaying of the 'five giants' of want, disease, squalor, ignorance and idleness. For older people, Beveridge offered the promise of freedom from fear of a future of poverty and ill health. The boldness of the vision of 'cradle to the grave' security fired the enthusiasm of the British, for whom war time living, with its fears and uncertainties, had followed all too quickly upon the insecurity and misery of the economic depression of the 1930s.

The values enshrined in the Beveridge Report informed the foundation, in 1948, of the National Health Service and the National Insurance and National Assistance Acts. Critically for older people, the values of the post-war welfare state underpinned an intergenerational contract: the state, through taxation of the younger, working population, would ensure the welfare of the older population and in later life be provided for in turn (Walker 1996). Arguably, these values enshrined the notion of reciprocity and interdependence between generations. However, these collectivist values certainly dovetailed with the collectivist methods that had recently been employed to mobilize Britain's wartime economy: mass consumption of state organized, funded and administered services. It was believed that the methods that had won the war could be employed to win the peace.

The legacy of the 1940s: attitudes to older people in the welfare state

The welfare state's principles and methods of standardization, mass production and mass consumption have subsequently been the targets of sustained criticism, for their perceived paternalism, inflexibility and inefficiency. However, the assumptions about older people that informed post-war welfare policy have received less attention.

'Disengagement theory' described the assumed natural process of decline, as the older person gradually disengaged from society (Gilleard and Higgs 2002). Ironically, what was seen as a natural, even desirable, process of disengagement would probably be seen today as a feature of social exclusion. Nevertheless there is evidence that the idea of disengagement has had a lasting influence on the delivery of health and social care in the United Kingdom. Although older people are the beneficiaries of 40 per cent of NHS spending on hospital and community health services (Howse 2007), quality of care has frequently been of a lower standard than that available to younger people (Kings Fund 2000). This was acknowledged as a problem by the Blair government, with the introduction of the *National Service Framework for Older People* (DH 2001). This promised to tackle age discrimination in health and social care services and has achieved some success (Healthcare Commission, Audit Commission and Commission for Social Care Inspection 2006). However, there is evidence that health care decisions can still be informed by a subjective notion of a 'fair innings': where older people deemed to have had a long life have been excluded from many treatments that could prolong life or increase well-being (Carruthers and Ormondroyd 2009).

Social care spending also appears to reflect the view that older people have fewer social needs than other groups. Social care interventions with older people are overwhelmingly focused on physical care needs (Clark 2009). In addition, although social care spending on older people has increased by 3 per cent since the mid-2000s, this must be compared with the 20 per cent increase for people with learning disabilities and 14 per cent for those with physical disabilities (Kings Fund 2011). If ageism is woven into the structures and processes of the health and social care system, the underpinning financial and organizational structures of the welfare state, conceived in the 1940s, can also be argued to have had a lasting impact on the experiences of older people.

The legacy of the 1940s: fragmentation and division in the welfare state

The National Assistance Act 1948 provided a legislative framework for a system of locally administered social care for disabled and older people. Crucially, these local arrangements existed in parallel with a national system of Social Security benefit payments. This separation of the provision of care from the provision of cash was a deliberate policy: it freed social work intervention from its inglorious nineteenth century origins as the arbiter of those deemed deserving or undeserving of poverty relief (Glasby et al. 2010). However, this division is not common elsewhere in Europe (McKay and Rowlington 1999). It can work to artificially separate poverty from other needs deemed to fall within the social care remit: poverty can be seen as 'another agency's problem' (Glasby and Littlechild, 2009: 7).

The division between the benefits and social care systems, established in the 1940s, still undermines holistic, person-centred practice. However, the differing funding frameworks for National Health Service and Local Authority social services have had a similar, lasting and problematic influence on the experiences of older people. The division between 'free at the point of delivery' health services and social care that is charged for has created an inequitable system that has persisted to this day (Lewis 2001).

Older people frequently have needs that straddle the specific responsibilities of health and social care agencies; yet, despite the rhetoric of partnership and multi-agency working, the experience of older people has been that these boundaries lead to confusion, uncertainty and anxiety (Glasby and Littlechild 2004). It is ironic that, once government created the divisions between health and social care agencies, the mission of successive governments has been to bind these divisions back together.

Resources, legislation, confusion

Lymbery (2006; 2010) has illustrated the extent to which governments have understood the health and social care divide in terms of conflicting organizational structures and professional rivalries. However they have consistently failed to address the consequences of a resource base that is simply inadequate to meet demand. Consequently, meeting older people's needs has often been characterized by financial 'cost-shunting' and conflict between agencies (Lewis 2001). The shifting distinction between a 'health need' and a 'social need' is defined in the ebb and flow of arcane and contradictory government guidance. Successive guidance has implied a boundary that is at odds with the law, setting a threshold for continuing health care below that specified in legislation (Clements 2010). This has resulted in a suspicion that governments have been complicit in the redefinition of 'free' health care as 'means tested' social care (Mandelstam 2005).

The fragmentation of agency responsibilities and insecurity of entitlement for older people has been exacerbated by the absence of an overarching legal framework for health and social care. In May 2011 the Law Commission published proposals to rationalize what has been termed a 'hotchpotch of conflicting statutes' (Clements

2004, para. 1.30). In proposing basic minimum entitlements for services the Law Commission has recognized that the existing legal and policy framework has offered older people little certainty and few absolute rights. Consequently, the apparent legal obligations of health and social service agencies have been subject to continuous review and challenge. The legal duties of statutory agencies have frequently been defined through the interpretation of case law, hardly the most accessible source of certainty for older people and practitioners.

Uncertainty concerning the rights of older people has had some foundation in the lack of a universally accepted definition of 'need'. Instead, 'need' has been a movable not an absolute concept. In social care need has frequently been interpreted as being synonymous with 'available resources' and thus subject to fluctuation with the financial fortunes of local authorities (Brammer 2010). Although this interpretation has been the subject of legal challenge, it is arguable that the needs of older people have not been subject to the firm foundations of moral entitlement: they have been addressed through a 'gift' relationship with the local authority and the taxpayer (Duffy 2005: 153).

The legacy of the 1980s: from collectivism to individualism

From its inception until the 1970s, the post-war British welfare state largely benefited from bipartisan political support. This consensus was challenged from the late 1970s by the emergence of the 'hard-edged, market-led, competitive world of "Thatcherism", and its recasting of British society into "winners and losers"' (Evans 2004: 49). The Conservative governments of the 1980s and 1990s maintained a hostility to the welfare state on economic and moral grounds. First, the tax-funded welfare state was seen as a drain on the economy and as a significant barrier to economic growth and prosperity. Publicly funded welfare services were portrayed as being inefficient, bureaucratic and self serving. However, the welfare state was also perceived as undermining the moral fabric of the nation. In a departure from the collectivist ideals of Beveridge, a new consensus focused on the need to discourage welfare dependency (Bochel and Defty 2007). Welfare provided a disincentive for self-reliance: the obligation of individuals and families to look after themselves and their own had been supplanted by the 'overweening nanny state'.

In a return to the Victorian moral landscape of the 'deserving and undeserving poor', government justified 'rolling back the state' by demonizing the 'feckless' and the 'scrounger'. Although not characterized in moral terms as 'undeserving', older people were caught in the cross fire of wider assaults on social welfare. Cuts to social services budgets and alterations to the state pension were part of a package of measures designed to facilitate tax cuts (Hills 1998). These were intended to reward Thatcher's 'winners' (Evans 2004) by providing incentives for the entrepreneurial engines of economic growth (Hills 1998). In contrast, many older people fell into the category of 'losers': relative poverty for older people more than tripled between 1984 and 1989 (Goodman et al. 2003).

The legacy of the Thatcher era has many identifiable strands and forms embedded in many aspects of British life. One aspect of this legacy was the supplanting of collectivism by individualism as a guiding principle of social action. The individual, freed from the paternalism of the state, is expected and empowered to make provision for his/her own welfare needs. State support should exist as a safety net, a residual service for those unable to take care of their own needs (Clarke 2005). However, individuals should first turn for support to their own family and community, the latter embodied in networks of friends, neighbours and voluntary groups (Griffiths 1988). Of course these philosophical principles merge with economic considerations of the health and social care requirements of an ageing population. These arguments have proven to be remarkably consistent over time; the words of the 1981 White Paper *Growing Older* can be compared with those of government's vision for social care in 2010: 'Care in the community must increasingly mean care by the community' (DHSS 1981: 3). 'We can transform care, not by looking upwards to the state, but outwards to open communities – by empowering individuals and unlocking the power and creativity of neighbourhoods to deliver the Big Society' (DH 2010: 9).

Case study

Mrs Woods lives on her own in a flat in London. She moved there following the death of her husband seven years ago. Her only son and his family live in Canada; she speaks to him weekly by telephone and stays in touch with her grandchildren by e-mail. Mrs Woods' mobility has decreased over the past two years; she is largely restricted to walking to the corner shop for her shopping. When she has been ill, the shop owners, Mr and Mrs Kohli, deliver Mrs Woods' shopping. On the last occasion they supplied her with cooked meals. Mrs Woods does not like to trouble her neighbours who, like many of the residents in the flats, are young professionals who have recently moved to the neighbourhood. They are out to work early in the morning and back late at night. Following a hospital admission, as the result of a fall, Mrs Woods did receive some social services home care support; but, this was removed after a few weeks. She then received support from a community based organization, but recent funding cut backs have led to the closure of that service; resources have been targeted at those deemed to be most 'vulnerable'. Mrs Woods has had further falls and is worried that, if she had a serious fall, no one would find her. She is fearful of immigrants and crime, stories of which appear to dominate her newspaper, and feels anxious when she leaves her front door. None of this she communicates to anyone else, to whom she appears as stoic, cheerful and independent.

Comment

The case study illustrates the sometimes ambiguous and contradictory experiences of 'community' and 'neighbourhood' for older people. However, policies for health and social care have provided rhetorically appealing visions of choice, independence and community. They are similarly presented as being transformational: defined as a radical departure from all that has gone before (Lymbery 2010). However, as the quotes from 1981 and 2010 policy illustrate, there has been a lasting ambition to unlock the power of communities as an alternative to the welfare state. That the same desires are being restated so forcefully, after an interval of thirty years, perhaps indicates the difficulty of realizing that ambition. The case study reveals some of the complexities that would need to be addressed to make the vision of a 'Big Society' a reality for many older people.

Community care in the 1990s

The community care reforms of the 1990s were built around a nexus of economic priorities and ideological assumptions. The ideological assumptions were that individuals, families and communities could and should do more to support themselves (Johns 2011). The economic determinants of policy were largely driven by a desire to cap the state's expenditure on residential care for older people (Lewis and Glennerster 1996). Changes to Supplementary Benefit entitlement in the early 1980s had the unforeseen consequence of making it relatively easy for older people to gain access to fully funded residential care. Funding was conditional on eligibility for benefits and not a question of whether the older person needed residential care, as opposed to community-based support (Means and Smith 1998). In fact, the latter was made more difficult to obtain by central government cuts to local authority social services budgets. Residential care was paid for by central government, through the benefits system, not through locally administered social services budgets. Consequently, this created what the Audit Commission (1986) referred to as a 'perverse incentive' for older people to enter residential care rather than be supported to remain in their own homes.

The White Paper *Caring for People* in 1989 set out a vision of community care, where individuals would be free to exercise choice in a market of private and voluntary sector care providers. Provision of 'in house' local authority services was to be discouraged: local authorities were to be 'enablers', rather than providers of care services. The role of local authority social services departments would be to assess needs and coordinate support to enable the person to live in their home for as long as possible. The perverse incentive for residential care would be abolished: a new funding structure would transfer funding to local level, for administration by local authorities. Access to state support would now be conditional on an assessment of need conducted by local authority, care management staff.

The intentions of the community care reforms were undermined by the fact that they contained within them contradictory objectives for local authorities and care managers. Older people were promised choice, independence and needs led services. However, the overarching aim of containing social care expenditure meant that this had to be achieved within a framework of targeting and resource constraint (Ellis et al. 1999; Tanner 2003).

The consequences of targeting and rationing

Despite its emphasis on the empowerment of service users through the exercising of choice, the experience of many older people has been of bureaucratic and inflexible services (Counsel and Care 2008). Similarly, it has proven increasingly difficult to gain access to state-funded support, unless one's needs are deemed to create imminent risk. Frequently, individuals are denied access to services until a crisis necessitates urgent, reactive and costly intervention (Audit Commission 2000; Glasby et al. 2010). Despite the rhetoric of needs led assessment and services, need has increasingly become equated with risk (Kemshall 2002).

The response of local authorities to the government imperatives to contain social care expenditure has been to restrict access to support by tightening eligibility criteria. A 3 per cent increase in social care expenditure has been entirely swallowed up by demographic changes: the population of older people has increased by 6 per cent, with a 25 per cent increase in those over 85 (Kings Fund 2011). Consequently, since 2006, tightening eligibility criteria has resulted in a 7 per cent fall in the number of older people receiving publicly-funded social care.

The aim of successive governments has been to promote preventative services for older people. However, almost by definition, a focus on high level risk implies immediate and reactive intervention as opposed to longer-term preventative work. It is perhaps unsurprising that social care provision is characterized by poor investment in preventative services (CSCI 2006).

The case for prevention

Early intervention and prevention, providing support for people's low level needs, can prove to be cost efficient. Primarily this is because the maintenance of older people's health and well-being through early intervention delays the necessity of expenditure on more expensive, reactive health and social care (Windle et al. 2009).

However, a purely economic rationale does not fully encapsulate the benefits of prevention: the overriding concern of the social care system, with a narrow reactive focus on risk and personal care needs, totally fails to capture the complexity of older people's lives. This is particularly illustrated by the failure of services to acknowledge the interrelationship of psychological well-being and physical health needs. There is a clear correlation between psychological well-being, subjective notions of quality of life and the prevention of ill health (Bowling et al. 1997).

Research by Clark et al. (1998) illustrated the psychological benefits of support in maintaining the 'home', an extension of the person's identity as well as a source of security. Its importance is evident when it is understood that avoiding the perception of decline is essential in maintaining older people's resilience to physical and emotional threats to well-being (Tanner 2003; Henwood and Hudson 2008). Therefore, there is a clear link between the maintenance of psychological well-being and the prevention of functional decline (Henwood and Hudson 2008).

It is therefore surprising that, despite the exhortations of successive governments, prevention is not more firmly established as a principle of health and social care provision. Glasby et al. (2010: 20) suggest the following reasons:

- The benefits of prevention are frequently long term, whereas the immediate priorities of government and health and social care budget holders are short term.
- It is difficult to prove that something has been prevented, particularly when mechanisms of cause and effect are complex.
- Prevention requires double funding, to ensure that crisis needs are still being met whilst preventative approaches are established.

Activity 2.4

Return to the case study of Mrs Woods. What preventative services might be helpful here?

The focus on high risk, short-term crisis work ensures that people like Mrs Woods are unlikely to receive social care intervention until a crisis occurs. In these circumstances, not only do the immediate physical and emotional consequences of the crisis have to be addressed, but also the longer term consequences of regaining and maintaining confidence and resilience. Even after the crisis of a hospital admission, there is evidence that services still fail to address psychological and social needs, including the need to reintegrate into social networks and to regain confidence (Richards and Coast 2003). It is therefore no surprise that failure to do so is linked to risk of hospital readmission, or admission to residential care (CSCI 2004, 2005)

The personalization agenda

Dissatisfaction with restrictive and inflexible arrangements for social care prompted younger disabled people to advocate for the opportunity to purchase and manage their own support. The Community Care (Direct Payments) Act 1996 provided a framework to enable cash payments to be made in lieu of local authority funded and coordinated services. Although initially restricted to those under 65, provision was extended to older people in February 2000. In 2003 it was made mandatory for local authorities to offer direct payments for those eligible for them.

The enthusiasm in central government for Direct Payments can be linked to the long standing critique of an inflexible, self-serving welfare state that was unresponsive to individual need. Direct Payments can therefore be seen within the context of 1990s community care policy, as an embodiment of its central principles of independence, choice and empowerment.

These principles were embraced and extended by the 1997 Labour government. Re-branding itself against an image of its old collectivist identity, New Labour channelled its historic commitment to social justice through the narrative of empowerment through individual choice. Users of public services were redefined as consumers or customers; the relationship between consumer and 'modernized' services would be revolutionized through the transformational metaphor of 'shopping' (Carey 2009). For policy makers definitions of citizenship have increasingly been viewed through the prism of the citizen as a consumer. It is argued that consumption provides psychological benefits to the individual; in terms of gratification and self-esteem, but also in terms of enhanced motivation and participation in social interaction (Edquist 2004). The citizen as consumer was therefore seen as an essential component of strategies to promote social inclusion.

Through the concept of 'personalization' New Labour was able to square the circle of using individualized, market solutions to address collective principles of social well-being; so, personalization is:

a new way to link the individual and the collective good: people who participate in creating solutions that meet their needs make public money work harder and help deliver public policy goals. Self-directed services work because they mobilise a democratic intelligence; the ideas, know-how and energy of thousands of people to devise solutions rather than relying on a few policy makers.

(Leadbeater et al. 2008: 81)

Although presented by government as a radical departure from previous practice (Lymbery 2010) the current 'personalization agenda' in social care provides a clear link to the original aims of the 1990s community care reforms, through its promise to consumers of, 'maximum choice, control and power over the support services they receive' (HM Government 2007: 2–3).

The original vehicle of personalization, Direct Payments, has since been extended. Individual Budgets were proposed in the *Strategy for an Ageing Population* (HM Government 2005), the Green Paper *Independence, Well-being and Choice*, and the White Paper *Our Health, Our Care, Our Say* (DH 2006). Individual Budgets aimed to combine money from a variety of funding streams, to give older people greater flexibility in meeting their individual needs.

In December 2007, *Putting People First* (DH 2007) stated that Personal Budgets would become the expected mode of delivering social services assistance. Personal Budgets consist of the total amount of money allocated by a local authority to meet an individual's social care needs. This can be taken as a Direct Payment, or local authorities can still be retained to commission services on the older person's behalf. Personal Budgets differ from Individual Budgets in that they only encompass social care funding. The difficulties, including legal ones, of weaving together the funding streams envisaged for Individual Budgets has meant that the term is no longer being promoted by the Department of Health (SCIE 2010a).

Will personalization work for older people?

The principles of personalization neatly align with the rejection of deterministic constructs of old age and ageing: they purport to recognize individual needs, aspirations and identity (Leadbeater 2004). Similarly, these principles resonate with the values of person-centred practice and it is tempting to accept them at face value. However, social care policy has also been informed by economic and ideological imperatives. These too are framed in the language of individual choice and self-determination. Personalization can therefore be seen as a convergence of the disability movement's struggle for independent living and the desire of successive governments to reduce welfare dependency through a discourse of personal responsibility (Ferguson 2007; McLaughlin 2009). This apparent convergence disguises the fact that the disability movement strongly recognizes the impact of structural inequality and the role of government in mediating its effects. This concern is less evident in government policy (Carey 2009) to the extent that the personalization agenda could be perceived as a manifestation of the government's attempt to shed itself of its obligations (Scourfield 2007).

There is evidence that there is less engagement with the personalization agenda by older people than with other groups, with only 2 per cent of those eligible receiving direct payments in 2006 (NHS Information Centre 2010). Clough et al. (2007: 76) suggest that 'being a competent consumer is not easy and demands energy and experience. The management of services by an individual is complex and personalisation through participation (Leadbeater, 2004) is not easy if you feel your cognitive or physical strength is fading'.

However, it would appear that many practitioners make judgements about whom they filter in and out of access to direct payments, based upon 'common sense' notions of risk and vulnerability (Ellis 2007; Taylor and Harris 2008). A key issue is the need to recognize that personalization is not restricted to the acceptance or rejection of Direct Payments (CSCI 2009). Yet, many local authorities have struggled to engage with the vision, beyond the enticing possibility of shedding long-term responsibility towards potential clients (Schwehr 2010). Nevertheless, the principles of personalization, sketched out by a Labour government, have become the basis of a new cross-party welfare consensus: they are the central theme of the Coalition government's vision for social care (DH 2010).

Coalition policies in an era of 'austerity'

The Coalition policies on the deficit reduction should be seen in the context of the relatively poor provision of income and services for older people. The basic state pension is low in relation to earnings and is only 16 per cent of average earnings or 31 per cent if the Second Pension is included. This is compared with 51 per cent in France, 62 per cent in Sweden and 82 per cent in the Netherlands (Walker 2011). The June 2010 Budget had a disproportionately negative impact on low income groups. Although older people are not hit as hard as some other poor people, they will nevertheless suffer a net loss of 3 per cent of their income from 2010 to 2014 (Brown and Levell 2010). Older people living in the private rented sector will be adversely affected by cuts in Housing Benefit. This will mean that older people receiving Local Housing Allowance will lose on average £12 per week nationally and in excess of £30 per week in London (Walker 2011).

One positive change is the Coalition decision to restore the link between the basic state pension and average earnings. This is change that has long been campaigned for. From April 2011 the state pension will rise in line with the higher of either average earnings, prices or 2.5 per cent. Prices have risen faster than average earnings so the state pension will rise by 4.6 per cent in April 2011. However, the price measure used for pension increases will be the Consumer Price Index (CPI) rather than the currently used Retail Price Index (RPI). CPI is usually lower that RPI and can be interpreted as a cost cutting measure, even though RPI is said to provide a superior coverage of goods and services (Brown and Levell 2010). A further assault on income will occur as the Coalition scales back the means-tested pension credit. Those receiving pensions credit will see these top-up payments frozen for four years, resulting in a significant cut in retirement incomes for about one in six older people.

A further change that will affect older people is the equalization of the state pension age from November 2018. This is 2 years earlier than planned with the pension age for both men and women increasing to 66 by April 2020. This will affect 5.1 million people and the vast majority of losers will be women, particularly those born after 1953, who will be unable to claim their state pension until they are 66 (Walker 2011).

The impact of austerity on social care services

Increasing privatization and marketization of services, alongside the gradual reduction of access to state services through ever tighter eligibility criteria, mean that older people needing services face an increased burden of costs, particularly for social care services. Policies to further reduce the range of available state services, and a shift towards payment for services, will place an even greater burden on those older people who are dependent on the state retirement pension as their only source of income.

In spite of significant increases in spending on adult social care between 1997 and 2009, which was mainly provided to older people, there is still considered to be a significant gap between what is needed and provided. Walker (2011) estimates that there are 4.1 million older people with low level needs and 0.9 million with high level needs. He claims that only 3 out of 5 with high level needs receive any formal support in their own or residential/nursing homes, and that there has been a decline of 70,000 receiving support in their own homes as eligibility criteria are tightened. This is only likely to increase as local authorities further restrict services to those deemed to be most in need.

Summary

This chapter has traced the evolution of the key themes that have underpinned the policy and practice of working with older people. There has been a steady progression towards a more individualized understanding of the needs of older people, and practice has evolved accordingly. Personalization offers a clear potential to address the bureaucratic and inflexible provision of support that is endured by many older people. However, this chapter has also highlighted the intractability of many of the concerns and issues that have dogged successive generations of government and policy makers. A particular concern must be the possibility that consideration of the impact of structural inequality gets lost in the superficial, rhetorical appeal of the power of consumerism. The reality is that today's bold visions are being enacted in a context where the dominant agenda is saving money, with 'doing more for less'. This agenda is reinforced by the current economic fashion for austerity; its consequences are budgetary reductions and their impact on services for older people.

Further reading

Glasby, J. and Littlechild, R. (2009) *Direct Payments and Personal Budgets: Putting Personalisation into Practice*. Bristol: The Policy Press.

References

Abbott, S., Fisk, M. and Forward, L. (2000) Social and democratic participation in residential settings for older people: realities and aspirations, *Ageing and Society* 20(3): 327–40.

Andrews, M. (1999) The seductiveness of agelessness, *Ageing and Society* 19(3): 301–18.

Andrews, M. (2000) Ageful and proud, *Ageing and Society* 20(6): 791–5.

Angus, J. (2006) Ageism: a threat to 'aging well' in the 21st century, *Journal of Applied Gerontology* 25(2): 137–52.

Audit Commission (1986) *Making a Reality of Community Care*. London: HMSO.

Audit Commission (2000) *The Way to Go Home: Rehabilitation and Remedial Services for Older People*. London: Audit Commission.

Audit Commission (2004) *Older People – A Changing Approach, Independence and Well-being*. London: Audit Commission.

Beresford, P. (2001) Service users, social policy and the future of welfare, *Critical Social Policy* 21(4): 494–512.

Beresford, P. (2005) Redistributing profit and loss: the new economics of social welfare, *Critical Social Policy* 25(4): 464–82.

Biggs, S., Phillipson, C., Money, A. and Leach, R. (2006) The age-shift: observations on social policy, ageism and the dynamics of the adult lifecourse, *Journal of Social Work Practice* 20(3): 239–50.

Birren, J.E., Kenyon, G.M., Ruth, J.C., Schroots, J.J.F. and Svensson, T. (eds) (1996) *Explorations in Adult Development*. New York: Springer Publishing.

Bochel, H. and Defty, A. (2007) MPs' attitudes to welfare: a new consensus?, *Journal of Social Policy* 36(1): 1–17.

Bowling, A., Grundy, E. and Farquhar, M. (1997) *Living Well into Old Age*. London: Age Concern.

Brammer, A. (2010) *Social Work Law*, 3rd edn. Harlow: Pearson.

Brown, J. and Levell, P. (2010) *The Distributional Effect of the Tax and Benefit Reforms to be Introduced between June 2010 and April 2014: A revised assessment*. Briefing Note 108, Institute of Fiscal Studies. www.ifs.org.uk/projects/346(accessed 16 April 2011).

Bytheway, B. (2000) Youthfulness and agelessness: a comment, *Ageing and Society* 20(6) 781–9.

Calnan, M., Badcott, D. and Woolhead, G. (2006) Dignity under threat? A study of the experiences of older people in the United Kingdom, *International Journal of Health Services* 36(2): 355–75.

Carey, M. (2009) Critical commentary: happy shopper? The problem with service user and carer participation, *British Journal of Social Work* 39(1): 179–88.

Carrigan, M. and Szmigin, I. (2000) Advertising in an ageing society, *Ageing and Society* 20: 217–33.

Carruthers, I. and Ormondroyd, J. (2009) *Achieving Age Equality in Health and Social Care*. London: Department of Health.

Carter, J. (1998) *Postmodernity and the Fragmentation of Welfare*. London: Routledge.

Clark, A. (2009) *Ageism and Age Discrimination in Primary and Community Health Care in the United Kingdom*. London: Centre for Policy on Ageing.

Clark, H., Dyer, S. and Horwook, J. (1998) *That Bit of Help: The High Value of Low Level Preventative Services for Older People.* York: Joseph Rowntree Foundation.

Clarke, A. and Warren, L. (2007) Hopes, fears and expectations about the future. What do older people's stories tell us about active ageing? *Ageing and Society* 27(4): 465–88.

Clarke, J. (2005) New Labour's citizens: activated, empowered, responsibilised, abandoned?, *Critical Social Policy* 25(4): 447–63.

Clements, L. (2004) *Community Care and the Law*, 3rd edn. London: Legal Action Group Publishers.

Clements, L. (2010) NHS Funding for continuing care in England: the revised (2009) guidance, *Journal of Social Care and Neurodisability* 1(1): 39–47.

Clough, R., Manthorpe, J., OPRSI (Green, B., Fox, D., Raymond, G., Wilson, P.), Raymond, V., Sumner, K., Bright, L. and Hay, J. (2007) *The Support Older People Want and the Services They Need.* York: Joseph Rowntree Foundation.

Cordingley, L. and Webb, C. (1997) Independence and aging, *Reviews in Clinical Gerontology* 7(2): 137–46.

Counsel and Care (2008) *A Charter for Change: Reforming Care and Support for Older People, their Families and Carers.* London: Counsel and Care.

CSCI (Commission for Social Care Inspection) (2004) *Leaving Hospital: The Price of Delays.* London: CSCI.

CSCI (Commission for Social Care Inspection) (2005) *Leaving Hospital: Revisited.* London: CSCI.

CSCI (Commission for Social Care Inspection) (2006) *Handled with Care? Managing Medication for Residents of Care Homes and Children's Homes: A Follow-up Study.* London: CSCI.

CSCI (2009) *The State of Social Care in England 2007–2008.* London: CSCI.

CSJ (The Centre for Social Justice) (2010) *The Forgotten Age: Understanding Poverty and Social Exclusion Later in Life.* London: The Centre for Social Justice.

Currie, J. (2004) *The Take Up of Social Benefits.* NBER Working Paper No. 10488. Cambridge, MA: National Bureau of Economic Research.

Davidson, S. (2005) *A Demographic Time Bomb? The Politics of Ageing and the British Media.* Paper presented to the 55th Political Studies Association Annual Conference, 4–7 April 2005, University of Leeds.

DH (Department of Health) (2001) *National Service Framework for Older People.* London: Department of Health.

DH (Department of Health) (2006) *Our Health, Our Care, Our Say: A New Direction for Community Services.* London: Department of Health.

DH (Department of Health) (2007) *Putting People First: A Shared Vision and Commitment to the Transformation of Adult Social Care.* London: Department of Health.

DH (Department of Health) (2010) *A Vision for Adult Social Care: Capable Communities and Active Citizens.* http: //www.dh.gov.uk/prod_consum_dh/groups/dh_digitalassets/@dh/@en/@ps/documents/digitalasset/dh_121971.pdf (accessed 7 September 2011).

DHSS (Department of Health and Social Security) (1981) *Growing Older.* London: HMSO.

Dominy, N. and Kempson, E. (2006) *Understanding Older People's Experiences of Poverty and Material Deprivation.* Research Report 363. Leeds: Department of Work and Pensions.

Duffy, S. (2005) *Keys to Citizenship: A Guide to Getting Good Support for People with Learning Disabilities*. Birkenhead: Paradigm.

DWP (Department for Work and Pensions) (2005) *Opportunity Age: Meeting the Challenges of Ageing in the 21st Century*. London: Department for Work and Pensions.

Edmonson, R. and Von Kondratowitz, H. (2009) *Valuing Older People: A Humanist Approach to Ageing*. Bristol: Policy Press.

Edquist, K. (2004) Cohesion through consumerism: the new European social model? Paper presented at the Annual Meeting of the International Studies Association, Montreal, 17 March.

Ellis, K. (2007) Direct payments and social work practice: the significance of 'street-level bureaucracy' in determining eligibility, *British Journal of Social Work* 37(3): 405–22.

Ellis, K., Davis, A. and Rummery, K. (1999) Needs assessment, street-level bureaucracy and the new community care, *Social Policy and Administration* 33(3): 262–80.

Estes, C.L. (1979) *The Aging Enterprise*. San Francisco, CA: Jossey-Bass.

Estes, C.L. (2001) *Social Policy and Aging: A Critical Perspective*. Thousand Oaks, CA: Sage.

Evans, E.J. (2004) *Thatcher and Thatcherism*, 2nd edn. London: Routledge.

Ferguson, I. (2007) Increasing user choice or privatizing risk? The antinomies of personalization, *British Journal of Social Work* 37(3): 387–403.

Ferguson, I. and Lavalette, M. (2005) 'Another world is possible': social work and the struggle for social justice, in I. Ferguson, M. Lavalette and E. Whitmore (eds) *Globalisation, Global Justice and Social Work*. London: Routledge.

Fineman, M.A. (1998) The inevitability of dependency and the politics of subsidy, *Stanford Law and Policy Review* 89: 91–3.

Foster, J., Dale, J. and Jessopp, L. (2001) A qualitative study of older people's views of out of hours services, *British Journal of General Practice* 51(470): 719–23.

Gibson, D. (1998) *Aged Care: Old Policies and New Problems*. Cambridge: Cambridge University Press.

Giddens, A. (1991) *Modernity and Self-identity*. Oxford: Polity Press.

Gilleard, C. and Higgs, P. (2002). The third age: class, cohort or generation?, *Ageing and Society* 22: 369–82.

Glasby, J., Ham, C., Littlechild, R. and McKay, S. (2010) *The Case for Social Care Reform – The Wider Economic and Social Benefits*. Birmingham: University of Birmingham.

Glasby, J. and Littlechild, R. (2004) *The Health and Social Care Divide: The Experiences of Older People*, 2nd edn. Bristol: The Policy Press.

Glasby, J. and Littlechild, R. (2009) *Direct Payments and Personal Budgets: Putting Personalisation into Practice*, 2nd edn. Bristol: The Policy Press.

Godfrey, M., Townsend, J. and Denby, T. (2004) *Building a Good Life for Older People in Local Communities: The Experience of Ageing in Time and Place*. York: Joseph Rowntree Foundation.

Goodman, A., Myck, M. and Shephard, A. (2003) *Sharing in the Nation's Prosperity? Pensioner Poverty in Britain*, Commentary 93. London: Institute for Fiscal Studies.

Greenberg, J., Shimel, J. and Martins, A. (2004) Ageism: denying the face of the future, In T.D. Nelson (ed.) *Ageism: Stereotyping and Prejudice Against Older Persons*. Cambridge, MA: MIT Press.

Griffiths, R. (1988) *Community Care: Agenda for Action*. London: HMSO.

Healthcare Commission, Audit Commission and Commission for Social Care Inspection (2006) *Living Well in Later Life: A Review of Progress Against the National Service Framework for Older People*. London: Healthcare Commission.

Henwood, M. and Hudson, B. (2008) *Prevention, Personalisation and Prioritisation in Social Care: Squaring the Circle*. London: Commission for Social Care Inspections.

Hills, J. (1998) *Thatcherism, New Labour and the Welfare State*. London: LSE.

HM Government (2005) *A Strategy for an Ageing Population*. London: The Stationery Office.

HM Government (2007) *Putting People First: A Shared Vision and Commitment to the Transformation of Adult Social Care*. London: HM Government.

Howse, K. (2007) *Health and Social Care for Older People in the UK: A Snapshot View*. Working Paper 607. Oxford: Oxford Institute of Ageing.

Hughes, C.M. and Goldie, R. (2009) 'I just take what I am given': adherence and resident involvement in decision-making on medicines in nursing homes for older people, *Drugs and Aging* 26(6): 505–17.

Inman, P. (2010) The left must tackle the baby boomers' timebomb, *Guardian*, 6 December.

Johns, R. (2011) *Social Work, Social Policy and Older People*. Basingstoke: Macmillan.

Jordan, B. (2001) Tough love: social work, social exclusion and the Third Way, *British Journal of Social Work* 31: 527–46.

Kemshall, H. (2002) *Risk, Social Policy and Welfare*. Buckingham: McGraw-Hill/Open University Press.

King's Fund (2000) *Age Discrimination in Health and Social Care*. Briefing note. London: King's Fund.

King's Fund (2011) *Social Care Funding and the NHS: An Impending Crisis?* London: King's Fund.

King's Fund (2005) *The Business of Caring: King's Fund Inquiry into Care Services for Older People in London*. London: King's Fund Publications.

Kite, M.E. and Wagner, L.S. (2004) Attitudes toward older adults, in T.D. Nelson (ed.) *Ageism: Stereotyping and Prejudice Against Older Persons*. Cambridge, MA: MIT Press.

Kumar, K. (1995) *From Post-Industrial to Post-Modern Society*. Oxford: Basil Blackwell.

Leadbeater, C. (2004) *Personalisation Through Participation: A New Script for Public Services*. London: Demos.

Leadbeater, C., Bartlett, J. and Gallagher, N. (2008) *Making it Personal*. London: Demos.

Levitas, R., Pantazis, C., Fahmy, E., Gordon, D., Lloyd, E. and Patsios, D. (2007) *The Multi-dimensional Analysis of Social Exclusion. A Research Report for the Social Exclusion Task Force*. London: The Cabinet Office.

Lewis, J. (2001) Older people and the health–social care boundary in the UK: half a century of hidden policy conflict, *Social Policy & Administration* 35(4): 343–59.

Lewis, J. and Glennerster, H. (1996) *Implementing the New Community Care*. Buckingham: Open University Press.

Lister, R. (1997) *Citizenship: Feminist Perspectives*. Basingstoke: Macmillan.

Llewellyn, A., Agu, L. and Mercer, D. (2008) *Sociology for Social Workers*. Cambridge: Polity Press.

Lymbery, M. (2006) United we stand? Partnership working in health and social care, *British Journal of Social Work* 36(7): 1119–34.

Lymbery, M. (2010) A new vision for adult social care? Continuities and change in the care of older people, *Critical Social Policy* 30(1): 5–26.

McKay, S. and Rowlington, K. (1999) *Social Security in Britain*. Basingstoke: Macmillan.

McLaughlin, H. (2009) What's in a name: 'client', 'patient', 'customer', 'consumer', 'expert by experience', 'service user' – what's next?, *British Journal of Social Work* 39: 1101–17.

Mandelstam, M. (2005) *Community Care Practice and the Law*, 3rd edn. London: Jessica Kingsley.

Means, R. and Smith, R. (1998) *From Poor Law to Community Care*. Bristol: The Policy Press.

Minichiello, V., Browne, J. and Kendig, H. (2000) Perceptions and consequences of ageism: views of older people, *Ageing and Society* 20: 253–78.

NHS Information Centre (2010) *Social Care and Mental Health Indicators from the National Indicator Set: Further Analysis 2009–10*. http//www.iconhs.uk/webfiles/publications/009_Social_Care/socmhi09–0final/Provisional_Report_Social_Care_and_Mental_Health_Indicators_200910.pdf (accessed 7 September 2011).

Oliver, M. (1990) *The Politics of Disablement*. Basingstoke: Macmillan.

Oliver, M. (1996) *Understanding Disability: From Theory to Practice*. Basingstoke: Macmillan.

Ottenheimer, H.J. (2008) *The Anthropology of Language: An Introduction to Linguistic Anthropology*. Belmont, CA: Wadsworth.

Pateman, C. (2000) The patriarchal welfare state, in K. Nash (ed.) *Readings in Contemporary Political Sociology*. Malden, MA: Blackwell.

Pensions Commission (2006) *Implementing an Integrated Package of Pension Reforms: The Final Report of the Pensions Commission*. London: The Stationery Office.

PIU (Performance and Innovation Unit) (2000) *Winning the Generation Game*. London: The Stationery Office.

Powell, J., Robison, J., Roberts, H. and Thomas, G. (2007) The single assessment process in primary care: older people's accounts of the process, *British Journal of Social Work* 37: 1043–58.

Price, D. (2006) The poverty of older people in the UK, *Journal of Social Work Practice* 20(3): 251–66.

Priestley, M. (1999) *Disability Politics and Community Care*. London: Jessica Kingsley.

Rees Jones, I., Hyde, M., Higgs, P. and Victor, C.R. (2008) *Ageing in a Consumer Society: From Passive to Active Consumption in Britain*. Bristol: Policy Press.

Richards, S. and Coast, J. (2003) Interventions to improve access to health and social care after discharge from hospital: a systematic review, *Journal of Health Service Research and Policy* 8(3): 171–9.

Scharf, T. (2007) The extremes of age: challenging poverty, promoting inclusion. Inaugural Lecture, Westminster Theatre, Chancellor's Building, Keele University, 15 May. www.keele.ac.uk/(accessed 20 December 2007).

Scharf, T., Bartlam, B., Hislop, J., Bernard, M., Dunning, A. and Sim, J. (2006) *Necessities of Life: Older People's Experiences of Poverty*. London: Help the Aged.

Scharpf, F. (1997) Economic integration, democracy and the welfare state, *Journal of European Public Policy* 4(1): 18–36.

Schmidt, V.A. (2002) Does discourse matter in the politics of welfare state adjustment?, *Comparative Political Studies* 35(2): 168–93.

Schwehr, B. (2010) Safeguarding and personalisation, *Journal of Adult Protection* 12(2): 43–50.

SCIE (2010a) *Personalisation: A Rough Guide*. London: Social Care Institute for Excellence.

SCIE (2010b) *SCIE Guide 15: Dignity in Care*. London: Social Care Institute for Excellence.

Scourfield, P. (2007) Social care and the modern citizen: client, consumer, service user, manager and entrepreneur, *British Journal of Social Work* 37(1): 107–22.

Sheehy, G. (1995) 'New Passages', *US News and World Report*, June 9.

Social Exclusion Unit (2005) *Excluded Older People*. London: ODPM.

Spicker, P. (2002) *Poverty and the Welfare State: Dispelling the Myths*. London: Catalyst.

Stevenson, O. (2008) Neglect as an aspect of the mistreatment of elderly people: reflections on the issues, *The Journal of Adult Protection* 10(1): 24–35.

Tanner, D. (2003) Older people and access to care, *British Journal of Social Work* 33: 499–515.

Tanner, D. and Harris, J. (2008) *Working with Older People*. Abingdon: Routledge.

Taylor, P.A. and Harris, J. (2008) *Critical Theories of Mass Media Culture: Then and Now*. Buckingham: Open University Press.

Thompson, P. (1992) 'I don't feel old': subjective ageing and the search for meaning in later life, *Ageing and Society* 12(2): 23–47.

Thornton, J.E. (2002) Myths of aging or ageist stereotypes, *Educational Gerontology* 28: 301–12.

Tinker, A. (1997) *Older People in Modern Society*. London: Longman.

Townsend, J., Godfrey, M. and Denby, T.J. (2006) Heroines, villains and victims: older people's perceptions of others, *Ageing and Society* 26: 883–900.

Vojak, C. (2009) Choosing language: social service framing and social justice, *British Journal of Social Work* 39: 936–49.

Walker, A. (1981) Towards a political economy of old age, *Ageing and Society* 1: 73–94.

Walker, A. (1987) The poor relation: poverty among old women, in C. Glendenning and J. Millar (eds) *Women and Poverty*. Brighton: Wheatsheaf.

Walker, A. (ed.) (1996) *The New Generational Contract, Intergenerational Relations, Old Age and Welfare*. London: University College London Press.

Walker, A. (1999) The future of pensions and retirement in Europe: towards a productive aging, *Hallym International Journal of Aging* 1: 3–15.

Walker, A. (2005) Towards an international political economy of ageing, *Ageing and Society* 25: 815–39.

Walker, A. (2011) Older people, in *Defence of Welfare: The Impact of the Spending Review*. Social Policy Association. www.social-policy.org.uk (accessed 16 April 2011).

Wilding, P. (2000) *The Welfare State 2000–2050*. Paper presented to the Political Studies Association-UK 50th Annual Conference, London, 10–13 April.

Williams, F. (2001) In and beyond New Labour: towards a new political ethics of care, *Critical Social Policy* 21(4): 467–93.

Windle, K., Wagland, R., Forder, J., D'Amico, F., Janssen, D. and Wistow, G. (2009) *National Evaluation of Partnerships for Older People Projects: Final Report*. Canterbury: Personal Social Services Research Unit, University of Kent.

Woolhead, G., Calnan, M. and Dieppe, P. (2004) Dignity in older age: what do older people in the United Kingdom think?, *Age and Ageing* 33(2): 165–70.

PART 2

Equality and diversity in working with older people

3 Working with older people from Black and ethnic minorities

Chris Gaine

After reading this chapter you should be able to:

- show informed awareness of ethnic, cultural, religious and linguistic variation in Britain;
- appreciate something of the life histories of older minorities, their work, connections with roots, family networks, experiences of discrimination, patterns of illness;
- critically engage with assumptions about the role of women, religion and of supportive extended families;
- apply this to issues of personalized care;
- feel confident about areas of knowledge and relative ignorance, and know how to seek advice, information and support.

Introduction

As a social worker 'race' is really only important because of the effects of *racism* on service users (and maybe on you). 'Race' itself has no inherent significance, though part of racism is the belief that groups that look different are significantly different under the skin. In fact they aren't. 'Race' is a simplistic nineteenth-century idea that's lingered on in everyday discourse because it makes superficial sense, though it's long past its scientific sell-by date. Skin colour – the most obvious 'racial' characteristic – is useless in *biological* terms at predicting sporting ability; however, if one thinks in *social* terms, skin colour can predict pretty well who has access to golf courses and swimming pools and hence why Black people in some sports are the exception rather than the rule.

'Race' is an imposed and superficial category, albeit one that has had a massive and oppressive historical impact; ethnicity is about culture, language, customs, religious practices, patterns of family relationships and how people choose to live their lives. This puts the matter very briefly, but it's crucial. 'Ethnic' does not mean dark-skinned. The white British are a *majority* ethnic group in the UK, unlike Indians and the Chinese, who are *minority* ethnic groups. The common abbreviation BME (Black and minority ethnic) is intended to be broad, inclusive of eastern Europeans, Jews and the Irish, and

Black is more often than not written with a capital to signify that it's a socio-political term rather than a simple description of skin tone.

Some issues arise for BME older people because of culture, and some arise because of discriminatory treatment and experience. This is something like the distinction made by Modood (1992) between someone's 'mode of being' and their 'mode of oppression'; the effects of culture and the effects of 'race'.

Problems of generalization and stereotyping

One of the things that bedevils popular perceptions, media discourse and professional training about BME groups is generalization: 'The Chinese are . . .', 'Africans are likely to . . .', 'one issue with Muslims is . . .' and so on. This happens to older people too: any lack of first-hand contact, compounded with a lack of voice for the groups in question, makes for fertile territory for generalizations and stereotypes. It's difficult for a social worker to be experienced enough to have good first-hand knowledge of all BME groups, so your starting point has to be some kind of generalization. The important skill to develop is a constant reflection on what is individual and what is common, both in terms of cultural patterns and also in people's experience of difference. It's not an appropriate or skilled approach to say 'everyone is an individual and there are no patterns or similarities', or to think 'they're all the same, this case will be typical and predictable'.

Activity 3.1

List what you consider to be the main minority ethnic groups in Britain.

How much first-hand familiarity do you have with each, and how much second-hand knowledge from study or the media?

Which groups are most prone to being stereotyped with regard to social care?

Ethnic diversity: context and history

Britain became the ethnically and racially diverse country it is today within the lifetime of anyone aged about 65. To enable you to have a shared understanding with someone you're working with, Table 3.1 divides this recent history into several phases. This inevitably over-simplifies a complex history, but there are three patterns.

First, relative concentration. Apart from Chinese communities in Soho and Bangladeshis in the Shoreditch/Whitechapel area of East London these two groups are widely dispersed around the whole UK because of employment in catering. Other groups are more concentrated in towns and cities (especially London) or in the former industrial centres to which they were drawn by (low paid) job opportunities.

Table 3.1 Immigration as a source of ethnic diversity since the 1930s

Rough dates	Countries of origin	Motive for migration
1930s	Countries occupied by Nazis	Jews fearing persecution and death
1940s	Italy	Some Italian prisoners of war stayed, other Italians invited under scheme for post-war reconstruction
1940s	Poland	Some Polish fighters stayed, some displaced by border changes
Late 1940s–early 1980s	Caribbean	Recruited by understaffed transport and health services. Temporary, but majority settled
Late 1950s, 1960s–present	India and Pakistan	First arrivals (overwhelmingly men) recruited to meet labour shortages; family reunification began 1960s
1950s–1970s	Irish	Work in construction, manufacturing, transport and health service, adding to nineteenth-century migration
Late 1960s, early 1970s	Indians born in East-Africa	Middle-class refugees with British passports, expelled by African leaders
1980s	Chinese; Bangladeshis	Catering and (for Bangladeshis) garment trade. Family reunification later than Indians
1980s–2000 on	Africans	Study; skilled employment opportunities; asylum
2004 on	Poland; other new EU	Higher wages, job opportunities

Second, apart from the beginning and end of the timeline people migrated from former colonies. While you may be unsure which countries were once part of the empire, in the late 1940s a quarter of the people on the planet were ruled from London. When older BME people first migrated there was no such doubt about the colonial connection: their education would have been heavily influenced by Britain's; many a Caribbean or Indian man now in his 80s will have fought in the war and many of their families will have older siblings who died fighting in it.

The third pattern is skin colour: by far the largest minorities are from outside Europe, and this has implications for their lives here.

Different age and gender structures

The dates above point to a distinctive feature of immigrant populations everywhere: their different age structure. People tend to migrate seeking a better life when they're young, so while in the 1960s schools were beginning to receive children of immigrant background either born here or reunited with parents, minority ethnic clients were unusual in old people's services. The same is true for health care: maternity services had to begin to deal with a changing population in the 1970s, but geriatric care was scarcely affected. A man from Pakistan who arrived aged 25 in 1960 only reached retirement age in the early 2000s, and any younger or later arrivals may still be working, so the immigrant population is younger than the majority, and the most recent arrivals are younger still. The largest group of migrants to have arrived since 2001 are about 700,000 Poles, overwhelmingly under 35, and while some have since had children and others have settled and brought their parents here, they will not appear for some years yet on social workers' caseloads of older people.

The most recent Annual Population Survey with relevant data (ONS 2010) shows that whereas 17 per cent of white British people are over 65, the only minority ethnic group that approaches this figure is Black Caribbean at 13 per cent. Only seven per cent of Indians in Britain are this age and only five per cent of Indians and Pakistanis. On the other hand, a higher percentage of the British Chinese, Indian and Pakistani population are in the 16–64 age range. These figures show that for some time to come social workers will meet fewer BME older people than they might expect. It's not because they die young and it's not always because less use is made of care services; there are just fewer of them, fewer still among the very old, and slightly fewer women than men in the older age groups, reflecting something of immigration patterns decades ago.

Returning to the earlier caution about generalization, it's worth remembering that of course one *will* meet older Africans and Chinese, and while a Polish man in his 80s may be one of the 1940s settlers, he might instead be the father or grandfather of a recent migrant worker.

As a country this age structure provides us with particular challenges and opportunities. A bulge in the younger age groups means more demands on schools because of numbers, but it also means we have a larger young workforce supporting the rising numbers of people who live longer because of better health. It will take decades before the percentage of BME older people matches that of the majority, so in that respect immigrants are a less expensive group (in contrast with the common rhetoric of immigrants being a burden).

Who's missing?

There are various groups not included in Table 3.1, because although they may be visible in particular towns, to the media, or to social workers, they aren't numerically significant. For instance, many Filipina nurses have been recruited into care homes, but it would be hard to find one as a care home resident.

Refugees are another group not featuring explicitly in the table, partly because they're a very disparate group from many different countries and partly because there are not nearly as many as tabloid newspapers suggest. In 2007 the Home Office reported that refugees made up just two per cent of immigrant numbers, and in 2009 the United Nations High Commissioner for Refugees estimated they made up half of one per cent of the British population. Few of these are old when they arrive, indeed the UNHCR estimates that 45 per cent of the people they are responsible for are under 18 (Migration Policy Institute 2010). Consider the kind of situations refugees escape from, and the means of doing so: younger people have a better survival rate.

The date when refugees came from a particular trouble spot is a guide to their likely age structure: Jews escaping the Holocaust are Britain's oldest group of refugees, followed by Hungarians fleeing a counter-communist uprising in 1956. Although not a numerous group, many of the Vietnamese refugees of the 1970s are now in their 60s and 70s.

Activity 3.2

What corrections can you make to your answers to Activity 3.1?

The relevance of culture and ethnicity

Family structure

A study in the late 1990s (Modood et al. 1997) showed little difference between ethnic groups in terms of contact between parents and adult children who didn't live with them: around 60 per cent of each group having been in personal and phone contact at least four times in the previous month (though minorities were frequently in touch with relatives abroad). On the other hand, living in the same household with different generations was more common among Pakistani, Indian and Bangladeshi families:

> The scarcity of small elderly households among minority groups is not just because the migrants have not yet reached old age. That is part of the explanation, but we have also found that minority elders, especially Asians, often lived with their sons and daughters [. . .] that means that the majority of elderly Asians live in large complex households . . .
>
> (Modood et al. 1997: 46).

Only about 20 per cent of Asians over 60 years old lived in small elderly households, compared with almost 90 per cent of whites of the same age. Another index of family closeness is how many people over 60 had an adult child living with them in the same household: only 13 per cent of whites did, compared with a third of Caribbeans and between 60 and 70 per cent for different Asian groups, reaching 72 per cent among the Chinese. The authors comment: 'Most of them were not yet of an age when they would require personal care; but when they reached that age, they would be much better placed to ask for help from their family than their white equivalents' (Modood et al. 1997: 45).

Various authors describe joint family structures more common among South Asians: 'An endogamous, kinship-based group with reciprocal relationships of moral, financial and social obligations, and it is an important source of identity and support' (Ahmad 1996: 55). It needs to be remembered, however, that these are not always harmonious units. There can be internal competition and conflict between siblings and generations (Ahmad 1996: 58), and, while it was a potential source of support, the 'community' was sometimes experienced as 'a somewhat oppressive presence in their lives, monitoring and judging behaviour' (Salway et al. 2007: 22). There are class dimensions in this too, with middle-class families being less closely involved, resulting in 'some distancing between kin occupying different class positions, which is usually [. . .] reflected in residential segregation' (Ahmad 1996: 59), and the largely Hindu and Sikh Indians tend to be better off than Pakistani and Bangladeshi Muslims and show more signs of family change. Women are likely to be regarded as guardians of different groups' culture and values, at least in the domestic sphere.

Not unrelated to the existence of the joint families described above, there is a clichéd and much criticized notion about ethnic minorities, especially south Asians: 'they look after their own' (Dominelli and Small 1988; Atkin and Rollings 1993; Ahmad 1996; Dominelli 2002). The problem for social workers is to disentangle when this serves as an excuse for shedding part of a busy workload (Walker and Ahmad 1994), or an avoidance of leaving a comfort zone of shared cultural expectations, or when it accurately describes a different set of cultural norms about who takes responsibility for elder family members.

With the largest, well-established groups – South Asian people – there is more networked family support than for the white majority, but this is not universally so, is much less true for Caribbean people, and is subject to change. One can see the risk of generalizing from the 2001 census finding that 10 per cent of White British and Irish adults were providing informal care to relatives, friends and neighbours, but so were 10 per cent of Indian adults, compared with 4 per cent of people from Mixed and Black African groups. This probably reflects the older age structures of White and Indian groups, but it shows that the present, let alone the future, is unpredictable.

It has been suggested that, counter to common assumptions, there was a higher take-up of residential care amongst minorities, that their health was rather poorer, and they perhaps did not live as long:

> which seems to indicate that they left it late to be admitted. This would imply that the low health expectancy of people in ethnic minorities means that care services are needed earlier, and that to achieve equity with the white group rather higher admission rates might be expected than at present.
>
> (Bebbington et al. 2001: 4)

Care home provision, or specialist accommodation, is therefore a growing and complex issue, requiring different assumptions about financial assessments if housing is jointly owned, and different provision in terms of linguistic, dietary and religious needs. Whereas it is relatively feasible for a widowed white property owner to sell a single-occupancy home to pay for residential care, it's more complicated if it's shared by other family members.

Other distinct issues emerge for ethnic minorities, even if families take on more daily responsibility than is common. For instance, in all groups carers are more likely to be women, though BME women carers may experience a greater sense of isolation (McCalman 1990) and probably because of higher rates of ill health among adults, Indian, Bangladeshi and Pakistani children are almost twice as likely to be carers as white children (Dunnell 2008).

There are also the extra economic costs of caring, for rooms set aside, special diets, sometimes additional laundry, higher heating bills and lost job opportunities. In

Identifying which language is used by an older person is not always straightforward, especially if you are not familiar with the intricacies of linguistic variation within a particular ethnic group. Bangladeshis speak the Sylheti dialect of Bengali, colloquially called Bangla, so what language do they speak?

Any printed guide to these intricacies will inevitably be inadequate, so one has to discover preferred family languages in as much detail as possible (including its alternative names). The Internet is a good source of specific information: the National Centre for Languages (CILT) has constantly updated and authoritative information (www.cilt.org.uk) and Wikipedia is a source of obscure detail not easily found elsewhere; it's not always totally accurate, but it's a good starting point.

Religion

While Chinese people are just as likely as white people to say they have no religion, '. . . religion is central in the self-definition of the majority of South Asian people' (Modood et al. 1997: 297). Caribbean people are more likely to be active Christians than white people, with a greater adherence to smaller, Black-majority churches than to Anglicanism or Catholicism (Modood et al. 1997: 305). You need to know the faith of anyone you work with if they have one, since it would be relevant if residential care was ever required, or if someone is fasting, or if you want to arrange an appointment on a non-Christian's equivalent of a Sunday.

Diet is an aspect of religion, and faith has a major influence on what various ethnic groups will and will not eat. Some universals are easy: never pork for Muslims or Jews and never beef for Hindus or Sikhs, but then individual and family variation comes into play. Though less common among Sikhs and very unusual for Muslims, some Hindus are completely vegetarian; some Muslims are quite relaxed about whether the meat they eat is *halal*, while others are very strict, as are some Jews with *kosher* provision. Though Islam prohibits alcohol (and Sikhism takes a strong line against tobacco) you'll find exceptions. With taboos about these things there is likely to be a greater shame in dependence and hence more reluctance to reveal it.

Gender roles are related to faith too, with impacts upon income and pension rights. Amongst working-age women, about a quarter of Christians, a third of Hindus and Sikhs and two thirds of Muslims are economically inactive (Open Society Institute 2005).

Table 3.3 'Religion is very important to how I live my life'

| Age | Percentage agreeing with statement | | | | | |
---	White	Caribbean	Indian	Pakistani	Bangladeshi	Chinese
All	13	34	47	73	76	11
16–34	5	18	35	67	67	7
35–49	13	43	56	81	92	8
50+	20	57	59	83	81	31

Source: Derived from data in Modood et al. (1997: 308).

Beliefs and customs to do with death and dying

> Allah has provided a cure for every malady, except one which is old age.
>
> (*Hadith*: Abu Dawud 183: 2).

Whatever a person's faith or ethnic group, religion is especially significant around dying. In supporting an older person or their family leading up to death it is crucial to consider the place of belief systems in plans for a 'good death', in making sense of it, or just dealing with it. It's therefore important to ask about these from a standpoint of some basic information, for instance knowing the titles of relevant religious officials (priest/pastor/imam, etc.), conventions and expectations as death approaches (family presence, prayers, rituals), and practices after death (washing, cremation, speed of burial, taboos about post-mortems).

For example, Muslim practice is generally for relatives and those known to the dying person to seek forgiveness before death occurs, which may entail many people present at the bedside. The bed should ideally face Mecca (south east in the UK). There are debates within Islam about when it is permissible to cease medical intervention, but assisted dying is unambiguously forbidden. A devout Muslim is expected to be resigned to death, accepting it as God's will. Afterwards relatives should thank God saying 'We are all of God and we shall return to Him' and the body should be washed and wrapped in a simple white shroud by two devout Muslims of the same sex. Ideally there should be no post-mortem, and the body should be buried facing Mecca within 24 hours, women traditionally seldom being present at funerals. Most older people die in either a care home or a hospital, and it is easy to see why a Muslim family may have anxieties about any of these details being taken out of their control.

Afterwards, it needs to be borne in mind that individuals in some faiths, including Christianity, may regard despair or anger at someone's death, and hence bereavement counselling, as irreligious, since relief should come from God. Some believers would not accept the Kübler-Ross model of a natural progression from denial through anger, bargaining, depression and final acceptance in response to the death of a loved one. Loss, in other words, is socially defined, and the idea of individual bereavement may not make sense to everyone. There is no formulaic strategy that can be applied here, except to be sensitive to this possibility and prepared to seek informed advice.

Health, illness and disability

There is a five times greater incidence of diabetes among South Asians, twice as many Pakistani men have cardiovascular disease than white men (the rate in Irish men and women is also high), and there are other conditions like high blood pressure with complex relationships to diet, exercise and stress. Less is known about mental health overall, since it is less culturally recognized in some communities, though 2008 data shows Black men have higher admission rates and are more likely to be compulsorily admitted.

In the 2001 census some ethnic groups reported higher rates of poor health. Pakistani and Bangladeshi women reported the highest rates and Chinese men reported

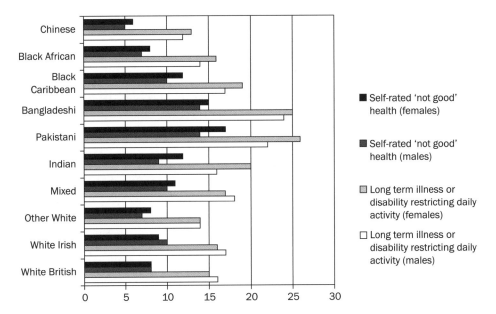

Figure 3.1 'Not good' health and long term illness or disability.

Source: Derived from data in 2001 census (ONS).

the lowest, which closely matches the relative proportions reporting long-standing illness or disability. Women reported higher rates of poor health than men in all Asian and Black groups.

Disability is a socially constructed phenomenon, so there will be different notions of which impairments disable people if they live in a joint family: consider for instance being partially sighted, or unable to walk unaided. But one only has to project Figure 3.1 into the future to see the likely scale of support needs as the least healthy groups become older, with added financial hardship through unclaimed benefits: 'reluctance to be identified as "disabled" or "incapacitated" made some unwilling to claim. However, the system itself was a barrier, being seen as unfair, stressful and complicated. Minority ethnic individuals were less likely than white people to receive sickness benefits'. (Salway et al. 2007, summary)

Experience of discrimination

Every minority ethnic older person does not have a history of struggling against racism, but many do. Some will have experienced it in the street, from neighbours or strangers; others will have received it from those in positions of power of various kinds: police, teachers, landlords, council officials, employers. As a social worker you may not perceive yourself as being in a position of power, but in some respects you are, so you might initially be treated with suspicion. Try to balance this unfairness against the years of unfairness that have led to it.

A 1970 study showed 65 per cent of British people thought they were inherently superior to Africans and Asians, and 42 per cent would make redundancy decisions solely on the grounds of colour. It's difficult to grasp today how overt racism was in the past, but you can hear first-hand accounts at www.generation3-0.org (see also Gill and Sveinsson 2011). Until 1968 it was perfectly legal to refuse housing or employment to someone on the basis of skin colour or ethnicity, and the first law to prevent it had few teeth.

> The pattern of discrimination . . . in British industry disclosed in these . . . studies appears to be so widespread and pervasive that an innocent stranger (or a frustrated black job applicant) could well believe that it is the result of a centralised directive, enthusiastically implemented, that the employment of coloured labour be restricted to those jobs that white men do not want.
>
> (Deakin 1970: 195)

A wealth of studies show systematic discrimination was routine in letting or buying accommodation, one in 1966 indicating a Black applicant would be refused six times out of ten (Daniel 1968). Council housing not designed for joint families inclined many south Asians to buy their own, and the segregation patterns we see today began in a past market restricted by discrimination and buying power. Those who trusted in council housing found themselves subject to the network of practices that led to Black Londoners' families being more often in old accommodation than new, in flats rather than houses, on less popular estates, and more likely to be on the higher floors of tower blocks (Smith 1977).

The police, too, were shown in numerous studies to have had explicitly racist attitudes which many didn't hesitate to express (Daniel 1968; Smith 1977) and several accounts of this were found in studies thirty years later (Modood et al. 1997: 281). Relations with the police, as perhaps the most visible manifestation of the state in people's lives, were at an all time low when riots in the 1980s

> highlighted the deplorable depths to which community–police relations had sunk in inner cities up and down the country where African-Caribbean people had settled. In Southall, with a high concentration of Asians, there was the clear and unmistakable view that the police were inordinately inactive in protecting Asian citizens from racist attacks . . .
>
> (Goulbourne 1998: 68)

This reached its climax with the death of Stephen Lawrence in 1993, subsequent investigation into the inadequate police response, the finding that the police were institutionally racist (MacPherson 1999) and ultimately the passing of a new and stronger discrimination law in 2000.

How much systematic discrimination still happens is not the point; there is no argument that it happened in the past. In dealing with a client group different from oneself it's always necessary to make an imaginative leap to see the world in a different way, to recognize different perspectives. This is self-evident when clients are much older, though perhaps it is more comfortable to value, for instance, the wartime experiences of older people than to recognize their struggle against widespread public racism. It can be hard to believe the state has one's best interest at heart when someone in the family has had no redress for discrimination, or when immigration policy has kept families apart for decades.

By the same token, older white people also grew up in a time when racial discrimination was routine, and they may indeed have practised it, so social workers from BME backgrounds may also encounter racism. They are entitled to support from employers (who are acting unlawfully otherwise) and in many metropolitan authorities there is likely to be a network of colleagues for informal support: they may be the only ones who understand the level of generosity, compassion and personal strength needed.

Outcome: economic inequality

As the accumulation of many past events and processes, minority ethnic people are generally poorer than the population as a whole: the 'ethnic penalty' (Modood et al. 1997). A compilation of data by the Home Office in 2003 showed that the risk of living in a low income household was lowest for white people at 17 per cent and highest for Bangladeshis and Pakistanis at 59 per cent (with Indians at 20 per cent, Black people at 27 per cent and Chinese at 23 per cent). The same study showed higher overall rates of unemployment were twice as high for minorities as white people and similar results were reported more recently by Palmer and Kenway (2008). At 2008 prices, household weekly expenditure was £502 per head for white people compared with £464 for Asians and £356 for Black people (ONS 2010). Decades of lower pay, greater risk of unemployment and – for some women – fewer contributions inevitably leads to a higher prevalence of low income and poverty among minority ethnic people. Even if there was no ethnic penalty nowadays, it lives on in pensions.

Outcome: are services open to all?

Formally receiving the Stephen Lawrence Report in Parliament, the Home Secretary said:

> We would all be deluding ourselves if we believe that the issues thrown up by this inquiry reflect only on the police. Indeed the implications of this report go much, much wider, and the very process of the inquiry has opened all our eyes to what it is like being Black or Asian in Britain today. And the inquiry process has revealed some fundamental truths about the nature of our society . . .
> (Straw, Hansard 24/02/1999)

We cannot therefore assume that just because the door to social care is not metaphorically locked, everyone feels free to walk through it – one may have to wedge the door open to prove it. In other words, services and the individuals who work in them have to be willing to uncover any personal and institutional barriers relating to language, food, ethos, unthought-out assumptions, and potentially inappropriate rules and structures. The task is to consider both culture and 'race'; how the way someone lives their life culture, community and family may hinder or help effective care (just as they can for ethnic majority people) and how racism may limit and constrain their options.

Some targeted services are clearly needed, though special provision can also marginalize, ghettoize, and allow mainstream provision to do too little to change. If too much emphasis is placed upon 'different' cultural practices minorities might be blamed for not being able to access services, or there could be an attempt to remedy someone's perceived cultural deficits by shifting them towards 'western values' (as if these were fixed). There is a balance to be negotiated.

Summary

This chapter has provided an overview of Britain's main minority ethnic groups and identified factors that might affect their social care, as well as their experience of the world as older people. It has also warned about over-generalizing and making assumptions based upon culture, language, religion or colour.

Further reading

Websites about caring support for BME people

Black and Minority Ethnic Carers' Support Service www.bmecarers.org.uk/
Carers' Federation www.carersfederation.co.uk/what-we-do/beconn/
Health Talk Online www.healthtalkonline.org/mental_health/mentalhealthcarers
Minority Ethnic Carers Support www.mecopp.org.uk/
Runnymede Trust filmed interviews with older people www.generation3-0.org
Social Care Institute for Excellence www.scie.org.uk/publications/guides/guide03/minority/index.asp
Swansea Local Authority www.swansea.gov.uk/index.cfm?articleid=16371
The Policy Research Institute on Ageing and Ethnicity, sells *Ethnicity, Older People and Palliative Care*, published jointly with National Council for Palliative Care in 2006 www.priae.org
www.movinghere.org.uk/galleries/histories/default.htm

References

Ahmad, W. (1996) The trouble with culture, in D. Kelleher and S. Hillier (eds) *Researching Cultural Difference in Health*. London: Routledge.
Atkin, K. and Rollings, J. (1993) *Community Care in Multi-racial Britain: A Critical Review of the Literature*. London: HMSO.

Bebbington, A., Darton, R. and Netten, A. (2001) *Care Homes for Older People (Volume 2): Admissions, Needs and Outcomes.* Canterbury: Personal Social Services Research Unit, University of Kent.

Daniel, W. (1968) *Racial Discrimination in England.* Harmondsworth: Penguin.

Deakin, N. (1970) *Colour Citizenship and British Society.* London: Panther.

Dominelli, L. (2002) *Anti-Oppressive Social Work Theory and Practice.* London: Palgrave Macmillan.

Dominelli, L. and Small, J. (1988) *Anti-racist Social Work: A Challenge for White Practitioners and Educators.* London: Palgrave Macmillan.

Dunnell, K. (2008) *Diversity and Different Experiences in the UK* (National Statistician's Annual Article on Society). London: ONS.

Gill, K. and Sveinsson, K.P. (2011) *Passing the Baton: Inter-generational Conceptions of Race and Racism in Birmingham.* London: Runnymede Trust.

Goulbourne, H. (1998) *Race Relations in Britain Since 1945.* Basingstoke: Macmillan.

Law, I., Karmani, I., Hylton, C. and Deacon, A. (1994) The provision of social security benefits to minority ethnic communities. Joseph Rowntree Trust Findings, *Social Policy Research* 59.

McCalman, J. (1990) *The Forgotten People.* London: King's Fund Centre.

Macpherson, W. (1999) *The Stephen Lawrence Inquiry: Report of an Inquiry by Sir William Macpherson of Cluny*, Cm 4262–1. London: The Stationery Office.

Migration Policy Institute (2010) Washington DC (www.MigrationInformation.org)

Modood, T. (1992; reissued 2011) *Not Easy Being British.* London: Runnymede Trust (with Trentham Books).

Modood, T., Berthoud, R., Lakey, J., Nazroo, J., Smith, P., Virdee, S. and Beishon, S. (1997) *Ethnic Minorities in Britain: Diversity and Disadvantage.* London: Policy Studies Institute.

ONS (Office of National Statistics) (2010) *Social Trends Vol. 40.* London: ONS.

Open Society Institute (2005) *British Muslims in the Labour Market.* Budapest: Open Society Institute, EUMAP.

Palmer, G. and Kenway, P. (2008) *Poverty Among Ethnic Groups: How and Why Does it Differ?* York: Joseph Rowntree Foundation.

Salway, S., Platt, L., Chowbey, P., Harriss K. and Bayliss, E. (2007) *Long Term Ill-Health, Poverty and Ethnicity.* Bristol: The Policy Press.

Smith, D. (1977) *Racial Disadvantage in Britain.* Harmondsworth: Penguin.

Walker, R. and Ahmad, W. (1994) Windows of opportunity in rotting frames: care providers' perspectives on community care and black communities, *Critical Social Policy* 40: 46–69.

4 Working with older people with mental health needs

David Gaylard

After reading this chapter you should be able to:

- discuss what is meant by good mental health and well-being in later life;
- identify the challenges to mental health and well-being and how might these be overcome;
- undertake activities that promote sound mental health, person-centred practice, and recovery with older people with mental illness;
- explore a case study of depression, suicide and alcohol abuse in an older person.

Introduction

There is a widely held view that older age is inevitably a period of physical and mental decline. However, only a minority of older people experience severe and enduring mental illness and much can be done to ameliorate both the risks and symptoms of the key mental disorders associated with later life (ONS 2004). The focus of this chapter is mental health and well-being in later life. In addition it also examines the links between depression and suicide among older people. It focuses on: identifying those at risk, working with people who have attempted suicide, how to challenge stigma and discrimination, BME perspectives, prevention and recovery. It concludes with a frequently overlooked field, that of older people and substance (alcohol) misuse.

Good mental health

Good mental health is as important in old age as it is at any other time of life. Everyone has mental health needs, whether or not they have a diagnosis of mental illness. Our mental health influences how we think and feel about ourselves and others, and our ability to communicate and manage change. It is central to health and well-being and has a significant impact upon our quality of life. Significantly, mental health is routinely identified by older people themselves as pivotal to ageing well (Bowling 2005).

Research consistently identifies that having a purposeful role, social status, good social relationships with family, friends and neighbours, an adequate income, remaining physically fit and living in a supportive neighbourhood, promote mental health (Age Concern 2003). Issues that older people identified as undermining mental health were their exit from the labour market (forced or planned retirement), deteriorating physical health, loss of independence, loneliness, fear of death, living in poor housing or neighbourhood and a decreased income (Victor 2005). The negative impact of losses tends to accumulate in later life, with physical illness being a key risk factor for developing mental health problems, particularly depression (Godfrey and Denby 2004). Loneliness is also a major factor leading to depression (Green et al. 1992) and an important cause of suicide and suicide attempts. How well older people adjust to late life challenges remains a key factor in determining ongoing mental health. Those older people who are able to adapt well tend to fare better (Robinson et al. 2005).

Activity 4.1

What is sound mental health?

Spend a few minutes thinking about how you would define what is good mental health and well-being.

What factors would you include?

Which factors might you exclude and why?

Key factors for sound mental health

Layard (2006) highlighted that in our knowledge economy, lifelong learning and sound mental health are increasingly vital to economic attainment and social cohesion. Layard identified eight key factors for a sound mental health: emotional and spiritual resilience; an underlying belief in our own worth and the worth of others; an ability to interpret the world around us as open to positive influences; realizing our own abilities; being able and willing to contribute to society as a citizen; creating positive relationships with the world around us; sustaining mutually satisfying relationships and taking control of our lives as much as possible.

The National Service Framework for Older People

In 2001, The National Service Framework for Older People (DH 2001) was published which initially had substantial influence on the development and direction of national standards to improve the quality and consistency of health and social care services for older people. It outlined eight key standards linked with overall aims to inform and support the key themes of the NHS modernization agenda of the time. For the focus of this chapter, three key NSF standards appear relevant:

Standard 2: Person-centred care aimed to ensure that older people are treated as individuals and receive appropriate and timely packages of care which meet their needs as individuals regardless of health and social care boundaries.

Standard 7: Mental health in older people aimed to promote good mental health in older people and to treat and support those older people with depression and dementia.

Standard 8: Promoting an active, healthy life aimed to extend the healthy life expectancy of older people.

In 2006, the Commission for Healthcare Audit and Inspection published a review of progress against the NSF for Older People titled *Living Well in Later Life*. They concluded there were three key areas that required further action without which sustainable improvement in the experiences of older people of public services are unlikely to be achieved. These were:

i   tackling discrimination, ageist attitudes and increased awareness of other diversity issues;
ii   ensuring that all of the standards set out in the national service framework (NSF) are met;
iii strengthening working in partnership between all the agencies providing services for older people to ensure that agencies work together to improve the experiences of older people that use public services.

(Commission for Healthcare Audit and Inspection 2006: 82)

Challenging stigma and discrimination

Older people with mental health problems face the combination of age discrimination coupled with the stigma of mental illness. The Social Exclusion Unit identified discrimination against people with mental health problems as the greatest barrier to social inclusion, quality of life and recovery.

There has been relatively little examination of the specific impact of age discrimination on mental health; it is well established that discrimination in any form is a risk factor for poor mental health (Thornicroft 2006). It can lower self-esteem, sometimes leading to feelings of worthlessness and despair. The result may be lowered expectations of rights and capabilities that prevent older people from contributing to society and enjoying life to the full.

There has been an established service delivery convention to organize mental health services separately for young, working age and older adults with an arbitrary service 'cut off' point being set at 65 years of age. Mental health services are unique in this approach which is becoming increasingly anachronistic, bearing in mind the cessation of the statutory retirement age coupled with an integrated health and social care system that is meant to be person centred and increasingly needs led based upon equality of access. The separation of mental health services could be viewed as discriminatory, however, there is also concern that a simplistic generic approach could lead to the loss of specialist mental health services that some older people require (Hurst 2009).

Our individual identities are not solely determined by our age but by many other factors, for example, our beliefs, race, gender, gender identity, disability, religion and sexual orientation. Although people may face discrimination as a result of any of these aspects of our identity or any combination of them, there is still a service provision tendency to 'classify', segregate and congregate older people together simply according to age. Yet all these factors can be as relevant to older people as younger people.

Older people are often perceived as being 'less worthy' than others. One result of such devaluation is social rejection, separation and exclusion. This can lead to older people being denied or having restricted access to things that we, as citizens, value and take for granted. In turn this becomes a vicious cycle; less opportunity leads to less participation, which in turn leads to an older person withdrawing and becoming isolated. The loss of valued relationships, respect, autonomy and participation are exactly the kinds of experiences that bring about depression, despair and isolation – factors which often consistently correlate with suicide in older people.

One way that we often respond to such claims is to express a view that older people choose to do these things as it's about them disengaging from the world and as such a part of growing old. Some people do prefer the company of other older people and do want space to reflect and look back on their lives; but not at the expense of all the other kinds of possible experiences they could have. Growing older is part of life but older people like everyone else have the right to engage and participate in all aspects of community life (Beeston 2006).

This may appear a somewhat bleak view but it is vitally important to recognize the possibility that discrimination, devaluation or rejection may lead to an older person believing that they are a 'burden' or a source of anguish to others.

Loneliness

Loneliness is a subjective, negative feeling related to the person's own experience of deficient social relations. Loneliness is most often defined on the basis of two causal models, one of which examines the external factors, which are absent in the social network, with the second model referring to internal factors such as personality and psychological factors. As people grow older the likelihood of experiencing age related losses increases and can impact the experience of loneliness. Living alone can be a cause of loneliness as can a lack of close family ties, or an inability to continue community related activities. This does not mean that all those who live alone are lonely or that family connections are more valued than friendships with people the same age. What is clear is that sociability plays an important role in protecting people from distress and enhances well-being and that social isolation is a major risk factor. Hansson and Carpenter's work (1994) suggests that people engaged in positive relationships have a greater resilience to the pressures and problems of everyday life, more so than those without relationships who can become isolated and subject to depression.

Those most affected by loneliness are very old people, widows and widowers, and people isolated by disability (Excell 2010). Older people who are caregivers may also be isolated and lonely; about a third of carers report feeling lonely, at least sometimes. If loneliness is described as an unwelcome loss or lack of companionship, or feeling that one is alone and not liking it, then most people including older people will feel lonely at some time. Where loneliness becomes overwhelming and is accompanied by a sense of lack of control or the opportunity to change it, it can descend into depression.

Prevalence and incidence of depression and suicide among older people

The mental health of older people is often a sorely neglected area. Mental ill-health is not an inevitable part of ageing as the majority of older people enjoy good mental health and well-being. But there are particular mental health problems associated with old age – specifically dementia and also depression, which although not a normal part of ageing is common. The prevalence of mental health problems among the 65+ age groups is however higher than in any other age group but these factors can be tackled; the problem is too often they are not. Older people are told too frequently (or may tell themselves): 'what can you expect at your age?' (Levenson and Jackson 2006: 57).

There are some 10.9m people aged 65+ in the UK. Of this 10.9m: 3 per cent will have severe and lasting depression; 15 per cent will have common mental health disorders such as depression, anxiety, panic attacks and neuroses (RCPsych 2006). It is estimated that mental ill health affects: 40 per cent of older people being treated by their GP; 50 per cent of older people receiving hospital treatment; 60 per cent of older people in residential care of whom 40 per cent will have depression (CSIP 2005). Older people are frequently the main carers for another older person, which of itself can make them more vulnerable to mental ill-health (Singleton et al. 2002).

Age Concern and the Mental Health Foundation reported on the UK Inquiry into Mental Health and Well-being in Later Life in 2006. Extracts of these reports provide an invaluable insight into depression among older people. There are currently up to 2.4m older people with depression severe enough to impair their quality of life. This will increase to at least 3.1m by the mid-2020s unless action is taken. There are very high levels of unmet mental health need amongst older people, with one in four (aged 65 and over) having symptoms of depression. Only a third of older people with depression ever discuss it with their GP. Only a half of them are diagnosed and treated, primarily with antidepressants.

Depression and suicide

Depression is not normal in later life but is common in later life; it is a significant factor causing severe health problems and it remains a major public health concern

(Godfrey 2009). Depression affects how people feel about themselves and the world around them, engendering a sense of worthlessness, the surrounding world as meaningless and the future as hopeless. The impact of depression can have global consequences on a person's daily life including sleep, appetite, energy levels, interest in social activities and participation. Later life depression prevents a person from enjoying things in which they previously found pleasure and can impact upon concentration. It has a negative effect on functional abilities, and is a major contributory factor in morbidity and mortality (Murray and Lopez, 1997).

Depression repeatedly features in research into suicide among older people. Hirsch et al. (2009) sought specifically to distinguish depression from physical health factors in suicide. Their study of almost 2000 older primary care patients found that 'happiness' – positive mental health – broke the link between physical health problems and suicidal feelings; with an association between physical health problems and suicidal thoughts, but those with positive mental health – despite physical illness – were less likely to feel suicidal (Jackson 2009).

One in four people aged over 66 suffer from depression, 22 per cent of older men and 28 per cent of older women. Of these, half are considered to meet the threshold for a severe depression diagnosis (Age Concern 2008). Two in five older people who live in care homes have depression, yet an Age Concern 2008 report comments they are all too often undiagnosed, untreated and at risk of physical health problems, premature death and suicide.

Risk factors for depression remain similar to those for suicide. Primary risk factors are money worries, stressful life events, bereavement, social isolation and loneliness. Older people often have fewer resources to do anything about these factors, inevitably remaining exposed to bereavement; physical frailty may limit their ability to stay socially active or meaningfully engaged with their communities. Beeston (2006) argues that older people also face greater obstacles in attempting to achieve positive mental health highlighting age discrimination and social exclusion.

Dennis et al. (2007) confirmed the association between depression and lack of social support networks, being widowed, poor self-rated general health and physical disabilities. Goldens et al.'s (2009) study of nearly 1300 older people from Dublin discovered that 35 per cent were lonely and 34 per cent had very little in the way of social support networks. A third of those with good social networks still described themselves as lonely. Poor well-being, depression and hopelessness were associated with loneliness and poor social networks; loneliness was strongly associated with depression and being widowed.

Working with people who have depression and suicidal ideas

It is important to distinguish between risk of suicide in the short term and risk in the longer term. It has been estimated that about 2 per cent of those who have made one attempt will succeed within a year of the first attempt with a particular risk occurring in the first three months (Butler and Pritchard 1983). The difficulty for clinicians and health and social care practitioners is in assessing just who are the people who fall into this category. It requires a balance between identifying those most likely to be at risk while not inappropriately intervening with those who are considered to be a lesser risk.

One of the major concerns when working with people who have attempted suicide is how or if this should be openly discussed at all. There are two main areas that are usually explored – one regarding the incident itself, the other the degree of intent. Questions tend to focus upon what their intent was. What is the relationship between depression and this attempt? What is the risk at the present of a further attempt? What kind of help would the older person be willing to accept? Questions about the degree of intent often tend to focus upon whether the attempt was planned or impulsive. Did the older person know they would be found soon after the attempt? What drugs were taken? How much alcohol was taken? Were there other drugs that were around but not taken? (Golightley 2008).

Mental health assessment

Throughout this book, all contributory authors endorse a 'person-centred' approach that puts older people at the centre of social work practice. However, studies have found that many assessments today are dominated by narrow functional capabilities, self-care needs or risks while individual life history, relationships and vital social networks remain neglected (Stanley et al. 1999). Assessments no longer appear 'holistic' in their focus as they have become perceived and practised in terms of their managerial function, for example, as a means of accessing scarce resources based upon risk, rather than in its professional sense of reaching an understanding of an individual within their social context.

Activity 4.2

How might listening to an older person's narrative help a practitioner carry out a mental health assessment?

From what you have read, or from your own experiences of working with older people with mental health needs, to what extent are they given the scope to tell their stories?

What could you do as a practitioner to increase the opportunities for older people to tell their own narratives or stories?

How might this improve their experience of mental health assessments and outcomes?

Working with an older person in this situation would need to focus on helping them identify positive factors or 'reasons for living'. Such an approach would assume that the older person will be able, with help, to identify reasons for their life (e.g. the love of their family, hope that life will change or moral objections about suicide) and be able to put these alongside more negative attributes. This helps older people identify their strengths rather than only deficits (Pritchard 1995).

Suicide rates

Rates of self-inflicted death among older people (and older men in particular) are considerable and rise sharply in the very old. The age-standardized suicide rate among young men aged 15–34 (the group considered at highest risk) totals some 261 per million; for men aged 65+ the rate is 414 per million, with the highest rate (175 per million) in men aged 85+. Older people are much more successful when they do decide to take their own life. The ratio of suicide attempts to completed suicides in the general population is 15:1; in older people it is approximately 4:1 (Beeston 2006)

Identifying those at risk

Older people who take their own lives either directly or indirectly often indicate their intentions to kill themselves to others. Unfortunately, family, friends, carers and professionals may play down or fail to recognize the real significance of what has been said or indicated to them. By recognizing certain signs and symptoms early on one may prevent suicide from occurring and greatly improve the circumstances and quality of life for an older person. The clues that an older person may be contemplating suicide can be verbal, behavioural or situational. The presence of depression or other mood disorders is also a significant factor. The Royal College of General Practitioners produced a checklist of factors that indicate high risk in older people.

Verbal: 'end centred talk', explicitly expressing a wish to die or take one's own life or indirect talk, e.g. talking about things as if they will not be around to see or participate in them;

Behavioural: accumulating or hoarding medication; making or changing a will; an interest in giving things away, putting one's affairs in order; sudden attendance or re-establishing contact with a religious faith; self-neglect or losing interest in life and household tasks; 'failure to thrive'; visiting a GP with non-specific medical symptoms;

Situational: sudden changes in personal circumstances, e.g. death of partner or close friend, retirement, moving home or a diagnosis of a serious illness (diabetes, dementia, cancer, stroke); depression or sudden recovery from depression, significant changes in eating or sleeping habits, the presence of tension, agitation or guilt; shunning company, intentionally isolating oneself or refusing to accept help.

Methods of suicide

The most common means of suicide amongst older people (across both sexes) is over-dose either by prescribed or over the counter medication – a total of 88.8 per cent outlined in the Hawton and Harriss 2006 study, of whom 49.3 per cent used paracetamol, 24 per cent minor tranquillizers and 15.9 per cent antidepressants.

The most common method of suicide among older men is hanging; among older women it is self-poisoning. Drowning is more common among older men than younger men; older women are more likely than younger women to end their lives by self-asphyxiation. Older people less frequently kill themselves by jumping from a high place or by carbon monoxide (e.g. poisoning from car exhausts). Tadros and Saleb (2000) suggest that the methods chosen by older people reflect the ease of access – older people are likely to be less physically mobile, may not own a car and have access to medication that is often being prescribed for other health-related problems. International studies support this hypothesis on the whole.

Suicide prevention

Suicide among older people often has multifaceted, complex dimensions; despite the commonly held view it is rare for a single event to cause an older person to take their own life. The challenge is to find effective means of preventing suicide from occurring. Interventions aimed at tackling suicide and self-harm among older people can take place at a number of levels (Beeston 2006). It involves identifying at risk individuals and groups while attempting to reduce access to means. Given the high number of older people who have contact with their GP in the months prior to taking their own life, it might be argued that primary care is an important setting to target interventions but these are likely to be different from those provided in secondary services to older people who may have already attempted to take their own life. Suicide prevention with older people is not a quick fix solution, as it requires action at primary, secondary and tertiary levels.

Black minority ethnic perspectives

Research into suicide and the specific factors affecting the mental health and well-being of older people from Black and minority ethnic (BME) communities is sparse as well as research into care and effective treatment (Sharif et al. 2008). The limited research to support practice was highlighted in a 2008 mapping literature review published by Sharif et al. (2008). This review concluded that depression in the BME communities is poorly understood or recognized by health and social care professionals and the potential for treatment or other interventions to make improvements is therefore not made available to those who might benefit.

The limited evidence highlights that key economic and social factors associated with depression (and suicide) are common among BME older people, e.g. poverty, poor housing and limited access to transport. The experience of migration and loss of contact with extended families also raises risks. Barriers to accessing treatment were also highlighted and included cultural insensitivity of services, for example, BME older people often 'somatize' symptoms by expressing mental ill health in physical terms, plus the use of culturally inappropriate diagnostic tools and interventions. BME older people sometimes lack knowledge about health and social care services and so are reluctant to seek help because of social stigma. BME older people commonly experience a 'triple whammy' of discrimination on the grounds of old age, race and mental illness (Jackson 2009).

SCIE suggests that social care practitioners consider a more proactive approach to ensuring culturally appropriate service provision while working with older people and local BME communities. It suggested the following person-centred practice considerations:

- ensure the older person and their family have all the information they need in the appropriate format they can understand;
- establish the older person's preferred language, arrange for a professional interpreter (as opposed to relying upon family/friends to interpret);
- find out about the person's cultural, religious beliefs and contact people from the local community (while respecting confidentiality) regarding particular cultural needs and local sources support;
- consider offering mainstream services – do not always assume it will be unacceptable to BME older people and discuss how they may be made more culturally acceptable.
- discuss with service providers about what they can do to make their services more culturally sensitive and acceptable while monitoring services clients receive.

Promoting recovery

Recovery is a personal (often unique) process so can sometimes be a contested term. McKnight (1995) argues that there are four central assumptions that characterize the traditional attitude and behaviour of health and social care professionals. These are:

- The service user is the problem, the professional is the answer.
- The professional 'remedy' or service defines the need.
- The 'problem' and the 'solution' are coded into comprehensible jargon.
- Professionals decide what help is effective.

Such needs-orientated assumptions are disempowering and disable the people with whom health and social care professionals come into contact. The alternative is to develop policies, approaches and activities that recognize and enable the development of people's capacities, skills, strengths and assets.

More recently users of mental health services and mental health professionals have come together to promote the idea of recovery (CSIP 2005, RCPsych 2006 and SCIE 2007). MIND (2001) reported findings of an extensive survey 'Roads to Recovery' in which over half of respondents said that they felt recovered or were coping with their mental distress. Respondents had various diagnoses, including depression, schizophrenia, bipolar, post-traumatic stress disorder and personality disorder. Such findings counteract the lack of serious positive messages about how people can learn to live with or 'recover' from mental distress. In this context 'recovery' is about people seeing themselves as capable of managing or finding a positive way forward out of their distress rather than as passive recipients of professional interventions. Tew (2005) argues 'recovery cannot be done to people; it cannot be led by experts who claim to know both the destination and route by which this is reached' (2005: 27).

Activity 4.3

Defining recovery

What does the term 'recovery' mean to you?

How might you try to define recovery with a mental health user?

What indicators (or signs) might you look for?

As opposed to accepting an illness diagnosis and learning to manage medication, the idea of recovery puts meanings, relationships and values at the heart of mental health care – it is a process not an event. The process of recovery may involve users learning to weave their illness experiences into a more integrated sense of his/herself, rather than bracketing off their illness experiences as 'alien' or 'other' (Coppock and Dunn 2010). The user-led Hearing Voices Networks encourage service users to develop strategies to take control of the voices they hear as opposed to eradicating them. User-led networks provide important opportunities for mutual support or reclaiming aspects of ordinary life while also providing a focus for campaign activities.

Older people and alcohol misuse

Substance misuse among older people is a neglected area of service provision, policy and research. Consequently, practitioners learn little about substance misuse problems amongst older people and thus often underestimate its seriousness. Practitioners sometimes incorrectly assume that older people are unlikely to respond to treatment, questioning why they should treat anyone with a drink problem at such a late stage. As previously highlighted, ageist assumptions can deter practitioners from effectively evaluating or identifying mental health, alcohol or drug problems among older people. The inattention to older people's substance misuse is particularly worrying given the strong statistical associations between substance misuse, suicide and chronic health problems.

The generation that is most likely to be associated with significant increases in illicit drug and alcohol abuse are the 'baby boomers' – those born in the two decades following the Second World War who are now approaching old age. The baby boomers have lived within an environment that has widely accepted and used alcohol, as it became more widely available, cheaper and less regulated (Excell 2010). Larger numbers of current users are expected to continue their habit as they reach 65 and beyond. A significant increase in demand on both health and social care services can be anticipated (Patterson and Jeste, 1999).

More research is published on alcohol misuse with older people than drug misuse due to the fact that alcohol remains readily accessible and more socially acceptable. There are still fewer studies about ageing populations when compared to those undertaken with younger people. International research suggests that women over 65 years drink less than older men of a similar age: Mishra and Kastenbaum (1980) in the USA and Neve (1993) in the Netherlands. Two distinct drinking patterns among older people emerge:

Early onset: older people who fall within this category traditionally experience a lifelong pattern of problem drinking, having probably been alcoholic most of their lives.

Late onset: this group tends to be highly educated and have had a stressful life event or emotional upheaval precipitating or exacerbating their drinking. Those in the late onset category typically have fewer physical and mental health problems (Brennan and Moos 1996). One third of older people fall into this category. Both groups fail to acknowledge their alcohol misuse and often drink secretly (Phillips and Katz 2001).

Excessive alcohol use in older people can also cause a range of physiological, physical and psychological problems with increased risks of coronary heart disease, stroke and hypertension. Alcohol may also exacerbate Parkinson's disease in older people (Feuerlein and Reiser 1986) while remaining a significant contributor in terms of reported accidents and falls (Wright and Whyley 1994). Another concern is that older drinkers often mix alcohol either with prescribed or over the counter medication. Eight out of 10 people (aged 65 and older) regularly take prescribed medication, one third taking four or more prescribed drugs a day. Therefore, there remains a greater possibility of interactions with prescribed medication (Dunne 1994). There is an abundance of evidence which suggests alcohol misuse goes under-recognized and undetected within the ageing population. Families, carers and professionals often deny any alcohol-related issues. This may be linked to the stigma attached to admitting dependency, or attitudes of certain professionals who consider there is little point in attempting to change such behaviours late in life.

Activity 4.4

How might generational differences affect substance abuse among older people?

What are the wider social policy implications of substance abuse in later life?

Assessment of substance misuse with older people: key practice do's and don'ts

- Don't assume that other professionals will always have assessed for alcohol or drug problems, e.g. do not adopt 'it's not my job' approach.
- Don't be afraid to ask; social work is all about dealing with sensitive personal issues.
- Don't be judgemental; no one starts drinking or using drugs intending to develop a problem.
- Don't worry if you don't understand what people say about their alcohol or drug use; they can explain more fully with helpful questioning. Alternatively, seek out appropriate basic or specialist training.
- Do expect there to be stigma and prejudice associated with alcohol and drug use among older people and the wider society.
- Do remember that even brief interventions from front line practitioners can help people change.
- Do routinely address alcohol and drug issues in your practice; the more you practise the better you'll get, and remember, anyone might be affected.
- Do seek out appropriate referral pathways for specialist alcohol and drug services or networks.
- Do your best to view alcohol and drug use in its wider context: is it making any problems worse or is it helping to reduce them?

(BASW 2010: 2)

Case study

Ethel is a 73 year old white British single woman with a long history of depression and alcohol dependency who lives alone in a housing association ground floor flat. Ethel recently absconded from an informal psychiatric admission after expressing suicidal intent. There are additional concerns around Ethel's self-neglect plus her poorly controlled medical conditions, namely angina, diabetes and Crohn's disease. When you visit Ethel at home she appears inebriated, but from your initial assessment you are unsure whether her presentation is due to her alcohol consumption or her diabetes. There is evidence of a recent fall; fresh cigarette burns on her clothing and furniture, urinary incontinence plus she is expressing suicidal thoughts.

What would be the first things you would consider doing to assist Ethel?

Comment

The first consideration would be to ensure Ethel is safe. You might consider calling the GP in to check Ethel's physical condition. From your knowledge of Ethel how might you aim to work with her in a person-centred way?

The above case study illustrates that mental health and alcohol misuse among older people remains a complex, multifaceted and only partially understood phenomenon. In contrast to the younger adult population, older people are also more likely to misuse over the counter medication, prescribed drugs and alcohol due to their increased physical, psychological and physiological needs. At the time of writing, national policy frameworks relating to this area remain vague and unchallenged coupled with a lack of accessible or meaningful evaluations that support assessment and treatment interventions with older people. Further research is urgently required to identify effective programmes and services based upon need (not age) to inform national policy, practice and interventions.

Summary

Promoting good mental health and well-being among older people has been a relatively neglected area in both research and policy. A UK inquiry into mental health and well-being in later life sought to fill in some of the gaps in the evidence base by seeking the views of older people, organizations and professionals on the key factors that either promote or hinder good mental health (Age Concern/Mental Health Foundation 2006). The responses from older people stated strongly that feeling valued, respected and understood was crucial for good mental health. Tackling age discrimination and improving public attitudes toward older people was therefore, unsurprisingly, a key priority for action. Therefore, society as a whole has to recognize that old age is not the final destination in our journey through life, but a point in our growth and progression. This chapter has sought to highlight some of the challenges of maintaining positive mental health in older age and key areas for further development.

Further Reading

Cattan, M. (2009) *Mental Health and Well-being in Later Life*. Maidenhead: Open University Press, McGraw-Hill Education.

Shepherd, G., Boardman, J. and Slade, M. (2008) *Making Recovery a Reality*, Sainsbury Centre for Mental Health Policy Paper. London: Sainsbury Centre for Mental Health.

Thompson, J., Kilbane, J. and Sanderson, H. (2008) *Person Centred Practice for Professionals*. Maidenhead: Open University Press, McGraw-Hill Education.

Williamson, T. (ed.) (2009) *Older People's Mental Health Today: A Handbook*. Brighton: OLM – Pavilion/Mental Health Foundation.

References

Age Concern (2003) *Adding Quality to Quantity: Older People's Views on Quality of Life and its Enhancement*. London: Age Concern.

Age Concern (2008) *Undiagnosed, Untreated, at Risk: The Experiences of Older People with Depression*. London: Age Concern.

Age Concern/Mental Health Foundation (2006) *Promoting Mental Health and Well-being in Later Life: A First Report from the Inquiry into Mental Health and Well-being in Later Life*. London: Age Concern/Mental Health Foundation.

BASW (2010) *Alcohol and Other Drugs: Essential Information for Social Workers – A BASW Pocket Guide*. Produced by British Association of Social Workers, the Alcohol Education and Research Council, NHS National Treatment Agency for Substance Misuse, Tilda Goldberg Centre, University of Bedfordshire.

Beeston, D. (2006) *Older People and Suicide*. Birmingham/Stoke on Trent: CSIP West Midlands/Staffordshire University.

Bowling, A. (2005) *Ageing Well: Quality of Life in Old Age*. Maidenhead: Open University Press.

Brennan, P.L. and Moos, R.H. (1996) Late life drinking behaviour, *Alcohol Health & Research World* 20: 197–205.

Butler, A. and Pritchard, C. (1983) *Social Work and Mental Illness*. Basingstoke: Macmillan.

Chan, J., Draper, B. and Banerjee, S. (2007) Deliberate self harm in older adults: a review of the literature from 1955 to 2004, *International Journal of Geriatric Psychiatry* 22: 720–32.

Commission for Healthcare Audit and Inspection (2006) *Living Well in Later Life: A Review of Progress Against the National Service Framework for Older People*. London: Commission for Healthcare Audit & Inspection.

Coppock, V. and Dunn, B. (2010) *Understanding Social Work Practice in Mental Health*. London: Sage.

CSIP (2005) *Everybody's Business: Integrated Mental Health Services for Older People*. London: DH.

Dennis, M., Baillon, S., Brugha, T., Stewart, R., Meltzer, H. and Lindesay, J. (2007) The spectrum of suicidal ideation in Great Britain: comparisons across a 16–74 years age range, *Psychological Medicine* 37(6): 795–805.

DH (Department of Health) (2001) *The National Service Framework for Older People*. London: DH.

DH (Department of Health) (2007) *Best Practice in Managing Risk: Principles & Evidence for Best Practice in the Assessment & Management of Risk to Self & others in Mental Health Services*. London: DH.

Dunne, F.J. (1994) Misuse of alcohol or drugs by elderly people, *British Medical Journal* 308 (6929): 608–9.

Ewing, J.A. (1984) Detecting alcoholism – the CAGE questionnaire, *Journal of the American Medical Association* 252: 1905–7.

Excell, S. (2010) Older people and dual diagnosis, in P. Phillips, O. McKeown and T. Sandford (eds.) *Dual Diagnosis: Practice in Context*. Chichester: Wiley-Blackwell.

Feuerlein, W. and Reiser, E. (1986) Parameters affecting the course and results of delirium tremens treatment, *Acta Psychiatrica Scandinavica Supplementum* 329: 120–3.

Godfrey, M. (2009) Depression and anxiety in later life: making the visible invisible, in T. Williamson (ed.) *Older People's Mental Health Today: A Handbook*. Brighton: OLM-Pavilion/Mental Health Foundation.

Godfrey, M. and Denby, T. (2004) *Depression and Older People*. Bristol: Policy Press.

Golden, J., Conroy, R.M., Bruce, I., Denihan, A., Greene, E., Kirby, M. and Lawlor, B.A. (2009) Loneliness, social support networks, mood and well-being in community-dwelling elderly, *International Journal of Geriatric Psychiatry* 24(7): 649–700.

Golightley, M. (2008) *Social Work and Mental Health*, 3rd edn. Exeter: Learning Matters.

Green, B.H., Copeland, J.R., Dewey, M.E., Sharma, V., Saunders, P.A., Davidson, I.A., Sullivan, C. and McWilliam, C. (1992) Risk factors for depression in elderly people: a prospective study, *Acta Psychiatrica Scandinavica* 86(3): 213–17.

Hansson, R.O. and Carpenter, B.N. (1994) *Relationships in Old Age: Coping with the Challenge of Transition*. New York, NY: Guilford Press.

Hawton, K. and Harriss, L. (2006) Deliberate self harm in people aged 60 years and over: characteristics and outcome of a 20 year cohort, *International Journal of Geriatric Psychiatry* 21: 572–81.

Hirsch, J.K., Duberstein, P.R. and Unutzer, J. (2009) Chronic medical problems and distressful thoughts of suicide in primary care patients: mitigating roles of happiness, *International Journal of Geriatric Psychiatry* 24(7): 671–9.

Hurst, P. (2009) What do you expect at your age?, in T. Williamson (ed.) *Older People's Mental Health Today: A Handbook*. Brighton: OLM-Pavilion/Mental Health Foundation.

Jackson, C. (2009) Older people, suicide and self harm, in T. Williamson (ed.) *Older People's Mental Health Today: A Handbook*. Brighton: OLM-Pavilion/Mental Health Foundation.

Layard, R. (2006) *The Depression Report: A New Deal for Depression and Anxiety Disorders*. London: LSE.

Levernson, R. and Jackson, C. (2006) Everybody's business: mental health in older people, in C. Jackson and K. Hill (eds) *Mental Health Today*. Brighton: Pavilion Publishing/Mental Health Foundation.

McKnight, J. (1995) *The Careless Society: Community and its Counterfeits*. New York: Basic Books.

Menninger, J.A. (2002) Assessment and treatment of alcoholism and substance related disorders in the elderly, *Bulletin of the Menninger Clinic* 66: 166–84.

MIND (2001) *Roads to Recovery*. London: MIND.

Mishra, B. and Kastenbaum, R. (1980) Alcohol and older age, in M. Ward and C. Goodman (eds) *Alcohol Problems in Old Age: A Practical Guide for Helping Older People with Alcohol Problems*. Surrey: Wynne Howard Publishing.

Moriarty, J. (2005) *Update for SCIE Best Practice Guide on Assessing the Mental Health Needs of Older People*. London: SCIE.

Murray, C.L. and Lopez, A.D. (1997) Alternative projections of mortality and disability by cause 1990–2020: global burden of disease study, *Lancet* 349: 1498–1504.

Neve, R. (1993) Developments in drinking behaviour in the Netherlands, *Addiction* 88: 611–21.

Office for National Statistics (2007) Mortality *Statistics for England and Wales Series DH2*, no. 32. London: ONS.

Office for National Statistics (2004) *Focus on Older People*. London: ONS.

Patterson, T.L. and Jeste, D.V. (1999) The potential impact of baby boom generation on substance misuse among elderly persons, *Mental Health and Ageing* 50(9): 1184–9.

Phillips, P. and Katz, A. (2001) Substance misuse in older adults: an emerging policy priority, *NT Research* 6: 898–905.

Pritchard, C. (1995) *Suicide: The Ultimate Rejection*. Buckingham: Open University Press.

RCPsych (2006) *Raising the Standard: Specialist Services for Older People With Mental Illness*. London: RCPsych.

Robinson, L., Clare, L. and Evans, K. (2005) Making sense of dementia and adjusting to loss: psychological reactions to a diagnosis of dementia in couples, *Ageing and Mental Health* 9(4): 337–47.

SCIE (2007) *Assessing the Mental Health Needs of Older People*. London: SCIE.

Sharif, N., Brown, W. and Rutter, D. (2008) *The Extent and Impact of Depression on BME Older People and the Acceptability, Accessibility and Effectiveness of Social Care Provision*, Systemic map report 03. London: SCIE.

Singleton, N., Mangu, N.A., Cowie, A., Sparks, J., Bumpstead, R. and Meltzer, H. (2002) *Mental Health of Carers*. London: HMSO.

Stanley, N., Manthorpe, J. and Penhale, B. (eds) (1999) *Institutional Abuse: Perspectives Across the Life Course*. London: Routledge.

Tadros, G. and Saleb, E. (2000) Age and methods of fatal self harm (FSH): is there a link?, *International Journal of Geriatric Psychiatry* 15: 848–52.

Tew, J. (ed.) (2005) *Social Perspectives in Mental Health: Developing Social Models to Understand and Work with Mental Distress*. London: Jessica Kingsley.

Thornicroft, G. (2006) *Actions Speak Louder: Tackling Discrimination Against People with Mental Illness*. London: Mental Health Foundation.

Victor, C. (2005) *The Social Context of Ageing: A Textbook of Gerontology*. Abingdon: Routledge.

Wright, F. and Whyley, C. (1994) *Accident Prevention and Risk Taking by Elderly People: The Need for Advice*. London: Age Concern Institute of Gerontology.

5 Working with older people with dementia

Sally Stapleton

After reading this chapter you should be able to:

- discuss how to promote person-centred practice with people with dementia;
- explore case examples of working with people with dementia, including positive interventions and practice solutions;
- describe an approach to enhancing communication with a person with dementia, including the use of life story work.

Introduction

It is a very exciting time within dementia care services. Since the 1990s the person-centred approach has moved from being a minority concept to one which has gained a broad consensus within health and social care practice. The person-centred approach is clearly stated as underpinning the NICE/SCIE clinical guideline *Dementia: Supporting People with Dementia and their Carers in Health and Social Care* (2006). This chapter begins by outlining a definition of the term 'dementia' and the National Dementia Strategy (DH 2009). It will then focus on the person-centred approach to working with people with dementia, their families and carers, including the use of dementia care mapping and life story books. The 'PAUSE for thought' approach is introduced as a way of bringing together ways of supporting communication. The chapter will use exercises and the case study of 'Elaine' to consider the application of person-centred practice. Consideration will also be given to the applications of the Mental Capacity Act (2005).

What is dementia?

Dementia is defined as a 'syndrome which may be caused by a number of illnesses in which there is progressive decline in multiple areas of function, including decline in memory, reasoning, communication skills and the ability to carry out daily activities'

(DH 2009: 15). Knapp et al. (2007) estimated that there are approximately 700,000 people living with dementia in the UK. This study also anticipated that by the 2040s this number will double to 1.4 million.

The most common subtypes of dementia are Alzheimer's disease, vascular dementia, 'mixed dementia' (a combination of both Alzheimer's disease and vascular dementia), Lewy body dementia, dementia in Parkinson's disease and frontotemporal dementia. There are numerous other conditions which cause dementia. These include other degenerative diseases (for example, Huntington's disease), prion diseases (for example, HIV related dementia), Creutzfeldt-Jakob Disease (CJD), and different types of toxic and metabolic disorders, such as alcohol-related dementia (NICE/SCIE 2006). The Social Care Institute for Excellence provides an excellent online resource, the 'Dementia Gateway', which summarizes the differences between the main subtypes of dementia. It is important to note that some subtypes of dementia do not involve memory difficulties in the early stages.

The National Dementia Strategy

The Department of Health published *Living Well with Dementia: A National Dementia Strategy* in 2009. It was introduced to ensure that significant improvements are made to services for individuals with dementia. There are 17 objectives in three key focus areas within the National Dementia Strategy: improved awareness, earlier diagnosis and intervention, and a higher quality of care.

The ethos of the National Dementia Strategy is underpinned by person-centred principles. However the term 'person-centred' is often used without a full explanation of its meaning (Brooker 2007). Therefore, this chapter summarizes key aspects of person-centred care.

The person-centred approach to dementia care: moving from 'people with DEMENTIA' to 'PEOPLE with dementia'

When thinking about the person-centred approach to dementia care, it is extremely important to have information about the PERSON with dementia, rather than just knowledge of the person's diagnosis of DEMENTIA (Kitwood 1997). With this principle firmly in mind, the case study of 'Elaine' will be referred to on several occasions during this chapter.

Case study

Elaine is 77. She lives at home with her husband. Elaine has a diagnosis of Alzheimer's disease. Her family are concerned that she is tearful and anxious during the day and she is getting frustrated with her husband. She has declined to go to a local day centre. Her husband is becoming very stressed and is asking for help.

Activity 5.1

Now you have read the case study, reflect on what further information you would need to help you understand Elaine's experiences and offer support to Elaine and her husband.

Dementia reconsidered: the person comes first

The late Professor Tom Kitwood, founder of the Bradford Dementia Group, was the first to use the term 'person-centred' with regards to dementia care. In his book *Dementia Reconsidered: The Person Comes First* (Kitwood 1997), he wrote about the beginnings of the model of person-centred dementia care. Having himself witnessed the potential in using psychotherapeutic ideas and practices with people with dementia, he came to the conclusion that more could be done to help people with dementia than had been previously believed. He and his colleague, Kathleen Bredin, drew on concepts from psychotherapeutic work, including person-centred psychotherapy (Rogers 1961) to form an approach to working with people with dementia: 'We called the whole approach "person-centred care", following the example of Rogerian psychotherapy' (Kitwood 1997: 4.)

The Enriched Model of dementia

In the 1980s, the dominant way of understanding the effect of dementia on a person was to concentrate on the degree of neurological damage. Kitwood called this 'the standard paradigm' (Kitwood 1989). However, Kitwood proposed that the way a person with dementia thinks, feels and acts is influenced by a number of factors. These included the degree of neurological impairment, the person's life history, personality and physical health, and their social and psychological environment. He called this the 'Enriched Model' of dementia (Kitwood 1993). This model explains how individuals with similar neurological damage can have a widely diverse experience of living with dementia. It also highlights how different social environments can have a major impact on a person with dementia.

Activity 5.2

Imagine that you are going to be moving into a care home and you are unable to give people any information about yourself. Using the Enriched Model, what information would you want the care home to know about you?

How would you want to spend your time?

How would you want people to treat you?

'Personhood' and psychological needs

Key to the person-centred model of dementia care is the concept of 'personhood'. Kitwood defined personhood as 'a standing or status that is bestowed upon one human being, by others, in the context of relationship and social being. It implies recognition, respect and trust' (Kitwood 1997: 8).

Kitwood gave numerous examples of how someone's personhood can be undermined within a care setting. He used the term 'Malignant Social Psychology' (MSP) to describe this phenomenon. In essence, episodes of MSP occur when a person with dementia is treated as a lesser human being, or not as a human being at all. Examples include ignoring a person with dementia, or treating a person with dementia like a child or an object. Kitwood (1997: 46–7) described a total of 17 categories of MSP which he called 'personal detractions'. MSP can happen to any human being, ourselves included. When you experience MSP it can have a profound effect on your well-being. However, most of the time, you will have the cognitive resources to help you cope with the experience. For example, you might speak up for yourself, seek social support or engage in other self-soothing strategies, such as going for a walk, etc. A person with dementia is less able to engage in ways of coping due to experiencing cognitive difficulties. MSP can therefore be particularly damaging to their personhood and well-being. Brooker (2007) provides an excellent chapter on the 'social environment', which outlines all 17 categories of personal detractions. Table 5.1 gives examples of personal detractions that might apply to the case study of Elaine. It also outlines examples that you might personally experience. As you read each example, consider the emotional impact that it might have.

Kitwood was always very clear to point out that episodes of MSP within dementia care services rarely occur as a result of malicious intent. Instead, they are part of a culture of care and are related to the value base of a society which prizes youth and intellect.

Table 5.1 Examples of personal detractions

Personal detraction (Brooker and Surr 2005)	Examples
Disempowerment: not allowing a person to use the abilities that they do have.	**Elaine:** A family member says to Elaine 'I'll do that for you' at the first sign that Elaine is beginning to find a task difficult. **You:** Your partner says 'oh give it to me' when you are not 100 per cent sure how to do something
Labelling: Using a label as the main way of referring to or relating to a person.	**Elaine:** When at the local shop with her husband, Elaine walks around several times, the shop assistant says to Elaine's husband, 'I think that she is a wanderer. My friend works in the dementia part of a care home and she says that many of them are wanderers.' **You:** You are picking up your child from a new school and you hear other parents mutter quietly 'she's one of those social work types'.

Maintaining personhood

Christine Bryden in her book *Dancing with Dementia* (2005) speaks about her own personal experiences of being diagnosed with dementia 10 years previously at the age of 46.

> How you relate to us has a big impact on the course of the disease. You can restore our personhood, and give us a sense of being needed and valued. There is a Zulu saying that is very true. '**A person is a person through others**'. Give us reassurance, hugs, support, meaning in life. Value us for what we can still do and be, and make sure we retain social networks. It is very hard for us to be who we once were, so let us be who we are now and realise the effort we are making to function.
>
> (Bryden 2005: 127)

Her book is truly inspirational and gives a huge insight into the experience of living with dementia. In recent years, other people with dementia have written about their own experiences. This has given further support for the need for person-centred practice.

Kitwood outlined the factors which he viewed as central to supporting and maintaining personhood. He used the term 'positive person work' to describe actions that support a person's psychological needs. Bradford Dementia Group have further developed Kitwood's ideas and list 17 categories of positive person work, called 'personal enhancers', which are alternatives to personal detractions. Examples of personal enhancers are being warm, respectful and enabling (Brooker and Surr 2005). Table 5.2 gives examples of personal enhancers that might apply to the case study of Elaine. It also outlines examples that you might experience. As you read each example, reflect on the emotional impact that it might have.

Brooker (2007) highlights that in order to engage in positive person work, staff members need to be supported in a person-centred way. Organizations who demonstrate

Table 5.2 Examples of personal enhancers

Personal enhancer (Brooker and Surr 2005)	Examples
Empowerment: Letting go of control and assisting a person to discover or employ skills and abilities.	**Elaine:** Elaine enjoys preparing lunch for the family. A family member says to Elaine 'Do you want to start washing the vegetables for our salad? I'll see if I can find anything else in the fridge.' **You:** You are not 100 per cent sure how to do something. Your partner says 'Would you like a hand?'
Acceptance: Entering into a relationship based on an attitude of positive regard or acceptance for a person.	**Elaine:** When at the local shop with her husband, Elaine walks around the shop several times, the shop assistant says to Elaine 'Hello Elaine, lovely to see you today. Have you found everything that you are looking for today?' **You:** You are picking up your child from a new school. Other parents smile and exchange greetings with you.

person-centred values in their support of staff are much more likely to encourage the use of positive person work with people with dementia and their families.

Well-being in people with dementia

Following many hours of detailed observations, Kitwood and Bredin (1992a) compiled a list of indicators of relative well-being and ill-being. Indicators of well-being included: showing pleasure; bodily relaxation; initiating social contact; assertiveness; sensitivity to others' needs; use of and responding to humour; helpfulness; showing signs of self-respect; demonstrating affection; expressing a range of emotions and creative self-expression. Indicators of ill-being included: withdrawal; physical discomfort; fear; intense anger; unattended despair; anxiety; bodily tension; unattended grief; apathy; agitation and boredom.

On a moment by moment basis, relative well-being and ill-being can be viewed as a combination of mood state and engagement, including engagement with others, activities or objects (Brooker and Surr 2005). Well-being is influenced by the type of activity that the individual is engaged in (or not). Certain types of activities have a higher potential for promoting well-being than others. For example, interacting with others and participating in leisure activities has a higher potential for promoting well-being than being withdrawn or being unresponded to by others.

The chapter now returns to the case study to explore how the Enriched Model of dementia might help to understand the impact of dementia on Elaine.

Activity 5.3

How does the following information help you to understand Elaine's current experiences of feeling anxious and tearful during the day and feeling frustrated with her husband?

How does it help understand why her husband is becoming very stressed?

What ideas would you have that could support Elaine's well-being?

Case study (continued)

Neurological impairment: Elaine has been diagnosed with Alzheimer's disease. She experiences difficulties with memory and planning difficulties which affect her ability to complete complex tasks. Elaine has clearly stated that she does not wish to attend a day centre. According to the Mental Capacity Act (2005) adults must be assumed to have capacity to make decisions for themselves unless it can be proven otherwise. Following an assessment, Elaine is able to fulfil the criteria for having capacity to make this particular decision. She is able to understand information relevant to the decision, retain the information for long enough to make a decision, weigh up the pros and cons and communicate her decision (Jones 2005).

Life history: Elaine grew up in a loving, hardworking family. She married at 19 and had two children. She is now a grandmother and has four grandchildren. She worked in the local post office and was a very popular member of the local community. She was a keen dressmaker and gardener. She used to arrange flowers for the local Church.

Personality: Elaine has always been a very kind, polite and reserved person. She has a strong work ethic. She has a strong Christian faith.

Health and physical fitness: Elaine is often prone to experiencing haemorrhoids which cause her discomfort and embarrassment.

Social and psychological environment: Elaine's family are very caring and supportive. As Elaine has found it increasingly difficult to complete the cooking, household tasks and flower arrangements for the local Church, her husband and daughter have taken on these roles. She therefore spends a lot of time during the day being unoccupied, apart from following her husband around the house.

Comment

Ways in which you could support Elaine might include the following:

- *Encourage Elaine's family to support Elaine in completing parts of household tasks that she is still able to do, and to see this as a meaningful way of spending time with Elaine, rather than focusing on doing tasks as quickly as possible. Explore if Elaine would like to do any other meaningful activities within or outside of the home.*
- *Consider the use of personalized support to help maintain Elaine's role of flower arranger for the Church.*
- *Suggest a visit to the GP to check for haemorrhoids or any other physical health problem.*
- *Offer a carer's assessment.*

Dementia Care Mapping

Dementia Care Mapping (Kitwood and Bredin 1992b) was developed to try to gain an insight into the viewpoint of the person with dementia, when the person is unable to express their own views. Dementia Care Mapping (DCM) has been revised and updated on a number of occasions by the Bradford Dementia Group (Brooker and Surr 2005). DCM is an observational method that looks at the experience of being in a care setting such as a hospital ward, day centre or care home, from the viewpoint of the person with dementia. The results of DCM provide information on person-centred care within a care setting as measured by relative levels of well-being and ill-being, the types of activities that a person with dementia is engaging in, and the social psychological environment that surrounds the person (episodes of positive person work and malignant social psychology). The process of a DCM can be used to help staff gain an insight into the lived experience of people with dementia within the care facility. Crucially, DCM enables staff to plan ways of enhancing the well-being of particular individuals with dementia, thus ensuring high quality person-centred care. DCM featured on the BBC2 documentary 'Can Gerry Robinson fix dementia care homes' which was first broadcast in 2010.

Research evidence supports the use of DCM as a developmental process to change care practice (Brooker 2005). DCM has also been recognized in key good practice guidance and policy documents (e.g. NICE/SCIE 2006; National Audit Office 2010). Its role in enhancing person-centred care has also been recognized by the British Standards Institution (2010).

Stapleton et al. (2010) reported on the multiagency use of DCM. Three projects were set up within county council day centres, NHS inpatient wards and independent sector care homes. The care homes project involved multiagency working and was led by a senior lecturer in social work from the University of Chichester. Across all service settings, DCM was found to be very helpful in implementing person-centred practice.

The main principles behind DCM have been incorporated into an observational tool that forms part of the regulatory process for care facilities by the Care Quality Commission. Therefore, concepts from DCM have become central to the current understanding of quality of care within dementia care facilities.

Supporting person-centred communication with people with dementia

Morton (1999) provides an excellent summary of the evolution of person-centred approaches to working with people with dementia. Following exploration of the origins of person-centred approaches by Rogers (1961), Morton considers the influence of Rogers' work on Feil, who trained in psychology and social work in the 1950s. Feil went on to develop 'Validation Therapy' (e.g. Feil 1993). The essence of this approach is to focus on the emotional content of a person's communication, rather than the 'facts' of what a person is saying. The caregiver then acknowledges and validates these emotions and feelings using verbal and non-verbal means.

Following the work of Feil (e.g. 1993), Stokes and Goudie (1990) developed 'Resolution Therapy'. This also involves paying attention to a person with dementia's verbal and non-verbal (i.e. behaviour) communications. The caregiver attempts to understand the meaning behind the communication by trying to identify the underlying emotions. The caregiver then makes an attempt at a response that reflects and validates the person's feelings. Following this, the caregiver makes practical attempts to meet the person's needs that have been highlighted and hence provide a 'resolution'.

Activity 5.4

Dilemma: A person with dementia says 'Where's my Mum': how could you respond?

If you concentrate just on the 'facts' you are limited to saying things like 'your Mum died 20 years ago' or you will need to lie and say 'she'll be here later'. How does this feel to say these things to a person with dementia? If you instead concentrate on the emotional meaning, you have other options. What is the emotion behind 'I want my Mum'? Is it:

anxiety, loneliness, missing their family, missing their home, grief, feeling lost, feeling hungry, cold, wanting to be hugged? Based on these, what could you say? How about . . . 'It sounds like you are feeling really worried?', 'it's really difficult being without your family isn't it?', 'it sounds like you are really missing your Mum, what would your Mum do if she were here?', 'it sometimes feels lonely here, would you like me to come and sit with you?'

Life story books

Life story books can greatly enhance communication between a person with dementia, their family, friends and carers. Powell (2000) provides an excellent approach to producing a life story book/memory book. In summary, a life story book can contain photographs or pictures accompanied by a sentence or two on topics that are relevant to the person. For example, it could contain information about a person's family members, friends and pets, where they have lived, their job, hobbies, interests, family holidays, important life events and information about the present, such as where the person lives now and activities that they enjoy doing. Woods et al. (2008) outline the positive benefits of life story books within care homes in particular:

- They provide information that the person and their family are happy to share with others
- They can be used to help staff get to know a person when the member of staff sits with the person and goes through their life story book with them.
- They can be used as a communication aid.
- They can help maintain a person's sense of identity.
- They can facilitate reminiscence.

Smyth (2006) used DCM to evaluate the use of life story books with people with dementia within an NHS continuing care ward. Life story books led to higher levels of well-being for most individuals compared to either 'general reminiscence' or 'life on the ward as usual'. In addition, staff reported feeling more positive about their ability to communicate when they used the book. Life story books also had a positive impact on family visits, including visits with grandchildren.

'PAUSE for Thought': bringing together person-centred approaches to communicating with a person with dementia

Since 2003 I have been facilitating sessions for health and social care staff about person-centred approaches to communicating with people with dementia, and have pulled together the different person-centred communication approaches that are outlined in this chapter into a model. I have called this 'PAUSE for Thought'.

PAUSE for Thought has two meanings. First, it is a prompt to stop and reflect. Secondly, the acronym 'PAUSE' also acts as a mnemonic that highlights the key aspects of person-centred approaches:

'P' stands for 'person', which represents the importance of knowing information about a person with dementia to aid positive communication.

'A' stands for 'activities and aids', which encourages the use of objects, pictures, photos, life story books and music to initiate conversation with the person with dementia.

'U' stands for 'you', which represents the necessity of working as part of a supportive team and organization, where person-centred communication is encouraged.

'S' stands for 'supporting self-esteem and psychological needs', which serves as a reminder that people with dementia have difficulty maintaining their own self-esteem and psychological needs. We need to use personal enhancers and avoid personal detractions.

'E' stands for 'emotions', which encourages us to think less about the facts and more about what the feeling and meaning is behind a person's communication.

We now return to the case study to explore how the PAUSE for Thought model could be used to help support communication with Elaine.

Activity 5.5

Three years have passed. You have been involved in organizing Elaine's recent move into a care home. The staff do not know Elaine very well. Elaine is tearful a lot of the time, saying that she needs to pick her children up from school.

Take a moment to go through the PAUSE for Thought model and consider how you might use it to give advice to the care home.

Ideas might include:

P – Person: Can a staff member meet with Elaine's family to find out about her life history and personality? Would a life story book help?

A – Activities and aids: The care home has just started using DCM to help to enhance the well-being of people with dementia. Elaine agrees to be part of the mapping process. DCM highlights that Elaine became tearful when she was unoccupied. She experienced well-being when she was sitting in the garden and when she was engaged in a reminiscence group about fashion.

From previous work with Elaine, you know that she has a strong work ethic and likes to feel occupied. She likes dressmaking, gardening and flower arranging. She has a strong faith and enjoys having a role within the Church and local community. Are there opportunities for her to engage in her interests, have a role within the care home and to practise her faith?

U – support for you: Is the team being supported in a person-centred way within the organization? Are there opportunities for training, supervision and reflection? Do the team work together and support each other?

S – Supporting self-esteem and psychological needs. DCM highlighted that Elaine's psychological needs were supported by being asked to help with tasks in the home (personal enhancer). Later, Elaine became quite distressed and said to a member of staff 'I have to go and pick up my children'. The mappers could see that it was difficult for the care worker to know what to say. The care worker looked very uncomfortable and did not respond to Elaine (personal detraction). The results of DCM were shared with the team and they were encouraged to build on the positive person work that they were starting with Elaine. The team were supported in generating alternative ways of responding to Elaine when she is distressed, focusing on the underlying emotions (see below).

E – Emotions: What is the emotion underlying Elaine's communication 'I have to go and pick up my children?' Is it feeling worried about being away from her family, or feeling she needs to be doing something important? What could possible responses be? One possible idea might be 'I can see that you are feeling really worried about your family'. One practical way of trying to provide a resolution might be to see if she would like to call her family on the telephone.

Summary

Dementia care has been highly influenced by the person-centred approach. One need only look to the title of the National Dementia Strategy *Living Well with Dementia* to see how current thinking has embraced the person-centred model. One of the most striking elements to emerge in recent years is the importance of person-centred practice at an organizational level. Providing person-centred care involves intensive emotional labour. Therefore, the organization needs to help staff members feel supported and valued to reduce stress levels (Brooker 2007). Such a concept has much to offer person-centred practice beyond the field of dementia care.

Further reading

Brooker, D. (2007) *Person-centred Dementia Care: Making Services Better.* London: Jessica Kingsley.

Bryden, C. (2005) *Dancing with Dementia: My Story of Living Positively with Dementia.* London: Jessica Kingsley.

Kitwood, T. (1997) *Dementia Reconsidered: The Person Comes First.* Buckingham: Open University Press.

Useful websites

Bradford Dementia Group, University of Bradford www.brad.ac.uk/health/dementia/

Social Care Institute for Excellence (SCIE) Dementia Gateway www.scie.org.uk/publications/dementia/index

References

British Standards Institution (2010) *PAS 800: 2010. Use of Dementia Care Mapping for Improved Person-Centred Care in a Care Provider Organization – Guide.* London: British Standards Institution.

Brooker, D. (2005) Dementia Care Mapping (DCM): a review of the research literature, *The Gerontologist* 45 (1): 11–18.

Brooker, D. (2007) *Person-centred Dementia Care: Making Services Better.* London: Jessica Kingsley.

Brooker, D. and Surr, C. (2005) *Dementia Care Mapping: Principles and Practice.* Bradford: Bradford Dementia Group.

Bryden, C. (2005) *Dancing with Dementia: My Story of Living Positively with Dementia.* London: Jessica Kingsley.

DH (Department of Health) (2009) *Living Well with Dementia: A National Dementia Strategy.* London: Department of Health.

Feil, N. (1993) *The Validation Breakthrough.* Cleveland: Health Professions Press.

Jones, R. (2005) *Mental Capacity Act Manual.* London: Sweet and Maxwell.

Kitwood, T. (1989) Brain, mind and dementia; with particular reference to Alzheimer's Disease, *Ageing and Society* 9: 1–15.

Kitwood, T. (1993) Discover the person not the disease, *Journal of Dementia Care* 1(1): 16–17.

Kitwood, T. (1997) *Dementia Reconsidered: The Person Comes First.* Buckingham: Open University Press.

Kitwood, T. and Bredin, K. (1992a) *Person to Person: A Guide to the Care of Those with Failing Mental Powers.* Loughton: Gale Centre Publications.

Kitwood, T. and Bredin, K. (1992b) A new approach to the evaluation of dementia care, *Journal of Advances in Health and Nursing Care* 1(5): 41–60.

Knapp, M., Prince, M., Albanese, E., Banerjee, S., Dhanasiri, S., Fernandez, J.L., Ferri, C., McCrone, P., Snell, T. and Stewart, R. (2007) *Dementia UK: The Full Report.* London: Alzheimer's Society.

Morton, I. (1999) *Person–centred Approaches to Dementia Care.* Bicester: Winslow Press.

NICE/SCIE (2006) *Dementia: Supporting People with Dementia and their Carers in Health and Social Care.* London: National Institute for Health and Clinical Excellence.

Powell J. (2000) *Care to Communicate: Helping the Older Person with Dementia.* London: Hawker Publications.

Rogers, C.R. (1961) *On Becoming a Person.* Boston, MA: Houghton Mifflin.

Smyth, S. (2006) A preliminary investigation into the use of reminiscence and life review books as aids to promoting well-being for individuals with dementia: single case experimental designs. Unpublished doctoral thesis, University of East Anglia.

Stapleton, S., Moore, D., Constable, G. and Jones, K. (2010) HOPE for the future: gaining an insight into the experiences of people with dementia, *PSIGE Newsletter* 111: 27–31.

Stokes, G. and Goudie, F. (1990) Counselling confused elderly people, in G. Stokes and F. Goudie (eds) *Working with Dementia.* Bicester: Winslow Press.

Woods, B., Keady, J. and Seddon, D. (2008) *Involving Families in Care Homes: A Relationship-centred Approach to Dementia Care.* London: Jessica Kingsley.

6 Working with older people with learning disabilities

Terry Scragg

After reading this chapter you should be able to:

- understand the changes in services, the definitions of learning disability and the numbers of individuals affected;
- identify the main physical and psychological problems which affect older people with learning disabilities;
- consider the circumstances of carers of older people with learning disabilities and some of the consequences of loss of this key relationship;
- reflect on the impact of *Valuing People* policies and the personalization of services and the important role for social work in the lives of older people with learning disabilities.

Introduction

Since the early 1980s there have been significant changes in policies and services for people with learning disabilities; alongside these changes there has also been a rapid increase in life expectancy for people with learning disabilities reflecting improved living conditions and quality of life alongside greater access to community services. Ageing brings greater exposure to a range of common health problems where effective treatments exist, but can be limited as a result of stereotyped and ageist attitudes towards people with learning disabilities. These attitudes can expose individuals to risk of poor quality treatment and neglect and increase risks of earlier mortality. Policy initiatives such as *Valuing People* (DH 2001b) have had a major influence on practice, particularly in the growth of personalization, personal budgets and the adoption of person-centred approaches, although these developments are still at an early stage of implementation. In this changing context social work has an important role to play in supporting individuals and their families and carers, working within the framework of *Valuing People* in providing expertise and support to enable people to access services that meet their individual needs and helping to build links with wider community support systems.

Evolution of service provision

The history of learning disability services is one of gradual change from large scale institutional care to more individualized provision placing the person and their needs at the centre of the support provided. Earlier models of service provision segregated people with learning disabilities from the wider society in hospital settings which were unable to meet the needs of the individual and where the quality of provision was often of extremely poor standard. The slow transformation of services began towards the end of the twentieth century with the policy to close all long-stay hospitals, replacing them with a range of local authority residential care homes, to be superseded by supported living arrangements. These developments in service provision have provided greater opportunities for personal choice and control, with greater access to ordinary community facilities, and more individually tailored support from a wide range of service providers.

Defining disability and issues of terminology

There is a range of different terminology and definitions of learning disability, including educational, medical and legal definitions, but for the purposes of this chapter we have adopted the definition used in *Valuing People* (DH 2001b: 14) which described learning disability as a: 'Significant deficit in understanding new or complex information in learning new skills (impaired intelligence), reduced ability to cope independently (social impairment), which started before adulthood and has a lasting effect on development'.

The adoption of the term learning disabilities by government is based on the need to avoid confusion with specific learning difficulties conditions found in the educational field (Williams 2010) and is the term adopted in official publications and used in health and social care services. However it is important to understand that those to whom the definition applies may have different views and the term 'learning difficulty' is preferred by many in the self-advocacy movement as this suggests the potential to learn and to be taught new skills, rather than 'disability' which they feel emphasizes inability to do things (Sutcliffe and Simons 1993).

Numbers of people with learning disabilities

The numbers of people with a learning disability are difficult to define accurately, but figures for the United Kingdom suggest that there are approximately 210,000 people with a severe and profound disability and 1.2 million with a mild to moderate disability (Emerson and Hatton 2004). This study also estimated that there are around 25,000 older people with learning disabilities. Individuals with a severe disability are likely to be known to a range of services, whereas many of those with a mild disability are less likely to come to the attention of the statutory services. Approximately half of all adults with severe learning disabilities live with their families, with a similar number accessing a range of services increasingly based on small residential facilities or supported living (Bramner 2007).

One of the difficulties in understanding the needs of older people with learning disabilities is the lack of information about their circumstance. Grant (2010) argues that those with higher support needs are often 'lost' from learning disability services having been 'retired' from day services, moved into generic older people's services, or lost in the system due to lack of active case identification. Consequently it is difficult to estimate accurately the numbers of older people with learning disabilities in most localities, making it more difficult to provide appropriate support, and may lead to individuals experiencing impoverished lifestyles. The crucial importance of long-term planning by social care services is clearly evident from Grant's comments.

Older people with a learning disability: increasing longevity and some of its consequences

We have seen in earlier chapters that older people are increasing as a proportion of the population. This trend can also be witnessed among people with learning disabilities, who are now living much longer, although the biological aspects of ageing may differ, with evidence of ageing seen at a much younger age than the general population. Improvements in the health and social care of people with severe learning disabilities increases life expectancy, whereas those with mild learning disabilities now have a life expectancy similar to the rest of the population (Hogg 2000). An interesting statistic that illustrates this change is the dramatic improvement in the life expectancy of people with Down's syndrome. At the beginning of the twentieth century life expectancy was less than 10 years, whereas it is now approaching 50 years (Turk et al. 2001). Thorpe et al. (2000) suggest that people with learning disabilities who live beyond their third decade are now likely to live into old age.

Researchers have forecast that the number of people with a learning disability will grow by 20 per cent between 2001 and 2020, with the growth among those over 60 as high as 50 per cent (Emerson and Hatton 2004). This forecast suggests that the care needs of this group will grow exponentially, as they tend to age earlier than average and are more prone to heart disease, stroke, mental health problems and dementia. The increased numbers of older people with learning disabilities is said to result from an increased life expectancy, including those with more complex needs living into adulthood and a bulge in children with learning disabilities born in the 1950s and 1960s which is now working its way through into the 50 plus age group.

The recognition that ageing begins earlier for older people with learning disabilities is acknowledged in the National Service Framework for Older People (DH 2001a). The White Paper sets out the framework for planning services for all people over the age of 65 years, and states that when planning services for older people with learning disabilities a more extended approach is needed for people age from 50 upwards.

Common health problems that affect older people with learning disabilities

As more people with learning disabilities live to older age, they experience the same age-related health conditions as the rest of the population, although those with more severe levels of disabilities tend to experience age-related ill health at an earlier age than those with less severe disabilities (Hatzidimitriadou and Milne 2006). For example, people with Down's syndrome may show signs of ageing in their 30s, and a higher incidence of heart conditions and dementia. For those with the most severe and profound disabilities longevity is much reduced. With the onset of ageing occurring earlier it is suggested that those planning services should identify the needs of older people at an earlier age, with 50 suggested as an age when monitoring of age-related changes may occur. For people with Down's syndrome this should commence at age 40 (Janicki et al. 2002). Because of the incidence of health problems affecting people with learning disabilities access to high quality health care is crucially important with evidence from Mencap (2007) and Micheal (2008) reporting negative attitudes on the part of health professionals that expose individuals to greater risk.

Activity 6.1

List some of the potential barriers for people with learning disabilities accessing health care.

The Michaels report (2008) listed a wide range of barriers facing people with learning disabilities when accessing health care. Read this report on the Department of Health website (www.dh.gov.uk). The Mencap report (2007) also raises important questions about discrimination against people with learning disabilities in the NHS and can be accessed at www.mencap.org.uk.

Physical conditions

The most common physical conditions are those seen in the general population with mobility problems, cardiac and respiratory conditions, and those associated with deterioration of hearing and sight most prevalent. It has been suggested by Bland et al. (2003) that people with learning disabilities have less opportunity to maintain fitness and prevent deterioration. A further factor is the lack of routine monitoring of older people's health needs which may lead to undiagnosed conditions that contribute to increased levels of disability and death.

A report by Kerr et al. (2006) describes the lack of awareness of professionals that older people with learning disabilities can experience pain as a result of conditions such as dementia and arthritis, but fail to receive pain relief. Behavioural changes, particularly those that challenged staff, and had pain at their root, could go unrecognized. The report recommended that social workers in community teams for people with learning disabilities (CTPLD) should be more aware of the impact of ageing when assessing individuals and when undertaking regular reviews of care arrangements.

People with learning disabilities are also susceptible to what are known as 'syndrome-specific conditions' whereby particular forms of learning disability can result in a greater risk of associated conditions (Janicki et al. 2002). This is seen in the relationship between Down's syndrome and congenital heart defects and early onset dementia. Other conditions such as epilepsy and cerebral palsy are associated with learning disability. Janicki et al. warn against assuming that the association between these conditions is inevitable and little can be done about them. The risks of this attitude was seen in a study of people with learning disabilities who were obese. Carers and staff in services did not recognize obesity as a problem, with excess weight being seen as the 'norm' for this population (Janicki et al. 2002).

Functional mental illness

Alongside these physical conditions there is a relatively high prevalence of mental health problems in people with learning disabilities, often remaining undiagnosed or poorly managed due to lack of knowledge (Deb et al. 2001). Depression and anxiety, and reactions to bereavement and behavioural problems have been identified (Day and Jancar 1994; Moss et al. 1998). In spite of a high incidence of mental ill health among people with learning disabilities relatively few are referred to psychiatric services (Moss et al. 1998; Cooper 1999).

Dementia

Dementia causes the impairment of higher mental functioning including loss of memory, problem-solving skills, the loss of social skills and emotional control. It is a progressive condition and usually irreversible (Alzheimer's Society 2010). Early onset dementia affects some people with learning disabilities when they are relatively young. Prevalence is thought to be the same or higher than in the general population, increasing from 6 per cent in the 40–60 years age group to 70 per cent in those aged 85–94 years. It particularly affects people with Down's syndrome with 25 per cent of the 50–59 age group and 50 per cent of those aged 60–69 years. Dementia symptoms are seen in impaired daily activities, abnormal emotional and social behaviours, aggressive behaviour and eating and sleeping disturbances. Co-morbidity, for example depression, can result in symptoms and demonstrates the need for early assessment and intervention. Older people with learning disabilities with early onset of dementia may not be recognized by health professionals and care workers can be ignorant of the signs of dementia. The need for greater awareness among those working with older people with learning disabilities is important in helping to recognize the early signs of dementia.

End of life issues

Increased life expectancy means that many more older people with learning disabilities are likely to develop illnesses with a long dying phase such as cancer. The diagnosis of a terminal illness means that the person affected will experience physical and psychological changes that require recognition in order that appropriate support and expertise can be provided. Hollins and Tuffrey-Wijne (2010) describe the complex range of issues that need to be addressed when an older person with learning disabilities is dying. These include understanding how illness affects the person and the changes they are likely to experience, feelings and reactions of family members, and the arrangements made by services to support the person and provide good partnership working across the range of professionals involved in end of life care. It is particularly important that health professionals working with people with learning disabilities with terminal illnesses are aware of the importance of palliative care and that staff supporting the person understand the importance of accessing such services. Research shows that many people with learning disabilities do not have access to palliative care during the final phase of their lives (www.respond.org.uk). Where the person with learning disabilities is living in a residential service end of life issues can include the level of support needed, the skills and resources required and the emotional involvement of those providing care for the person. Support staff, particularly young carers, may not have experienced death before and this can raise fears. The needs of staff supporting the person demand sensitive support by managers to help their staff express grief where there has been longstanding involvement with the person dying and anxieties about death (Hollins and Tuffrey-Wijne 2010). Overall, the important message from these authors is that the person with learning disabilities should remain firmly in the centre of decision making and the subsequent choices made.

Psychological and social aspects of ageing

Little is known about how people with learning disabilities respond psychologically and socially to ageing. Factors could include cognitive limitations where the person has difficultly comprehending the ageing process, or where people are prevented from experiencing normal life events (Janicki et al. 2002). The importance of mortality which is an integral part of ageing can be denied to people with learning disabilities who are denied opportunities for involvement in rituals such as funerals which can help grieve the loss of loved ones (Thorpe et al. 2000). Often well-meaning actions by staff and carers protect the person from unpleasant events which it is thought may harm their development. As people with learning disabilities live longer they are increasingly likely to outlive their parents and friends. How a person copes with the death of someone close with no basic understanding of the life cycle and the concept of death can be challenging to staff supporting the person. Older people with learning disabilities should be supported to participate in family and community rituals and helped to make sense of natural events such as death and bereavement, through reminiscence and life story work (Johnson 2010).

Older people with learning disabilities and their family carers

Half of adults with learning disabilities live with a family carer, and a third live with a carer who is aged 65 and over, the majority being parents, with the remainder grand-parents or siblings (Hatzidimitriadou and Milne 2006). A study by McConkey (2005) found that one in six carers were rated as being in poor health. The health of family carers may also have an influence on the access to health care for their son or daughter with a learning disability. McGrother et al. (1996) found that carers had 40 per cent more limiting health disorders compared with the general population, with depression four times more common among female carers.

Another consequence of the increasing longevity of people with learning disabilities is that many older parents believed that their son or daughter would die before them and this has left families without plans for the future (www.respond.org.uk). It is often a crisis, such as the death of parent, or when a parent becomes too frail to continue living at home, that the family becomes visible to social care services. This can lead to the person with learning disabilities leaving the family home for the first time, often when grieving for a loved one (Blackman 2003).

Carers also tend to have limited social networks as a consequence of relatives or friends dying or moving away and many are widows. After providing intensive care and support over many years to their loved ones, their own health may be at risk. As some carers age they may be supported by the previously 'cared for person' taking on domestic tasks that used to be done by the carer although this is often unrecognized (Walker and Walker 1998).

As the age profile of people with learning disabilities changes loss of the primary carer can occur during the middle or later years of the cared for person's life. The death of the carer, or where the carer is no longer able to cope, can precipitate a crisis, often with the loss of the most intense relationship the person with learning disability has experienced, accompanied by bereavement and loss of home. The consequences of this event can be immense, with multiple losses and a 'crisis point' reached, with the involvement of formal services (Hatzidimitriadou and Milne 2006).

Case study

Mr and Mrs Brown are both in their 80s and live with their daughter, Sheila, who is 52 and has Down's syndrome. They have recently moved from a large house to a two bedroom flat as they want to prepare for the time when they are unable to care for Sheila. For much of Sheila's life after leaving school she has had no connection with social care services and no relationships outside the family. Her parents have recently contacted the local authority and a social worker has met with Sheila and her parents several times, supporting them to plan for Sheila's future care. Sheila has the potential to be more independent, but has become reliant on her parents for her everyday needs. The social worker supported Sheila and her parents in describing their needs and explored the potential range of support. The social worker arranged for Sheila to receive a personal budget, administered by her parents, enabling her to access services that would help her gain skills using community services, improving daily living skills and introducing her to a wider range of relationships and circles of support. The aim of these changes is to prepare for the time when Sheila will live independently in the flat. The social worker has also put Sheila's parents in touch with MENCAP as they were interested in discretionary trusts where they could invest a sum of money to be administered on behalf of Sheila after their deaths. This would enable a person to administer the trust on her behalf and arrange for funds to support her. In this way any money left for Sheila would not compromise her benefits or social care funding, and could be used to maintain her property.

Comment

This case study illustrates the important role of social work in helping Sheila and her parents to plan for the future. It recognizes the importance of supporting Sheila to extend her circles of support and develop those skills that will be essential for her future. It also provides reassurance to her parents that the service is aware of Sheila and her needs and is actively involved in planning for the future when they will no longer be able to provide support.

Vulnerability and abuse

Older people with learning disabilities are particularly vulnerable to abuse and exploitation (Brown 1999), with a long history of abuse in institutional and community settings (Cambridge 2007). The evidence of widespread abuse resulted in the publication of *No Secrets* (DH 2000) which made adult protection a national policy. A study by Action on Elder Abuse (2006) on the reporting of incidents to local authorities found that over a quarter concerned adults with learning disabilities. As individuals choose their own support arrangements this can bring associated risks, as some of the responsibilities currently monitored by local authorities shift to the service user. Brown and Scott (2005) consider that social workers should play a vital role in continuing to scrutinize service arrangements.

Since *No Secrets* local authority adult social care services have been required to introduce local policies and procedures in conjunction with health agencies and the police to ensure a coordinated approach to investigating reported abuse. Dependent on the agency involved, and the level of abuse reported, the investigation may be conducted by the social worker. This means that social workers need to be aware of their responsibility under the local adult protection arrangements, working effectively with partner agencies and most of all with sensitivity and awareness of the risks faced when older people with learning disabilities are at risk of abuse.

Activity 6.2

Does the drive for greater personalization mean that people with learning disabilities are exposed to greater risk? Why is it essential to build protection into the lives of people with learning disabilities?

There is a fine balance between overprotection and underprotection. Brown and Scott in Cambridge and Carnaby (2005) have described the importance of a continuing social work role in the lives of people with learning disabilities.

Positive and successful ageing

In spite of a range of health problems related to ageing which may affect older people with learning disabilities, evidence suggests that many view old age positively and engage in opportunities that make their lives richer and more meaningful (Johnson 2010). In a discussion of how individuals adapt to change in old age Bigby (2010) identifies a range of factors that can combine to reduce the positive experience of ageing, including systematic low expectations, limited opportunities and poor access to support for older people with learning disabilities. These factors stem from age-related discriminatory social attitudes and structures rather than the inherent characteristics or the ageing process itself. These attitudes are sometimes held by staff where low expectations become self-fulfilling prophecies that can be challenged by evidence that suggests older people with learning disabilities are able to adapt as they age and can be more skilled in terms of adaptive behaviour and functional skills, and have greater competence than at any other stage of their lives. How individuals are able to adapt positively to ageing will depend on the support provided. Bigby describes a range of activities that are central to support, including maintenance and strengthening of social networks, participation in community activities, the maintenance of skills and opportunities for self-expression and reflection. Underpinning all these activities is the promotion of a healthy lifestyle particularly where lack of exercise, poor diet and weight problems increase the risk of ill health.

Valuing people: the policy context

The most recent policy initiative for people with learning disabilities was the publication in 2001 of the White Paper *Valuing People* (DH 2001b). *Valuing People* is intended to address some of the longstanding disadvantages they have experienced over many years in segregated and poor quality services. The message of *Valuing People* is that people with learning disabilities are among some of the most vulnerable and socially excluded people in society, and this new policy initiative was intended to transform services to enable fuller and more independent lives as part of local communities. It is interesting that *Valuing People* makes little reference to the needs of older people, with the exception of one short section. This omission was further reinforced in *Valuing People Now* (2009b). Nevertheless *Valuing People* is based on the premise that people with learning disabilities should have equal legal and civil rights, should be supported in ways that promote their independence, and have increased choice and control over decisions in their lives and inclusion in their communities.

Personalization

To achieve the aims of *Valuing People* the previous Labour government promoted the concept of personalization set out in *Putting People First* (DH 2007). This publication and subsequent guidance (DH 2009a) describe a vision for social care which enables the individual to have maximum choice and control over how their needs are met and to directly manage their own support through a personal budget. This policy has the long term aim of offering individuals and their carers the ability to shape and commission their own services, tailoring their support more closely to their needs, rather than relying exclusively on services provided by local authorities, voluntary or private providers. A number of pilot programmes throughout the UK have tested the potential for personal budgets and the 'in control' project with its model of self-directed support is an example where this has been most extensively tested for people with learning disabilities (Duffy 2007). Currently a small minority of people with learning disabilities have a personal budget, although this figure is expected to rise as more local authorities introduce personal budgets and the policy becomes the mainstream practice in adult social care services.

Person-centred planning

Central to *Valuing People*, and underpinning the main principles of this new policy is the development of person-centred planning (PCP) as the main focus of work with people with learning disabilities. Although PCP offers the potential to transform the lives of individuals Mansel and Beadle-Brown (2005) make the point that there is also the risk that PCP can become another bureaucratic process that works on paper, but does not connect with the 'real life' of the person with a learning disability. Like all previous individualized planning systems the process can be time consuming, complex and resource intensive, with the need for leadership in services that is committed to its implementation and with staff trained to understand the purpose and processes of PCP which focuses on the implementation of plans, rather than finely honed paperwork.

The promotion of PCP as a key part of the personalization agenda has raised concerns about how this approach relates to care management (Cambridge and Carnaby 2005). Care management remains the formal mechanism for the assessment of an individual's needs and arrangement of services under the NHS and Community Care Act 1990. It was originally envisaged that care management focused on the person's needs, with the social worker able to access a devolved budget to purchase a range of services. Care management is now increasingly constrained by local authority financial arrangements and ever tightening eligibility criteria which means that social workers have little flexibility when it comes to designing services around people's needs. Cambridge (2008) has argued persuasively that to achieve the aims of *Valuing People* care management needs to be transformed to take account of the central tenets of PCP focusing on developing a supportive relationship with the service user, understanding their needs and wants, and lobbying and negotiating on their behalf to access a range of support services. In practical terms the social worker would help the service user to organize direct payments, support them to choose and purchase services, and monitor the effectiveness of support in meeting the person's needs. Cambridge's argument recognizes that some service users will need their social worker to arrange services for them, but also to ensure that they are not at risk of abuse and exploitation.

In suggesting some specific areas where social workers can make a positive contribution Duffy and Sanderson (2005) identify a number of areas where they can support individuals with learning disabilities. These include:

- systems knowledge, where the social worker is in a strong position to support the individual to navigate the service system, with its rules, policies and procedures;
- planning skills, where the social worker's knowledge of planning enables them to facilitate good decision making by the individual;
- community knowledge, where social workers can complement and extend the individual's own knowledge through their expertise;
- individual insight, acknowledging that the individual may be an expert on their own needs, but other perspectives offered by the social worker can offer something different and contribute valuable insights.

Sanderson (2002) has described PCP as rethinking the role of the learning disability professional, with the disabled person in control and the professionals providing problem-solving skills and acting as critical allies in making things happen. This has considerable implications for social work if it is to develop practices that incorporate the goal of personalization for people with learning disabilities.

The social worker's contribution

From the evidence on ageing and the physical, psychological and social circumstances and their impact on older people with learning disabilities, social work has an important role to play in supporting individuals. In helping them to identify their needs, supporting them in making choices about the care arrangements that best suit them and arranging services where required, usually through local authority multidisciplinary teams (Community Team for People with Learning Disability: CTPLD). This makes the contribution of social work particularly satisfying as it offers a range of approaches that support and enhance the quality of life of the individual with a learning disability. *Valuing People* (DH 2001b) has described the devaluation and exclusion that can be experienced by people with learning disabilities so it is important that the structural factors in society that may exacerbate the problems experienced by the older people with learning disabilities are recognized and understood in social work interventions.

Personalization has considerable implications and challenges for social work in the future as it fundamentally changes the way that professionals and people using services need to work together. Reframing social work practice in the context of *Valuing People,* the policy of personalization and adopting a person-centred approach could liberate practitioners to use their skills in ways that provide better outcomes for individuals who need their support. It also releases social workers from the straightjacket of care management where they are perceived as the gatekeepers or rationers of services, driven by increasingly restrictive eligibility criteria and resource constraints. Drawing on social work values, a reframed practice would enable practitioners to support older people with learning disabilities in taking greater control of their lives and providing support for the choices that matter to them, and provide ideas and information that enables individuals to commission services more closely tailored to their needs.

This would also support an approach to social work practice that encompasses working directly with individuals in both problem-solving and therapeutic ways, mobilizing resources to meet particular needs through liaison and coordination of services, and working with groups and communities to construct new types of response to problems, including the development of new services where gaps in provision are identified (Lymbery 2005).

Social work also has an important role to play in ensuring that older people with learning disabilities, who through the drive to increase personalization can be exposed to greater risk. Because of the ever present risk of exploitation, abuse and neglect, individuals need the support of family, community and services that make up the fabric of their lives. Brown and Scott (2005) recognize the important role played by social workers among other professional workers in supporting vulnerable people and containing situations of risk.

We can see how social work with older people with learning disabilities, incorporating a person-centred approach, can support the vision of a more personalized service. Social workers using this approach have the potential to get to know the individual, to understand their life experience and empower them to make their own choices, within the framework of anti-oppressive practice. PCP offers a more satisfying approach than the current care management practice which emphasizes a bureaucratic process, separation from the person requesting services, and driven by a narrow perspective of an individual's needs.

Summary

We have seen in this chapter how the lives of older people with learning disabilities have been transformed through the development of services that are more individualized and tailored to their personal needs. Along with greater life expectancy has come a range of needs including health, social and psychological, affecting older people and requiring the support of service systems. The introduction of *Valuing People* (DH 2001b) has provided impetus for a new approach to working with people with learning disabilities which has the potential to transform their lives through personalization and person-centred planning. Social work has an important role to play in supporting the implementation of these policy initiatives, and promoting the greater control by those people using services in order that the support they receive is more closely tuned to their needs.

Further reading

Cambridge, P. and Carnaby, S. (eds) (2005) *Person Centred Planning and Care Management with People with Learning Disabilities*. London: Jessica Kingsley.

Carnaby, S. (ed.) (2007) *Learning Disabiilty Today*, 2nd edn. Brighton: Pavilion Publications.

Grant, G., Ramcharan, P., Flynn, M. and Richardson, M. (eds) (2005) *Learning Disability: A Life Cycle Approach*, 2nd edn. Maidenhead: Open University Press.

Williams, P. (2006) *Social Work with People with Learning Difficulties*. Exeter: Learning Matters.

References

Action on Elder Abuse (2006) *Adult Protection Data Collection and Reporting Requirements*. London: Action on Elder Abuse.

Alzheimer's Society (2010) *Leaning Disabilities and Dementia*. www.alzheimers.org.uk (accessed 25 July 2011).

Bigby, C. (2010) Growing old: adapting to change and realizing a sense of belonging, continuity and purpose, in G. Grant, P. Ramcharan, M. Flynn and M. Richardson (eds) *Learning Disability: A Life Cycle Approach*, 2nd edn. Maidenhead: Open University Press.

Blackman, N. (2003) *Loss and Learning Disability*. London: Worth Publishing.

Bland, R., Hutchinson, N., Oakes, P. and Yates, C. (2003) Double jeopardy? Needs and services for older people who have learning disabilities, *Journal of Learning Disabilities* 7(4): 323–44.

Bramner, A. (2007). In context: policy and legislation, in S. Carnaby (ed.) *Learning Disability Today*. Brighton: Pavilion Publishing.

Brown, H. (1999) Abuse of people with learning disabilities: layers of concern and analysis, in N. Stanley, J. Manthorpe and B. Penhale (eds) *Institutional Abuse: Perspectives Across the Life Course*. London: Routledge.

Brown, H. and Scott, K. (2005) Person centred planning and the adult protection process, in P. Cambridge and S. Carnaby (eds) *Person Centred Planning and Care Management for People with Learning Disabilities*. London: Jessica Kingsley.

Cambridge, P. (2007) In safe hands: protecting people with learning disabilities from abuse, in S. Carnaby (ed.) *Learning Disability Today*. Brighton: Pavilion.

Cambridge, P. (2008) The case for a new case management service for people with learning disabilities, *British Journal of Social Work* 38(1): 91–116.

Cambridge, P. and Carnaby, S. (eds) (2005) *Person Centred Planning and Care Management with People with Learning Disabilities*. London: Jessica Kingsley.

Cooper, S.A. (1999) Psychiatric disorders in elderly people with developmental disabilities, in N. Bouras (ed.) *Psychiatric and Behavioural Disorders in Developmental Disabilltiies and Mental Retardation*. Cambridge: Cambridge University Press.

Day, K. and Jancar, J. (1994) Mental and physical health and ageing in mental handicap: a review, *Journal of Intellectual Disability Research* 38: 241–56.

Deb, S.M., Holt, T.G. and Bouras, N. (2001) *Practice Guidelines for the Assessment and Diagnosis of Mental Health Problems in Adults with Intellectual Disability*. Brighton: Pavilion.

DH (Department of Health) (2000) *No Secrets: Guidance on Developing and Implementing Multi-disciplinary Policies and Procedures to Protect Vulnerable Adults from Abuse.* London: Department of Health.

DH (Department of Health) (2001a) *National Service Framework for Older People.* London: Department of Health.

DH (Department of Health) (2001b) *Valuing People: A New Strategy for Learning Disability for the 21st Century.* London: Department of Health.

DH (Department of Health) (2007) *Putting People First: A Shared Vision and Commitment to the Transformation of Adult Social Care.* London: Department of Health.

DH (Department of Health) (2009a) *Transforming Adult Social Care.* LAC (DH) (2009)1. London: HMSO.

DH (Department of Health) (2009b) *Valuing People Now.* London: Department of Health.

Duffy, S. (2007) Care management and self-directed support, *Journal of Integrated Care* 15(5): 3–14.

Duffy, S. and Sanderson, H. (2005) Relationship between care management and person centred planning, in P. Cambridge and S. Carnaby (eds) *Person Centred Planning and Care Management with People with Learning Disabilities.* London: Jessica Kingsley.

Emerson, E. and Hatton, C. (2004) *Estimating Future Needs/Demands for Support for People with Learning Disabilities in England.* Lancaster: Lancaster University.

Grant, G. (2010) Healthy and successful ageing, in G. Grant, P. Ramacharan, M. Flynn and M. Richardson (eds) *Learning Disability: A Life Cycle Approach*, 2nd edn. Maidenhead: Open University Press.

Hatzidimitriadou, E. and Milne, A. (2006) Providing care for older people with learning disabilities, in S. Carnaby and P. Cambridge (eds) *Intimate and Personal Care with People with Learning Disability.* London: Jessica Kingsley.

Hogg, J. (2000) *Improving Essential Health Care for People with Learning Disabilities: Strategies for Success.* Dundee: University of Dundee.

Hollins, S. and Tuffrey-Wijne, I. (2010) End-of-life issues, in G. Grant, P. Ramcharan, M. Flynn and M. Richardson (eds) *Learning Disability: A Life Cycle Approach.* Maidenhead: Open University Press.

Janicki, M.P., Davidson, P.W., Henderson, C.M. and Davidson, P.W. (2002) Health characteristics and health services utilization in older adults with intellectual disability living in community residences, *Journal of Intellectual Disability Research* 46: 287–98.

Johnson, K. (2010) A late picking: narratives of older people with learning disabilities, in G. Grant, P. Ramcharan, M. Flynn and M. Richardson (eds) *Learning Disability: A Life Cycle Approach.* Maidenhead: Open University Press.

Kerr, D., Cunningham, C. and Wilkinson, H. (2006) *Responding to the Pain Experiences of People with a Learning Difficulty and Dementia.* York: Joseph Rowntree Foundation.

Lymbery, M. (2005) *Social Work with Older People: Context, Policy and Practice.* London: Sage.

McConkey, R. (2005) Fair shares? Supporting families caring for adult persons with intellectual disabilities, *Journal of Intellectual Disability Research* 49: 600–12.

McGrother, C.W., Hauck, A., Bhamumik, S., Thorp, C. and Taub, N. (1996) Community care for adults with learning disability and their carers: needs and outcomes from the Leicestershire register, *Journal of Intellectual Disability Research* 40: 183–90.

Mansel, J. and Beadle-Brown, J. (2005) Person-centred planning and person-centred action: a critical perspective, in P. Cambridge and S. Carnaby (eds) *Person Centred Planning and Care Management with People with Learning Disabilities*. London: Jessica Kingsley.

Mencap (2007) *Death by Indifference: Follow up to the Treat me Right Report*. London: Mencap.

Micheals, J. (2008) *Healthcare for All: Report of the Independent Enquiry into Access to Healthcare for People with Learning Disabilities*. London: Department of Health.

Moss, S., Lambe, L. and Hogg, J. (1998) *Ageing Matters: Pathways for Older People with a Learning Disability – Manager's Reader*. Kidderminster: British Institute of Learning Disabilties.

Sanderson, H. (2002) A plan is not enough: exploring the development of person centred teams, in S. Holborn and P. Vietze (eds) *Person Centred Planning: Research, Practice and Future Directions*. Baltimore, MD: Paul H. Brookes.

Sutcliffe, J. and Simons, K. (1993) *Self-Advocacy and Adults with Learning Difficulties*. Leicester: National Institute of Adult Continuing Education.

Thorpe, L., Davidson, P. and Jancar, M. (2000) *Healthy Ageing – Adults with Intellectual Disabilities: Biobehavioural Issues*. Geneva: World Health Organization.

Turk, V., Dodd, K. and Christmas, M. (2001) *Down's Syndrome and Dementia: Briefing for Commissioners*. London: Foundation for Learning Disabilities.

Walker, C. and Walker, A. (1998) *Uncertain Futures: People with Learning Difficulties and their Ageing Family Carers*. Brighton: Pavilion Publishing.

Williams, P. (2010) *Social Work with People with Learning Difficulties*. Exeter: Learning Matters.

7 Working with older people with long term conditions

Rick Fisher and Terry Scragg

After reading this chapter you should be able to:

- understand the main government policies related to people with long term conditions and some of the more common long term conditions;
- understand the needs of informal carers who are supporting a person with a long term condition;
- recognize the growing importance of assistive technology in supporting people with long term conditions;
- recognize the importance of effective collaborative working with professionals supporting people with long term conditions;
- appreciate the limitations of current services and some of the areas for change needed to develop more effective services.

Introduction

This chapter provides an overview of long term conditions that affect older people, including the main government policy initiatives and a description of those conditions social workers are likely to witness in their work with older people. It will also discuss carers' issues and the importance of supporting carers. The chapter will then briefly consider assistive technology and its role in supporting independence. Finally the value of collaborative working is explored recognizing the multidisciplinary nature of work with older people with long term conditions.

What is a long term condition?

Long term conditions are the largest single cause of poor health and mortality in the UK and make the greatest demands on health care resources. They have the power to limit the capacity of those who experience them; and may affect individuals physically or psychologically, and in many cases will impact on both these aspects of their lives. For the purpose of this chapter the following definition is adopted: 'A long term condition is one that cannot be cured, but can be managed through medication and/ or therapy' (www.dh.gov.uk.en/Heathcare/Longtermconditions)

For the Department of Health (2010) a long term condition is one that is both enduring (long term) and currently has no cure. Important distinctions also exist between conditions that are inherited, congenital, acquired and degenerative. The Department of Health estimates that long term conditions affect in excess of 15.4 million people in the United Kingdom, with three out of five people aged over 60 (DH 2010). Eighty per cent of primary care consultations and two thirds of emergency hospital admissions in the UK are related to long term conditions. Levels of chronic illness are predicted to increase as the population ages. As well as putting pressure on health and social care services chronic illness has a significant impact on older people's quality of life and well-being (Audit Commission 2004). Consequently, it is likely that a social worker involved with older adults will work with a number of service users who have long term conditions. These are likely to be varied and complex in their nature and as such will offer considerable challenge to those with the condition, their carers, and professionals.

Activity 7.1

You are a student on placement in an adult services team and are visiting an older person who requires an assessment.

How can an understanding of long term conditions that are likely to affect older people help make you aware of the person's wider needs?

An understanding of long term conditions is important in understanding how an older person may have difficultly managing many aspects of their personal care and day living tasks, and also mean that they are likely to be dependent on others, and need the support of a range of professionals, to support them in their preferred choices about their independence and quality of life.

Long term conditions model

The Department of Health's long term condition model (www.dh.gov.uk/en/ Healthcare/longtermcondtions) categorizes the population with long term conditions into those that have the most complex needs, those with medium needs and those whose condition is relatively easy to control. The management of long term conditions is based on four broad interventions:

- case management, with dedicated one to one support from skilled health professionals such as community matrons, who have regular face to face contact;

- personalized care planning, using a person-centred approach with the individual at the centre of decision making about their care and how services will be delivered;
- supporting people to self care, by providing information and skills to enable the individual to manage their own health (for example, the Expert Patients Programme);
- assistive technology, using emerging telecare and telehealth technology to support people to remain independent and self care for as long as possible.

Government policies in the care of people with long term conditions

The government has produced policies in response to the specific needs of people with long term conditions, policies related to older people and policies related to people with disabilities generally, all of which have reflected a shift towards empowering people to have more control over their lives:

Managing the complexity of long term conditions

Supporting People with Long Term Conditions (DH 2005a) recognized that there is a need for a joint health and social care approach to these conditions. It further stated that such conditions were likely to result in complex needs that required careful assessment and management, if those with the conditions were to realize their full potential. It also recognized that the most appropriate way to approach these conditions was to support the individual to manage their daily lives in their own homes wherever possible. The document further explained the need for services to be delivered on a local basis and the need for staff training to ensure the delivery of appropriate care.

The *National Service Framework on Long Term Conditions* (DH 2005b) built on *Supporting People with Long Term Conditions* but also focused particularly on the needs of those with neurological conditions. It was particularly concerned with:

- improving health outcomes for people with long term conditions by offering a personalized care plan for vulnerable people most at risk;
- reducing emergency bed days by 5 per cent by 2008 through improved care in primary care and community settings for people with long term conditions;
- improving access to services, ensuring that by 2008 no one waits more than 18 weeks from GP referral to hospital treatment, including all diagnostic procedures and tests.

To achieve these aims it identified 11 quality requirements for service provision which were based upon the experiences of people with long term conditions and their carers (see Box 7.1).

Box 7.1

11 quality requirements for service provision

- Quality requirement 1: A person centred service. People with long term neurological conditions are offered integrated assessment and planning of their health and social care needs. They are to have the information they need to make informed decisions about their care and treatment and, where appropriate, to support them to manage their condition themselves.
- Quality requirement 2: Early recognition, prompt diagnosis and treatment. People suspected of having a neurological condition are to have prompt access to specialist neurological expertise for an accurate diagnosis and treatment as close to home as possible.
- Quality requirement 3: Emergency and acute management. People needing hospital admission for a neurosurgical or neurological emergency are to be assessed and treated in a timely manner by teams with the appropriate neurological and resuscitation skills and facilities.
- Quality requirement 4: Early and specialist rehabilitation. People with long term neurological conditions who would benefit from rehabilitation are to receive timely, ongoing, high quality rehabilitation services in hospital or other specialist settings to meet their continuing and changing needs. When ready, they are to receive the help they need to return home for ongoing community rehabilitation and support.
- Quality requirement 5: Community rehabilitation and support. People with long term neurological conditions living at home are to have ongoing access to a comprehensive range of rehabilitation, advice and support to meet their continuing and changing needs, increase their independence and autonomy and help them to live as they wish.
- Quality requirement 6: Vocational rehabilitation. People with long term neurological conditions are to have access to appropriate vocational assessment, rehabilitation and ongoing support, to enable them to find, regain or remain in work and access other occupational and educational opportunities.
- Quality requirement 7: Providing equipment and accommodation. People with long term neurological conditions are to receive timely, appropriate assistive technology/ equipment and adaptations to accommodation to support them to live independently, help them with their care, maintain their health and improve their quality of life.
- Quality requirement 8: Providing personal care and support. Health and social care services work together to provide care and support to enable people with long term neurological conditions to achieve maximum choice about living independently at home.
- Quality requirement 9: Palliative care. People in the later stages of long term neurological conditions are to receive a comprehensive range of palliative care services when they need them to control symptoms, offer pain relief, and meet their needs for personal, social, psychological and spiritual support, in line with the principles of palliative care.

- Quality requirement 10: Supporting family and carers. Carers of people with long term neurological conditions are to have access to appropriate support and services that recognise their needs both in their role as carer and in their own right.
- Quality requirement 11: Caring for people with neurological conditions in hospital or other health and social care settings. People with long term neurological conditions are to have their specific neurological needs met while receiving treatment or care for other reasons in any health or social care setting.

Source: National Service Framework for Long Term Conditions (Department of Health 2005a).

In *Improving the Health and Well-being of People with Long term Conditions* the Department of Health (2010) developed further the notion of the individual at the heart of care. It promoted the need to embed personalization across all public services, with personal budgets under the control of individuals, who would purchase the care that helped them manage their condition. The introduction of the Health Act 2009 allowed pilots of personal health budgets for people with long term conditions.

The care of older people

The *National Service Framework for Older People* (www.nhs.uk/NHSEngland/NSF/Pages/Olderpeople) sets out eight standards in the care of older people. The standards aimed to ensure that care is based on clinical need, not age, and that services treat older people as individuals, promoting their quality of life, independence, dignity and their right to make choices about their own care. They focused on common conditions and problems for older people, for example, strokes and falls and preventing crisis and emergency admissions occurring. They also aimed to improve intermediate care, speeding up hospital discharge and helping people get better in their own homes or in supported community settings.

The personalization agenda

Our Health, Our Care, Our Say: A New Direction for Community Services (DH 2006) provided a new direction for community services, with a vision for community-based care, with the aim of enabling people to live more independently and to exercise greater personal choice. To achieve this will need greater flexibility in service provision, improved access, prompt interventions and a broader range of service provision from which individuals can select the care that enables them to live with minimal disruption to their daily lives. More recently *High Quality Care for All* (DH 2008) has further reinforced the need for all services to be personalized (see www.scie.org.uk for more information on personalization).

The person as expert in their condition

Closely related to these policy initiatives is *The Expert Patients Programme* (DH 2002). This initiative recognizes that the person with a long term condition often understands their condition better than professionals and becomes an expert in learning how to cope. The aim of the programme is to support people who have a chronic condition by increasing their confidence, improving their quality of life and helping them manage their condition more effectively. The programme provides group-based generic training delivered by a network of trainers and volunteer tutors, all of whom have a long term condition. The programme offers training courses which teach people how to manage their condition using core skills, including making the best use of resources, developing effective partnerships with service providers and taking appropriate action when this is needed. Currently over 100,000 people have participated in the programme, with some positive results, although there has been no reduction in service use (Ham 2011).

Each of these policy initiatives point to the need to create and provide services that augment individuals' lives, with service users empowered to make choices about how they want to manage their condition and how they want to be supported by health and social care services. To achieve this requires a fundamental shift from a 'one size fits all' approach, often relying on hospital care, to a community based, responsive, adaptable and flexible service, requiring whole system change. The challenge for local systems is the need for large scale change, not only in location of delivery, but also in behavioural change of service users and professionals providing services to create the individualized care that both the government and users of services demand (Singh and Ham 2006).

Case study

In a recent controversial case which reached the Supreme Court, 70-year-old Elaine MacDonald took her local authority, Kensington and Chelsea, to court to overturn a decision on the level of funding it provided for her. Ms MacDonald has a number of long term conditions, including the consequences of a stroke, as well as arthritis and a heart condition. She had been admitted to hospital on several occasions following falls and after her third hospitalization in 2007 her medical consultant advised a night carer would be helpful in the initial stage following her last stay in hospital. Following her discharge from hospital her local authority provided a personal budget which included sufficient funding for night time care as she needed to use a commode at night and was at risk of further falls. Following several re-assessments of her needs, this culminated in 2008 with her care funding being reduced and she was no longer funded for night time care, but instead provided with funding for the purchase of incontinence pads.

Ms Macdonald issued a claim for judicial review with the case eventually reaching the Appeal Court and finally the Supreme Court where the judges found in favour of the local authority and its decision to reduce funding to Ms MacDonald.

Comment

This is a very important case which dramatically highlights the tension between the aspirations of policies on personalization for older people with long term conditions and the resources local authorities are willing to make available to fund care packages. At the heart of this case is the Resource Allocation System (RAS) and how the local authority had used this to quantify Ms MacDonald's needs and her personal budget, which left her dissatisfied and felt that it undermined her quality of life. The following websites have detailed accounts of the case and the court decisions:

www.ardenchambers.com
www.fightingmonsters.wordpress.com
www.headoflegal.com/supreme-court-judgements

Long term conditions commonly affecting older people

While the term long term condition covers a wide spectrum of conditions, the focus is on those which most commonly affect older people. It should also be noted that a person may suffer from more than one condition. In that case the symptoms may exacerbate those of the other condition and/or medication for one condition may aggravate the symptoms of the other. It should also be recognized that by the very definition a long term condition cannot be 'cured' or reversed and is therefore rarely a goal for treatment.

Long term conditions affecting the respiratory systems

Long term respiratory conditions include chronic obstructive pulmonary diseases (COPD), such as chronic bronchitis, emphysema and asthma. A common feature of the ways in which they present is the debilitating effect they have on those who experience them. Shortness of breath is the most marked feature in all of these conditions. This is not a situation in which an individual becomes weary after climbing several flights of stairs; rather it is where the person struggles to cope with many of the more mundane activities of daily living that most take for granted. This may mean that the individual is unable to fulfil personal hygiene needs, and has very restricted mobility. Each breath is an effort and this consequently means that all activities must be planned in advance if the older person's safety is to be maintained.

Long term conditions affecting the cardiovascular system

Long term conditions which affect the circulatory or cardiovascular system primarily concern heart conditions and stroke. Long term heart conditions are usually referred to as 'heart failure' and these are closely related to respiratory conditions. As a result, a person who is in heart failure will experience shortness of breath that produces a consequent reduction in mobility and capacity to undertake the usual activities of daily life. A stroke or 'cerebro-vascular accident' occurs when there is an interruption to the blood carrying oxygen and nutrients to the brain. Strokes may be described as 'dense' and have long lasting effects, or they may be very minor 'transient ischaemic attacks '(TIA) which may pass almost unnoticed. There is a considerable range of effects from strokes that extends from being catastrophic, with complete loss of consciousness and residual loss of bodily functions such as paralysis, incontinence, loss of or impaired communication, to minor lapses in consciousness that may have very little residual impact.

Long term conditions affecting the nervous system

Long term conditions relating to the nervous system include Parkinson's disease, multiple sclerosis and motor neurone disease. These are very different conditions about which there is sometimes confusion. Parkinson's disease occurs where there is a deficiency in the chemical dopamine. This results in tremors, rigidity and slowness of movement and can affect all of the muscles in the body. The condition is thought to exist in 120,000 people in the UK (www.parkinsons.org.uk).

Multiple sclerosis (MS) is a degenerative condition of the central nervous system (the brain and spinal cord). The central nervous system controls the body's actions and activities, such as movement and balance. As MS affects the protective sheath around nerves, transmission of messages to and from the brain is disrupted. As a result it manifests in a variety of ways and sometimes appears to mimic the symptoms of stroke, in that those who experience the condition may have slurred speech and difficulties with bladder continence.

Motor neurone disease (MND) is a progressive degenerative disease that attacks the upper and lower motor neurones. This leads to weakness and wasting of muscles, causing increasing loss of mobility in the limbs, and difficulties with speech, swallowing and breathing. MND progresses, usually from the muscles of hands, feet and mouth. The effects of MND can vary enormously from person to person, from the presenting symptoms, the rate and pattern of the disease progression to the length of survival time after diagnosis. By contrast with multiple sclerosis it does not usually affect the bladder or bowel. The incidence or number of people who will develop MND each year is about two people in every 100,000 and the number of people living with MND at any one time in the UK is approximately seven in every 100,000. Breathing and production of mucous and saliva are affected in MND and a major risk to the patient is that of choking. It is important to note that in all of these conditions there is little change in cognition or understanding, and in the case of MND the individual may be fully aware of all of their surroundings, yet be unable to communicate in any way (MND Association 2002).

Long term conditions affecting the metabolic system

Diabetes mellitus is a major long term metabolic condition that occurs when there is a disruption in the body's ability to metabolize carbohydrate and sugar effectively. There are two types: Type 1 where the body produces no insulin or insulin of insufficient quality or quantity to metabolize sugars and Type 2 where the body is unable to use insulin produced in the body effectively. The number of people with diabetes in the

UK is thought to be 2.6 million. Between 10 and 15 per cent are those with Type 1 diabetes who rely on insulin (Diabetes UK 2010). There are many causes of this common disease and although it is frequently recognized that lifestyle factors such as diet, alcohol consumption and exercise have considerable impact on the development of the condition, these are only part of the picture. There should also be acknowledgement of the necessity of constant monitoring, not only of blood sugar levels but of skin condition, particularly that of the feet, and of the importance of regular eye tests. Impaired vision and even total blindness is a common complication of diabetes.

Dementia

Dementia has been discussed in Chapter 5 and it is suggested that readers refer to this chapter for more information on this condition.

Risk of falls for those living with a long term condition

Falls in themselves do not constitute a long term condition; rather they may be a consequence of such a condition. A 'fall' is defined as 'an event whereby an individual comes to rest on the ground or another lower level with or without loss of consciousness' (American Geriatric Society/British Geriatric Society and American Academy of Orthopaedic Surgeons Panel on Falls Prevention 2001). It is estimated that in a primary care trust (PCT) or local authority (LA) with a population of 320,000, that there would be approximately 45,000 people aged over 65 in 2009 experiencing falls (Southwest Falls and Fractures 2010). Falls vary considerably in their severity. When faced with a situation where the person who has sustained a fall is socially isolated several factors come into play. These may be considered to be both physical and psychological aspects and a combination is highly likely where social isolation exists. In all the long term conditions discussed in this chapter, there is the potential for falls to occur. Those with COPD may have restricted movement due to trailing oxygen tubing. Those suffering from MS may experience dizziness or inability to control muscle spasms. Similarly, disorientation may affect those with diabetes or dementia; in the case of diabetes there may also be visual impairment. Sustaining a fall is at best unnerving and at worst it is extremely frightening for the person who has fallen and for their carer. A person who falls and is undiscovered for several hours may rapidly develop hypothermia which can quickly lead to death. Clearly this is a serious situation and one which has considerable impact upon the planning and organization of care for individuals in their own homes. Guidance issued by the National Institute for Health and Clinical Excellence (NICE) in 2004 and updated in 2010 addressed the assessment and prevention of falls in older people. NICE guidance sets out ideas about the assessment of risk when individuals first come into contact with the caring services.

Informal carers and long term conditions

Older people with long term conditions rely substantially on informal care, and it is estimated that this provision is valued at approximately £70 billion, and constitutes a 'third frontier' in care delivery (Berry 2011). The majority of long term care of older people is still provided informally by families with one in eight adults providing this care. It is estimated that there are 3.3 million women and 2.4 million male carers, with over half of all carers supporting a person over 75 years of age (www.ageconcern.org. uk). A survey of carers in households in England in 2009/10 (www.ic.nhs.uk/pubs/ carerssurvey) found that a quarter of all carers were themselves over 65 years, and were likely to be providing care for over 20 hours a week. In addition half the carers reported that their health had been affected by caring, and that their social and leisure activities were restricted. In spite of the significant contribution of informal carers to older people with long term conditions, they still receive very limited support from public services, with caring responsibilities creating a series of severe problems for many carers.

A survey of research concerned with the needs of carers of people with long term conditions (Harris et al. 2003), although concerned with adults up to the age of 65, found a number of factors that applied across a range of long term conditions and caring situations. These included:

- services for the cared for person were patchy and that carers were not seen as a priority area;
- carers frequently had a negative experience of service provision and felt they were not listened to;
- the health status of the cared for person could have a dramatic effect on the health of the carer;
- carers experienced more distress about behavioural and social problems which had an adverse effect on families;
- some carers did not want to be involved in some of the practical and emotional aspects of caring and similarly the person with a long term condition did not want carer involvement in this area;
- carers experienced grief for the loss of the person's potential and personality.

Although some caution is required in interpreting these findings across all informal care with older people with long term conditions, they nevertheless point to some generic factors that professionals need to take into account when working with older people and who are supported by informal carers.

Case study

William Jones, aged 80, lives with his daughter Jennifer, and his son-in-law Graham, along with their four children. Mr Jones moved to live with his daughter a year ago when he could no longer manage on his own. He has a severe respiratory condition that requires a constant oxygen supply and he also has an associated heart condition. Due to his dependency his daughter, who has given up her job, and son-in-law provide a significant amount of informal care, including getting up at night to assist him to the toilet. The increasing demands of caring is having an effect on Graham and Jennifer's relationship as well as causing concern that their children are neglected and resentful of their grandfather. Graham and Jennifer have discussed with Mr Jones his entering a nursing home, but he adamantly refuses to consider it. Family life has also been disrupted by the need to call the emergency services several times when Mr Jones collapsed and found breathing difficult, with paramedics providing treatment in the home. Graham has contacted the social services department as he is concerned about the family situation and particularly the demands on his wife and the effects on their children. You have been asked to visit the family. What issues do you need to consider?

Comment

This case study demonstrates the complexity of situations where an older person with a long term condition is reliant on informal care to support them and the pressure this places on the family. Social work in such situations requires an understanding of the impact of a long term condition on the person, and the pressures this can place on informal carers. It demands both support for the service user's independence and recognition of the needs of informal carers. The following points should be considered in relation to the case study:

- *How does the cared for person feel about being dependent on their family for support?*
- *What services would the cared for person feel would support them and their carers?*
- *Do the carers have sufficient time for themselves and the children?*
- *What is the impact on their health of the caring role?*
- *What is the impact on their relationship with the cared for person?*
- *Do the carers feel they are receiving sufficient support?*
- *Does caring have an impact on their personal and social life?*
- *What impact does caring have on their financial situation and whether they are receiving the Carer's Allowance, Disability Living Allowance and Attendance Allowance?*
- *Have the carers been offered the opportunity to manage a personal budget on behalf of their relative which would potentially provide the opportunity to personalize a care package more effectively?*
- *What other sources of information and help are available through local organizations that could support them?*

The growing importance of assistive technology

The prevalence of an ageing population with long term conditions is a principal driver of the need for assistive technology that embraces a range of equipment and processes, with the primary aim of supporting independent living. In his review of recent developments in chronic illness policy in the UK, Ham (2010) identified ten key characteristics of a high performing chronic care system, with information technology underpinning the provision of care. Everyday items such as kettle tippers and tap turners can enhance independence as can furniture raisers, and heightened toilet seats. Similarly grab handles and stair rails will be invaluable aids to many frail older people.

Where the older person with a long term condition is particularly at risk, is living alone or has a history of falls, a variety of more complex assistive technology products is increasingly being developed, designed to improve the quality of life of those who use them often through remote monitoring. These devices were originally concerned with home safety and security monitoring, but have grown to include a wide range of sensors and devices that are capable of being personalized to the needs of the service user. The range of assistive technologies include telecare, where environmental sensors indicate the movement of an older person or use of equipment in the home, and tele-monitoring where devices are used to monitor clinical parameters or 'vital signs' in a person's home and transmit data to a central monitoring service. A study in Sheffield (Soady and Day 2011) identified the changing demographics of the city. The popula-tion of older people age 65+ will continue to grow, but the most rapid increase will be in the 85+ age group and those with dementia, and these will become the main drivers for future demand and the deployment of telecare devices and services. The study predicted a significant growth in the number of older people with long term condi-tions, particularly in the 85+ age range who are also frail and dependent and at risk of falls and have difficulty with self-care tasks, including those with dementia.

Activity 7.2

When assessing a service user who lives alone and is at risk, can you identify how assistive technology could assist them to retain their independence?

When involved in assessing a person's needs, a familiarity with the range of assistive technology available to support an older person with a long term conditions is helpful as this can provide guidance in spotting areas of their everyday activities that could be enhanced by simple equipment, or their security and health improved by telecare products and processes.

The need for professionals to work collaboratively

Working with people with long term conditions is an area of practice that requires a number of professionals to coordinate their activities and use their knowledge and understanding of the contribution of other professions and agencies, as well as main-taining an awareness of the skills needed for effective multi-professional working (Goble 2009). The routine management of long term conditions is delivered by primary care teams, particularly nurses, with examples of case management and the deploy-ment of community matrons (Hutt et al. 2004; Singh and Ham 2006) improving the care for older people and reducing the use of emergency admissions to hospital. In his review of what is needed to achieve a high quality service for people with long term conditions Ham (2010) identifies a number of key elements that services need to consider. Three that are particularly important to social workers are the need to ensure that service users are able to self-manage their condition with support from carers and families, that social care is fully involved in work with people with long term conditions alongside professionals from primary care services, and that no single intervention is sufficient and demands a range of contributions from different professionals.

If services are to support the vision of a person-centred approach to people with long term conditions there needs to be a commitment to supporting the person in a way that encourages maximum independence and autonomy, not only in self-care, with support where needed, but in their choice and control in decisions about their care and treatment. Even where an older person with a long term condition lacks capacity they should be involved as much as possible about any decision that affects them. Assessing capacity often benefits from the contribution of members of the multi-disciplinary team rather than one profession (for a discussion of the Mental Capacity Act 2005 and implications for work with people with long term conditions see Mantell and Clarke 2011). Collaboration then is the cornerstone for multi-professional teams working to support people with long term conditions (Goble 2009). The value of professionals working from a shared value base and communicating that value base is regarded by Beresford and Trevillion (1995) as the foundation of effective multi-professional practice.

Some of the key issues in services for older people with long term conditions

Although there has been an increasing recognition of the need to improve services for older people with long term conditions, articulated through successive government policy statements and programmes of innovation, particularly in the primary care field, with emphasis on more personalized support, progress has been painfully slow and uneven (Ham 2010), with developments too often reliant on one-off projects rather than embedded across all services. Furthermore the current organizational arrangements and service structures are seen as a barrier to change, with the current reorganization in the NHS likely to further impede effective service delivery. It is recognized that there is still a considerable amount of development needed to achieve the type of service that would meet the expressed needs of individuals, with evidence from users' groups and research findings that the present levels of funding and service provision are inadequate (Beresford and Shaping Our Lives 2010), and that there is a significant gap between the rhetoric of improvement and change, and the reality faced by many older people and their carers.

Services for people with long term conditions are influenced by a number of factors, including the population growth of older people, the prevalence of dependency levels, assumptions about the continued availability of informal care, the structures and cost of services, and decisions about public expenditure, which is seen to be chronically inadequate in relation to the extent of need, which is central to maintaining current levels of provision and supporting future developments. Services for older people with long term conditions, along with other groups, is at a crossroads with urgent need to consider the funding of services, and to ensure that social care is accorded the priority it demands by government, politicians and policy makers, if it is to achieve a truly person-centred service (Standards We Expect Consortium 2011).

Practice points for work with people with long term conditions

Effective social work with older people with long term conditions requires knowledge and understanding of a wide range of factors. Some we have briefly covered in this chapter, but above all remember the following points:

- Acknowledge the challenges that the individual faces as they manage their long term condition.
- Recognize small adjustments to the professional approach, such as negotiating the timing of support, that facilitate minimum disruption to family life, as this may have considerable impact upon the ongoing relationship between the service user and providers.
- Recognize that the older person's care needs may fluctuate and/or deteriorate, so monitor and record changes carefully – sometimes it can be difficult for those living in the situation to notice gradual changes occurring.
- Be flexible and ready to alter or adapt care arrangements. Remember that the service user will develop expertise and knowledge about their condition, and ensure that they are at the centre of their care planning.
- Recognize the demands long term care also makes on informal carers and ensure they receive their entitlements.
- Where possible enable the older person, or their carer, to manage an individual budget, so that they have more flexibility to tailor services to their particular needs.
- Acknowledge the value of working collaboratively where the person with a long term condition is often managing a complex range of personal issues and needs the support of a range of professionals who each bring their own particular expertise.

Summary

This chapter has summarized the main government policies concerned with long term conditions, and described common long term conditions and how they can impact on older people. Many people with long term conditions rely on informal care for their main support and the chapter has explored some of the pressures and demands on carers. As more older people are supported to maintain their independence in their own homes the role of assistive technology is discussed which will be of growing importance in the future. Finally the chapter has briefly discussed collaborative working and its importance in work with people with long term conditions, with a brief comment on some of the key issues facing services.

Further reading

Beresford, P., Fleming, J., Glynn, M., Bewley, C., Croft, S., Branfield, F. and Postle, K. (2011) *Supporting People: Towards a Person-centred Approach*. Bristol: The Policy Press.

Resources

Department of Health website on long term conditions. Advice for professionals and those with long term conditions.
www.dh.gov.uk/en/Healthcare/Longtermconditions

DH (2005) *Independence, Well-being and Choice*. A booklet about ideas for better social care services for adults. www.dh.gov.uk/publications

Information of particular long-term conditions. Examples:
Diabetes www.diabetesuk.org.uk
Dementia www.alzheimers.org.uk
Multiple sclerosis www.nhs.gov.uk/Conditions/Multiplesclerosis
Parkinson's disease www.parkinsons.org.uk
The King's Fund www.kingsfund.org.uk/longterm_conditions

NHS Choices. Web pages on the needs of carers, both looking after a partner and a parent with a long term condition.
www.nhs.uk/CarersDirect/young/caring-and-illnesses

Royal College of Nursing. Webpages with resources and publications on the assessment and prevention of falls in older people.
www.rcn.org.uk/development/practice/clinicalguidelines/falls

Social Care Institute for Excellence. Webpages on personalization with implications for staff. www.scie.org.uk

References

American Geriatric Society, British Geriatric Society and American Academy of Orthopaedic Surgeons Panel on Falls Prevention (2001) Guideline for the prevention of falls in older persons, *Journal of the American Geriatric Society* 49: 664–72.
Audit Commission (2004) *Supporting Frail Older People*. London: Audit Commission.
Beresford, P. and Shaping Our Lives (2010) *Funding Social Care: What Service Users Say*. York: Joseph Rowntree Foundation.
Beresford, P. and Trevillion, S. (1995) *Developing Skills for Community Care: A Collaborative Approach*. London: Arena.
Berry, C. (2011) *Past Caring? Widening the Debate on Funding Long Term Care*. London: International Longevity Centre. www.ilcuk.org.uk (accessed 9 August 2011).
DH (Department of Health) (2002) *The Expert Patient: A New Approach to Chronic Disease Management for the 21st Century*. London: Department of Health.

DH (Department of Health) (2005a) *The National Service Framework for Long Term Conditions*. London: Department of Health. http://www.dh.gov.uk/en/Publicationsandstatistics/Publications/PublicationsPolicyandGuidance/DH_4105361 (accessed 9 August 2011).

DH (Department of Health) (2005b) *Independence, Wellbeing and Choice*. http://www.dh.gov.uk/en/Publicationsandstatistics/Publications/PublicationsPolicyAndGuidance/DH_4106477 (accessed 9 August 2011).

DH (Department of Health) (2006) *Our Health, Our Care, Our Say: A New Direction for Community Services*. London: Department of Health.

DH (Department of Health) (2008) *High Quality Care for All: NHS Next Stage Review Final Report*. London: Department of Health.

DH (Department of Health) (2010) *Long Term Conditions*. Available at: http://www.dh.gov.uk/en/Healthcare/Longtermconditions/index.htm (accessed 5 January 2011).

DH (Department of Health) (2010) *Improving Health and Well-being of People with Long Term Conditions. World Class Services for People with Long Term Conditions: Information Tool for Commissioners*. London: Department of Health.

Diabetes UK (2010) *Small Errors but Large Implications for Diabetic Patients Relying on Insulin Doses*. http://www.diabetes.co.uk/news/2010/Oct/small-errors-but-large-implications-for-diabetic-patients-relying-on-insulin-doses-91654106.html (accessed 8 August 2011).

Goble, C. (2009) Multi-professional working in the community, in J. McCray (ed.) *Nursing and Multi-professional Practice*. London: Sage.

Ham, C. (2010) The ten characteristics of the high performing chronic care system, *Health Economics, Policy and Law* 5(1): 71–90.

Ham, C. (2011) *Recent Developments in Chronic Illness Policy in the UK*. London: King's Fund.

Harris, J., Piper, S. and Morgan, H. (2003) *Experiences of Providing Care to People with Long Term Conditions*. York: Social Policy Research Unit.

Hutt, R., Rosen, R. and McCauley, J. (2004) *Case-managing Long Term Conditions: What Impact Does it Have in the Treatment of Older People?* London: King's Fund.

Mantell, A. and Clark, A. (2011) Making choices: The Mental Capacity Act 2005, in A. Mantell and T. Scragg (eds) *Safeguarding Adults in Social Work*, 2nd edn. Exeter: Learning Matters.

MND (Motor Neurone Disease) Association (2002) *Symptoms*. http://www.mndassociation.org/life_with_mnd/what_is_mnd/symptoms.html (accessed 9 August 2011).

Singh, D. and Ham, C. (2006) *Improving Care for People with Long-Term Conditions, A Review of UK and International Frameworks*. Birmingham: University of Birmingham, NHS Institute for Innovation and Improvement.

Soady, J. and Day, F. (2011) *Assistive Technology Needs Assessment*. Sheffield: NHS Sheffield.

South West Falls and Fractures (2010) *The Challenge of Fractures*. http://www.southwestfallsandfractures.org.uk (accessed 9 August 2011).

Standards We Expect Consortium (2011) *Transforming Social Care: Sustaining Person-centred Support*. York: Joseph Rowntree Foundation. Download summary at www.jrf.org.uk

8 Working with loss and bereavement in older people

Terry Scragg

After reading this chapter you should be able to:

- recognize the importance of transitions in the life of older people, particularly those leading to loss and bereavement;
- understand models of grief and loss and their application to social work practice;
- identify ways of working with people experiencing loss and bereavement;
- re-appraise the potential role for social work in loss and bereavement.

Introduction

This chapter will examine how older people experience major life transitions that accompany loss and bereavement, and the important role social work can play in supporting individuals who are experiencing loss. The chapter will describe models of grief work which have the potential to guide practitioners in working with the bereaved person, and those facing death, with suggestions for good practice that meets the psychosocial needs of older people. Finally, the chapter will argue that social work with older people offers a challenging and worthwhile area of practice, and that people experiencing loss should be given higher priority, at a time when social work is increasingly ignoring the wider needs of older people.

The older person, transitions and loss

Social work with older people often results from practitioners becoming involved at a point where the person is experiencing a significant life transition and an intervention is required. The concept of transitions is important in social work as it is concerned with the impact of change and adjustment which happens when a person experiences a major transition, such as declining health, the onset of a terminal illness or bereavement following the loss of a loved one (Lymbery 2005). Such major life transitions can be accompanied by intense personal and emotional feelings which often go unrecognized when there is pressure to respond to urgent practical issues. This is where a broader view of social work is helpful in recognizing that it can encompass both immediate help, alongside engaging with the person's grief and supporting them through the emotional upheaval that is symptomatic of the bereavement process.

Older people experience numerous transitions in later life, often resulting in multiple losses, such as health, status, close friends, relations and spouses (Kerr et al. 2005), with the risk of becoming overwhelmed or numbed by grief. The bereaved person's grief, although a universal response to loss, will be a uniquely personal experience that can dominate their lives for a considerable time. For most people the support of family and friends will be enough to enable them to manage the transition and there will be no need for professional support with help focused on those who are more vulnerable. For the older person who may be socially isolated, or has less access to a support network, or where there may be risk factors such as depression, professional help can be important. Social work involvement is also more likely where a transition is tipped into crisis, for example, where grief is intensified by other pressures such as poverty and deprivation, or where strained family relationships intensify or prolong the process of grieving. Other issues that create vulnerability at times of loss include belonging to a Black or ethnic minority group, discrimination on grounds of sexuality and having mental health problems or a learning disability (Croft 2011). In these situations social work can play a valuable role in providing support to the older person enabling them to come to terms with their loss and bereavement through the use of skills derived from counselling, while at the same time helping them to deal with some of the practical problems that undermine their personal resources.

Activity 1

Consider some of the losses that might be presented to you when working with an older person. Reflect on the ones that might make you reluctant to engage with the person on that issue.

What losses might you be less comfortable working with and why?

Do you have the opportunity to discuss your reactions to loss and bereavement in a professional setting, such as supervision?

Understanding grief and loss

Grief is a natural response to loss and describes the emotional pain that a person feels when someone or something they love is taken away. It is normally associated with the death of a loved one and this can cause the most intense grief, but any significant loss can cause grief including the onset of serious ill health, the loss of a close friend or the loss of a pet. Understanding different models of grief offers a framework for effective intervention with service users who are bereaved following loss.

Attachment theories

Much of the development of theories about grief work have evolved from the research of Bowlby (1980) whose original work was concerned with the attachment between mothers and children and grief as an instinctive response to separation. Later research by Bowlby's colleague Parkes (1996) indicated that patterns of attachment formed in childhood influenced bonds in adult life and in turn patterns of bereavement. The relationship with the deceased was considered important in determining the ability of the individual to negotiate the grieving process, and give some indication as to the nature of the grieving response.

Stage/phase model of grief

An important part of understanding grief is the notion of 'working through' or 'resolving grief' or what has been described as the 'stage or phase' model of grief. These models focus on the idea of letting go of the deceased in order to be able to move on with life. Here the work of Kubler-Ross (1970) and later Parkes (1996) are important milestones. They described the different stages of grief, moving from initial shock and numbness, through yearning and searching, to disorganization and despair, and eventually reorganization (Parkes 1996). The stages identified the feelings that accompanied them and were never, as with subsequent models, intended to be taken literally, or describe a linear timetable with no deviations, setbacks or regressions. An oversimplistic interpretation of these models by professionals can result in blindness to the individuality of grief.

Tasks of grieving

An alternative view of grieving is provided by Worden (2003) who conceptualized grief as a series of tasks, with an approach which suggests that bereavement is an active process rather than a passive state. Worden argues that the individual needs to work through their reactions in order to make a complete adjustment to their loss. Here the tasks of bereavement consist of working through the emotional pain of loss, while simultaneously adjusting to the changes in their circumstances, role, status and identity. These tasks are complete when the individual has integrated the loss into their life and loosened the intense emotional attachments to the deceased, allowing them to focus on the present and the future, rather than the past.

Continuing bonds

A further development in grief theory, which challenged conventional thinking, is provided by the work of Klass et al. (1996) which suggests that resolving grief involves having a continuing bond and a relationship with the deceased, and that these can be a healthy aspect of the survivor's ongoing life and not 'break the bonds' with the deceased as suggested in earlier theories. This approach is concerned with the bereaved person emotionally relocating the deceased as part of moving on with their life. Klass et al. provide examples of where parents still talk to their dead son, or a widow talks to her husband, and the comfort derived from these 'conversations'.

Dual processes

The contribution of Stroebe and Schut (1999) provided an important stage in the development of grief work with their dual process model which suggests that avoiding grief can be both helpful and detrimental, depending on the circumstances of the bereaved person. This model recognizes that both expressing and controlling feelings are important, and describes behaviour that alternates between a focus on the loss of the person (loss orientation) and avoiding the focus (restoration orientation). The loss orientation concerns grief work, while the restoration orientation involves dealing with secondary losses such as attending to the practical tasks of day-to-day living. Both orientations are seen as necessary for future adjustment. Stroebe and Schut argue that a person is unable to live in a state of constant grief, and that there are opportunities to balance feelings, such as sadness and anger, with hope and the ability to undertake new things. This included denial, even though previous thinking had suggested that to deny the situation was unhealthy. They recognized that for limited periods it could be a positive position to adopt, enabling the individual some respite from the intensity of their feelings.

Range of responses to loss

More recently Machin (2009) has argued that the individual can show bias towards particular dimensions of loss, such as feeling overwhelmed (deeply sunk into the distress of grief), or feeling the need to retain control (needing to manage emotions and retain a primary focus upon ongoing life demands); whereas the balanced/resilient dimension (capacity to face the emotional, social and practical consequences of loss with equilibrium) suggests that the individual is able to manage both the emotional and control aspects. Machin's approach has some similarities to the dual process model of Stroebe and Schut in identifying the need for a range of responses during the process of grieving, that stress resolving painful emotions as well as social adaptation.

Ambiguous loss

The grieving process can be complicated where there is loss that cannot be resolved or the loss cannot be acknowledged. Grief can be unresolved where the loved one is 'taken away' due to illness or injury, or where the deceased's body is lost (missing person) or where the person is still physically present, but is psychologically absent (parent with dementia). Boss (1999) describes this as 'ambiguous loss' where there is no resolution of the grieving process and where it is possible that the person will never 'get over' their grief, and a healthy way to adjust to this situation is to learn to live with their unresolved grief.

Disenfranchised grief

Where grief is not recognized or socially accepted, it can be difficult to deal with the loss as it may not be acknowledged, and the griever excluded from the rituals of death. Dota (2001: 4) describes this as 'disenfranchised grief' where 'the grief the person experiences when they incur a loss is not, or cannot be openly acknowledged, publicly mourned or socially supported'. Dota suggests that the loss of the loved one can be compounded by lack of recognition of the relationship, lack of acknowledgement of the loss and exclusion of the grieving person in discussion of rituals and grieving styles. This disenfranchisement consequently reduces the potential for access to sources of support by excluding the mourner from an active role in the dying and funeral rites. This can be particularly powerful where the bereaved person cannot be open with others, or their loved one publicly mourned, due to the stigma associated with the deceased, for example, the death in a same sex partnership where there is cultural disapproval of homosexuality or lesbian relationships.

Ambivalent grieving

An individual's experience of grief will depend greatly on their relationship with the deceased. The degree of closeness within a relationship can determine the degree of loss felt on the death of a partner or spouse. Where there has been a close loving relationship it can make grieving harder and the grief can be intense. Where relationships have been less fulfilling the immediate reaction can be relief, although over time guilt and despair can surface as even where relationships have been unsatisfactory, feelings of attachment and affection may have coexisted. The complications arising from ambivalence in the grieving process can result in delayed grief and as a consequence recovery (Scrutton 1999).

Risk factors in grief

A valuable help in identifying those likely to be at risk of poor outcomes in loss and bereavement, including risks of physical and mental health problems, has been developed by Sanders (1993) whose work on factors that contribute to risk is important. Two key factors contributing to potential risk is predisposing vulnerability and resourcefulness of the grieving person – stemming from life events and personality, and second, the nature of the external circumstances – which have resulted in the loss experience. Sanders identified a number of factors which can contribute to greater risk including sudden unexplained death, ambivalence or dependency in the relationship between the survivor and the deceased, lack of social support in the bereaved person's network and poverty of material resources. None of these will come as a surprise to the experienced social worker, but remind us that reactions to loss can be complex and influenced by a wide range of personal and environmental factors.

Applying models of grief to practice with older people

Most social workers will be familiar with the stage/phase models of grief, while more recent research has provided additional insights into the grieving process. The emphasis on a more balanced approach, with focus on an active process, recognizing both the depth of personal loss and the need to focus on practical issues, is a helpful approach. New insights have also recognized the value of integrating the deceased into the future life of the bereaved by means of a continuing bond.

All researchers stress the importance of recognizing the uniqueness of each individual's response to grief, and that there is no one right or wrong way to grieve. Models of grieving suggest that the bereaved person has to engage with their loss and work through it, so that their life can be reordered and meaningful again. Each of these models offers the social worker a framework to help them guide the bereaved person in their grief work. The social worker meeting a bereaved person for the first time has to find ways of helping and supporting which helps them most effectively. Therefore no single model of grieving is recommended above the rest as all have components which may be helpful. Above all, as Dent (2005: 23) has stated 'the most important part of supporting a bereaved person lies in "being with them", listening intently to their story, acknowledging their feelings and guiding them towards a new, different and meaningful life without the deceased'.

Activity 8.2

After reflecting on the different models of grief work, which approach seems to be most useful in informing your practice?

How could you incorporate knowledge of the grieving process into your work with older people experiencing loss?

Have any of the models of grief work led you to reconsider your approach to work with loss?

Social work practice in loss and bereavement

Social workers have an important and unique opportunity to work with older people experiencing loss as many are referred to services at a point where they are in transition following the death of a loved one, or some other significant loss that results in a grief reaction. Practitioners located in general or specialist health settings or palliative care services are particularly well placed to identify the needs of older people and their carers for support and intervention at times of crisis and change (Kerr et al. 2005), whereas local authority social workers in adult services teams can find that the pressure for speedy assessment and the arrangement of practical services under a narrow interpretation of care management may encourage them to miss or ignore the important psychosocial needs of an individual (Postle 2002). This situation has been exacerbated with the ever tightening eligibility criteria, concerned primarily with formal assessment, risk management and rationing of resources, implying a further withdrawal of social workers from adopting an holistic person-centred approach.

Ironically, however, the current focus on responding to those older people who are presenting the most urgent and complex needs provides an opportunity for social workers to reframe their practice as one which encompasses the totality of the social work role and in turn improves the practitioners' satisfaction with their role (Lymbery 2005). Older people interviewed for research into service users' satisfaction with social workers (Manthorpe et al. 2007) valued a more person-centred approach that recognized the feelings and worries of the older person through a personal relationship with the social worker, which complemented the assessment and provision of services within the care management process.

Supporting the older person coming to terms with loss and bereavement

Social work with older people potentially encompasses a wide range of activities, including administrative and practical tasks associated with statutory requirements, including formal assessments and the mobilization of resources to meet immediate needs, and those activities that have been variously described as reflexive/therapeutic (Payne 2005) and individualistic/therapeutic (Lymbery 2005). For the purpose of this section the emphasis will be placed on these latter activities which are concerned with supporting the older person experiencing loss and bereavement, where techniques derived from counselling and therapy underpin the social work practitioner's approach.

The starting point for work with a person who has experienced loss is person-centred practice using a non-directive approach, emphasizing empathy, genuineness and unconditional positive regard, and where the relationship is itself of intrinsic value (Rogers 1961; Egan 2007). Using this approach and listening to the person's story, in their own words, provides an understanding of how they view their loss and encourages them to express their grief in whatever way is most helpful to them. It is important that the older person is not denied the right to grieve; this is particularly important where well meaning relatives and friends try to protect the person from grief. According to Scrutton (1999) grief following loss can only be postponed, not avoided. Where grief is denied the bereaved person may continue to grieve for many years, paying an emotional price for being protected by kindness.

Supporting the person through the stages of grief

When working with an older person who is experiencing loss a knowledge of some of the stages of grief and the range of reactions is helpful as this can reassure the person that their thoughts and feelings are not abnormal. It is important to be able to reassure the person that it is normal initially to experience a state of shock and numbness and an inability to fully grasp what has happened in the first weeks after a death. Once the

Table 8.1 Some possible responses to grief

Feelings	Physical sensations	Behaviours
Shock	Hollowness in the stomach	Difficulty sleeping
Numbness	Tightness in the chest	Appetite disturbance
Sadness	Tightness in the throat	Absent mindedness
Yearning	Over-sensitivity to noise	Social withdrawal
Anxiety	Breathlessness	Dreaming
Anger	Muscle weakness	Searching
Guilt	Lacking energy	Crying
Self-reproach	Dry mouth	Sighing
Loneliness	Confusion	Irritability
Detached	Preoccupation	Restlessness
Fatigue	Sense of presence	Easily startled
Helplessness	Hallucinations	Visiting old haunts
Relief		

Source: based on Worden (1993).

initial shock subsides it can be followed by expressions of intense emotional and bodily distress. This can be a painful period of upheaval but is a necessary part of grieving and again quite normal. Not all these symptoms of grief will necessarily be experienced, but understanding that they are well established reactions to grief can be reassuring (see Table 8.1). Eventually, and this can vary with individual circumstances, the person will begin to focus on daily activities and some of the emotional turmoil will feel more under control. Although the loss and hurt may never completely recede it will gradually take its place alongside life's other demands. This is where supporting the older person to develop a new relationship with the deceased incorporating memories of the past into the present is a healthy late stage of grieving.

When grief persists

Where reactions are more extreme, grieving can persist over a long time period, or the person may find it difficult to adjust to life without the deceased (Stroebe et al. 2001). They may also have disturbing memories of the events surrounding the death, or may blame others for the death, or have feelings of guilt or shame as a result of their own behaviour (Parkes 2006). These reactions may indicate that the person is at risk and referral to specialist services may be necessary, for example, if there is concern that the person is harbouring suicidal thoughts. Where the older person talks about 'ending it all' these threats should not be ignored as suicide rates increase with age (see Chapter 4 for a more detailed discussion of suicide risk among older people). On the other hand concerns about older people at risk when their grief seems prolonged or extreme should be viewed with some caution as in Machin's (2009) view grief in Western society is seen as abnormal if it is anything other than fairly reserved and short term.

When social work contact closes it is important that a good ending to the relationship is planned so that the vulnerable older person does not have a further experience of loss to deal with. Without denying the pain of grief, helping them recognize ways in which they have coped well through the stages of bereavement is helpful. Finally, reviewing with the older person what has been achieved and helping them look forward to the future is also important (Machin 2009).

End of life care

Social work with older people who are terminally ill is a particularly sensitive and demanding area of practice and one that has been neglected by the profession (Lymbery 2005; Beresford et al. 2007). Apart from those social workers in specialist palliative care settings, who will mainly work with younger people with cancer (Leadbeater and Garber 2010), this is not an area of practice that most social workers will have experienced, and goes largely unrecognized as a result of other priorities in adult care services.

Work with older people with terminal illness has derived considerable value from the original work of Kubler-Ross (1970), who conceptualized the end of life stories of terminally ill people into a series of stages of grief experienced by people who were dying, which in turn has led to a new openness to talking about death. As in other stage/phase models of grief the concepts have increasingly been questioned, with the main criticism that human functioning is too multi-faceted to be reduced to a series of discrete stages (Bandura 1998). However, as in other stage models of grief Kubler-Ross never intended them to be seen as a linear trajectory of the dying person. It is also recognized that some older people will want to die, particularly where there is rapid physical decline or pain, and actively work to ensure that their life is not prolonged, while others may not wish to talk about how they want to die (Leadbeater and Garber 2010). Others may approach their death with calm acceptance that does not fit with the introverted and emotion-focused activity of grief described by Kubler-Ross (Machin 2009). A further consideration is that people from different faiths and cultures may have a wide range of perceptions about what makes death bearable. All this points to individuals having very different versions of what counts as a good death and similarly many variations in the process of dying.

In spite of these caveats there are some helpful approaches derived from counselling techniques which give guidance in supporting the dying person (Scrutton 1999). These start from the premise that the dying person will want to maintain as much normality for as long as possible, ensuring that their wishes are respected and that they feel they have control of their situation, and that others do not assume control. They will want to be at home, with those they want to be with, and where they may wish to discuss any anxieties and come to terms with their imminent death. This is also a time when they may wish to express their fears and feelings of loneliness, and discuss any religious or spiritual feelings with appropriate support where this is needed. It is also a time when they can discuss the practical issues concerned with what will happen after their death, such as the administration of a will and their funeral arrangements.

Case study

John aged 80, a widower who has terminal cancer and only a short time to live, is a very independent man with a strong personality. He has become increasingly frail, but was determined to remain in his own home for as long as possible with domiciliary support and visits from a Macmillan nurse from the local hospice. His social worker is Paul, who had originally been involved in assessing his need for domiciliary support. John valued Paul's visits and asked him to continue weekly contact. John's son Gary, who had not been close to his father, was informed that his father was dying and had made contact by telephone and was intending to visit him. John wanted to spend time with his son and asked Paul to meet with Gary and explain his wishes to heal any rifts with his son before he died. Paul was also able to support Gary as he dealt with the emotions around his father's imminent death. During Paul's visits John reminisced about his life and they looked at family photographs. John also wanted to talk about his approaching death, where he wished to die and what arrangements he wanted for his funeral. At his request Paul had made contact with a funeral director who had visited John and talked about his wishes. Not being a religious person he had been particularly insistent that the funeral director was clear about his wish for a brief ceremony followed by cremation. Paul also arranged for a solicitor to visit John to discuss his will and the disposal of his assets. As John's cancer spread he agreed to move to the hospice where he could receive more effective pain control and where he subsequently died. During John's short time in the hospice Paul visited him, although his pain control made conversation more difficult and he gradually weakened physically. Gary was at John's bedside when he died.

Comment

This case study illustrates some aspects of social work with a person who was terminally ill. Discussion of end of life issues can be important to older people, with the opportunity to review their life and its achievements, and what will happen after their death. Paul's approach could be described as 'being with John', showing respect, listening to the story of his life and his memories and taking time to look at photographs that marked the passage of time. This 'life review' work was a way that John was able to look back on his life in a positive way. Paul also enabled Gary to understand his father's wishes and encouraged him to establish contact with his father. This demonstrates how end of life care needs to take account of 'unfinished business' in family relationships. Each of these activities helped John make sense of his life and its meaning and approach his death with some equanimity. Throughout this work with John it raised issues for Paul about his own experience of loss, which he was able to discuss in regular supervision with a senior practitioner who had experience of end of life work.

What service users value about social work support

It is important to understand what older people experiencing loss and bereavement value, as it provides suggestions for how social workers can provide the most effective support. Research into service users' view of social work in palliative care (Beresford et al. 2008) identified the things they valued, including:

- their relationship with the social worker, particularly the kindness, warmth, compassion, sensitivity and empathy shown by the practitioner towards the service user;
- being able to determine their own agenda and work in partnership with the social worker;
- being listened to by a practitioner who was non-judgemental and respectful;
- a practitioner being reliable and delivering on promises.

Beresford et al. (2007) argue that what service users valued about the social work practice they had experienced was that it was truly psychosocial, in addressing both their individual personal and psychological needs and their wider social circumstances, recognizing that the two were inextricably linked. This view was reinforced by the feeling that the social worker was a 'friend', and that there was an informality (in contrast to other health care professionals) and flexibility in their approach which the service user valued.

These responses by people who are terminally ill and receiving social work mirror the earlier findings of Machin's (2007) research where a voluntary agency providing a specialist counselling service which focused on the psychosocial consequences of loss reported that service users felt confident in a service where counsellors were familiar with loss reactions, adopted a person-centred approach, and where they felt able to give an unedited account of their experience of loss. Research by Avis et al. (1999) on the delivery of palliative care services to nursing homes reinforces the findings of Beresford et al. and Machin that the personal qualities of the care worker were crucial to the older person's quality of life in the final stages of terminal illness. Here participants described the importance of the sense of friendship with the worker, and the sense of reciprocal giving and receiving, with the care workers communicating gentleness, safety and respect.

Practitioner issues: working with loss and grief

Working with loss and grief and being open to the pain of bereavement can bring to the surface personal losses, or raise questions about the future and what it might hold. To be an effective practitioner means achieving a balance between professional objectivity and human subjectivity (Machin 2009). Achieving this balance can be challenging so supportive consultation and supervision is essential for good practice. Where social work is narrowly focused on the practical activities of service delivery, ensuring loss and grief is discussed with managers and colleagues can enable all team members to have a clear sense of how loss is impacting on those older people using a service.

Four factors have been identified by Papadatou et al. (1998) as important in supporting practitioners working with grief and loss, and although these were originally applied to work with dying children they have equal value in work with older people:

- information: understanding all the factors relevant to the care giving role;
- practical support: collaborative and supportive team work that recognizes each practitioner's needs;

- emotional support: recognition of the impact of working with loss and grief on the practitioner;
- meaning-making support: providing debriefing and reflection on practice, with practitioners having the opportunity to reach a shared sense of meaning about their work with loss and grief.

It is also important that social workers have information on local resources for those experiencing grief as well as the services provided by national charities whose helplines, and in some cases local services, can be an additional support (see Resources below). Access to professional organizations such as the Association of Palliative Care Social Workers and courses offered by palliative care services can inform and improve practice.

The future of social work with older people experiencing loss

While the future of social work with older people remains uncertain, at least in the form that would meet the wider needs of older people, it is important to stress that social work has a vital, if under-developed role to play in supporting older people experiencing loss and bereavement. The demand for social work support will grow with an ageing population with more people wishing to die at home rather than in hospital (70 per cent of older people wish to die at home, although currently only 20 per cent achieve this) (DH 2008).

The growing importance of listening to the service user's voice and the increasing emphasis on person-centred practice and personalization points the direction for social work with older people, contradicting the narrow concept of the social worker as 'navigator' (DH 2006). Manthorpe et al. (2007) pose the important question of how far a commitment to anti-discriminatory practice, which is a central tenet of social work, is seen to encompass the issue of ageism, where negative attitudes towards older people which permeate society are reinforced by the services designed to support older people, and where second-rate treatment is rarely questioned.

Because social work with older people has become increasingly task orientated there has been little opportunity to develop therapeutic approaches to practice which Lymbery (2005) argues is an expression of the low value accorded to older people within society as well as within social work. An alternative discourse would argue that social work has an important role in supporting older people who have to make complex and life changing decisions about their future, which in turn needs knowledgeable, experienced and skilled practitioners (Richards 2000), with the profession 'asserting its continued relevance to the needs of older people in order to clarify its current and future role' (Lymbery 2005: 150).

Summary

This chapter has described models of grief which can inform social workers, who, with an understanding of the processes of loss and bereavement, can provide a framework which can help them in working with older people. Suggestions for direct work with the older person using a counselling approach provides a basis for social work practice that focuses on the key areas of support for the bereaved person, including those with terminal illness. Finally the chapter argues that social work with older people who are experiencing loss and bereavement is an important and professionally challenging area of practice that has long been neglected, and needs a more central role in social work, rather than a marginal activity in some specialist settings.

Resources: organizations that offer support to bereaved people

There is a wide range of national organizations which provide support to the bereaved. In addition many local care services provide access to support services. The main national organizations are:

AgeUK (formerly Age Concern) a national charity focused on helping and supporting older people which can offer practical advice on what to do when someone close to you dies. Has a helpful publication *Bereavement, Support after Death*. Can be downloaded from their website www.ageuk.org.uk

Bereavementinfo.com is an online service providing practical help and guidance on what to do when someone has passed away. It has a list of organizations that provide support to the bereaved person. Website: www.bereavementinfo.com

The Bereavement Trust offers an evening telephone helpline providing a sympathetic listening ear to anyone who is struggling with bereavement. Their helpline is open every evening between 6pm and 10pm, and includes Asian and Chinese language helplines. Helpline: 0800 435 455. Website: www.bereavement-trust. org.uk

Cruse Bereavement Care which works with and supports people who have been bereaved. Its services are free. Helpline: 0844 477 9400. Website: www.cruse.org.uk

The London Friend helpline offers support and practical information to lesbian, gay, bisexual and transgendered callers who have been bereaved or who are preparing for bereavement. Helpline open Tuesdays 7.30pm–9.30pm: 020 7837 3337. Website: londonfriend.org.uk

The Terrence Higgins Trust provides practical support, counselling and advice to anyone concerned about AIDS or HIV. Helpline: 0207 2421010 (noon–10pm daily). Website: www.tht.org.uk

The National Association of Widows provides information, advice and support to widows, including support through local branches. Helpline: 024 7663 4848. Website: www.widows.uk.net

The Samaritans offers confidential, non-judgemental support through a telephone helpline for people experiencing severe distress or despair. Helpline: 08457 909090. Website: www.samaritans.org.uk

Resources: organizations that provide information to professionals

The Association of Palliative Care Social Workers has a useful bibliography of publications, and other resources on its website for the social worker. Website: www.apcsw.org.uk

The Social Care Institute of Excellence (SCIE) provides access to a wide range of resources on loss, bereavement and end of life care. Website: www.socialcareonline.org.uk

Further reading

Beresford, P., Adshead, L. and Croft, S. (2007) *Palliative Care, Social Work and Service Users: Making Life Possible*. London: Jessica Kingsley.

Machin, L. (2009) *Working with Loss and Grief*. London: Sage.

Scrutton, S. (1999) *Counselling Older People*, 2nd edn. London: Arnold.

References

Avis, M., Jackson, J.G., Cox, K. and Miskella, C. (1999) Evaluation of a project providing community palliative care support to nursing homes, *Health and Social Care in the Community* 7(1): 32–8.

Bandura, A. (1998) Health promotion from the perspective of social cognitive theory, *Psychology and Health* 13: 623–49.

Beresford, P., Adshead, L. and Croft, S. (2007) *Palliative Care, Social Work and Service Users: Making Life Possible*. London: Jessica Kingsley.

Beresford, P., Croft, S. and Adshead, L. (2008) 'We don't see her as a social worker': a service user case study of the importance of the social worker's relationship and humanity, *British Journal of Social Work* 38: 1388–407.

Boss, P. (1999) *Ambiguous Loss, Learning to Live with Unresolved Grief*. Cambridge, MA: Harvard University Press.

Bowlby, J. (1980) *Attachment and Loss, Vol. 1, Attachment*. Harmondsworth: Penguin.

Croft, S. (2011) *Social Work to the Grave: The Role of Social Workers in the End of Life Care, St John's Hospice*. www.communitycarelive.co.uk (accessed 24 July 2011).

Dent, A. (2005) Supporting the bereaved: theory and practice, *Heathcare Counselling and Psychotherapy*. www.bacworkplace.org.uk/journal (accessed 24 July 2011).

DH (Department of Health) (2006) *Our Health, Our Care, Our Say: A New Direction for Community Services*. London: The Stationery Office.

DH (Department of Health) (2008) *End of Life Care Strategy*. London: The Stationery Office.

Dota, K.J. (ed.) (2001) *Disenfranchised Grief: Recognizing Hidden Sorrow*. New York: Lexington.

Egan, G. (2007) *The Skilled Helper*, 8th edn. Belmont, CA: Thompson.

Kerr, B., Gordon, J., Macdonald, C. and Stalker, K. (2005) *Effective Social Work with Older People*. Edinburgh: Scottish Executive Education Department. www.21csocialwork.org.uk (accessed 24 July 2011).

Klass, D., Silverman, S. and Nickman, S. (eds) (1996) *Continuing Bonds: New Understandings of Grief.* Philadelphia, PA: Taylor and Francis.

Kubler-Ross, E. (1970) *On Death and Dying.* London: Tavistock.

Leadbeater, C. and Garber, J. (2010) *To Allow People the Deaths they Want, End of Life Care Must be Radically Transformed . . .* London: Demos.

Lymbery, M. (2005) *Social Work with Older People.* London: Sage.

Machin, L. (2007) *The Adult Attitude to Grief Scale as a Tool of Practice for Counsellors Working with Bereaved People*, a study sponsored by Age Concern, Tameside, and Keele University.

Machin, L. (2009) *Working with Loss and Grief.* London: Sage.

Manthorpe, G., Moriarty, J., Rapaport, J., Clough, R., Cornes, M., Bright, L., Illiffe, S. and OPRSI (Older People Researching Social Issues) (2007) There are wonderful social workers but it's a lottery: older people's views about social workers, *British Journal of Social Work* 38(6): 1132–50.

Papadatou, D., Papazoglou, I., Petraki, D. and Bellali, T. (1998) Mutual support among nurses who provide care to dying children, *Illness, Crisis and Loss* 7: 37–48.

Parkes, C.M. (1996) *Bereavement: Studies in Grief in Adult Life.* London: Routledge.

Payne, M. (2005) *Modern Social Work Theory*, 3rd edn. Basingstoke: Palgrave Macmillan.

Postle, K. (2002) Between the idea and the reality: ambiguities and tensions in care managers' work, *British Journal of Social Work* 32: 335–51.

Richards, S. (2000) Bridging the divide: elders and the assessment process, *British Journal of Social Work* 30(1): 37–49.

Rogers, C.R. (1961) *On Becoming a Person.* London: Constable.

Sanders, C.M. (1993) Risk factors in bereavement outcomes, in M.S. Stroebe, W. Stroebe and R.O. Hansson (eds) *Handbook of Bereavement.* Cambridge: Cambridge University Press.

Scrutton, S. (1999) *Counselling Older People*, 2nd edn. London: Arnold.

Stroebe, M., Hansson, R., Stroebe, W. and Schut, H. (2001) *Handbook of Bereavement Research: Consequences, Coping and Care.* Washington, DC: American Psychological Association.

Stroebe, M. and Schut, H. (1999) The dual process model of coping with bereavement: rationale and description, *Death Studies* 23: 197–224.

Worden, W. (2003) *Grief Counselling and Grief Therapy*, 1st edn. London: Tavistock.

9 Work with older people and sexuality

Chris Gaine and Andy Mantell

After reading this chapter you should be able to:

- analyse and sometimes challenge common notions about sexuality;
- recognize some social changes with regard to sexuality that older people have experienced and their potential impact;
- critically apply insights in recognizing barriers to personalized care;
- recognize the importance of being able to effectively handle these issues with fellow professionals;
- reflect upon your assumptions and training needs about older people's sexuality.

Introduction

Older people are often assumed to be retired heterosexuals who have gradually become asexual, repressed prudes, and sexually well behaved. It follows from this that sexual orientation is taken for granted, that older people have no sexual needs or desires, that discussion or (worse still) joking about sex is offensive, and that lives of heterosexual monogamous rectitude are moving into their final decade or two of respectable behaviour.

Such assumptions make it hard for anyone involved in caring to deal appropriately with gay, lesbian, bisexual or heterosexual clients who would like to be sexually active with another, masturbate, have a taste for pornography, or who say or do things judged to be inappropriate. As Smith et al. (2010: 2) put it, 'everyone has sexuality, regardless of whether they are sexually active' or in the words of one older woman 'If I didn't have sex at all with another woman for the rest of my life I would still be a lesbian.' Heath (1999) argues that recognizing the sexuality of older people has payoffs in terms of general psychological well-being and preventing depression, just as it does for younger people.

Case study

Violet, aged 80, became depressed following the death of her husband. She would not eat, found it difficult to manage her house and started neglecting her personal care. She developed a chest infection and was admitted to hospital. Her daughters became concerned and after a social worker's assessment she moved into a warden-supported apartment. Three months later her eldest daughter contacted the social worker saying she was concerned that as a vulnerable adult her mother was 'being taken advantage of' by a neighbour, aged 78. The daughters, initially pleased that she was making friends, were less so upon discovering one morning that he had stayed the night.

What questions should a social worker ask about this situation?

Comment

'Vulnerable adult' is an emotionally loaded term. For social workers there are clear policies to be followed when a person is assessed as being in this category and at risk (see the Dept of Health Guidance, 2000, No Secrets). Yet while the term is applied to an individual, it is often their circumstances that cause the vulnerability. We can all be vulnerable in certain circumstances and changing a situation – for instance by providing better support – can significantly reduce vulnerability. Violet may be viewed as vulnerable, but this does not mean that she no longer has the right to be sexually active. Violet and her neighbour may have just sought the reassurance of intimate contact with each other or they may be having a sexual relationship. Our own expectations of how a person should behave can easily lead to conclusions that different behaviour must be wrong. In this situation Violet's daughters' concerns about their mother may be shaped both by their views of older people (especially their mother) having sex, but also by the loss of their father.

Assumptions and expectations

Physical changes of course account for some assumptions about the sexuality of older people. A whole range of physical ailments are more common with ageing but not inevitable; aside from specifically genital ageing in the form of vaginal dryness or erectile dysfunction, conditions such as arthritis, incontinence, breathing problems, muscle atrophy and strokes can make the activity of sexual intercourse more difficult. But this is not the whole story. In an era where people live longer and healthier lives, youth is still valorized and highly sexualized in a great deal of media output. At the same time, one survey (Saga 2010) indicated that 46 per cent of over 50s say they have sex at least once a week, and a Swedish survey showed that some stereotypes of older people are just out of date:

> From 1971 to 2000 the proportion of 70 year olds reporting sexual intercourse increased among all groups: married men from 52% to 68% . . ., married women from 38% to 56% . . ., unmarried men from 30% to 54% . . ., and unmarried women from 0.8% to 12% . . . Men and women from later birth

cohorts reported higher satisfaction with sexuality, fewer sexual dysfunctions, and more positive attitudes to sexuality in later life than those from earlier birth cohorts.

(Beckman et al. 2008: a279)

While advances in clinical treatment such as Viagra have extended the sex lives of some older people, societal changes have also affected 'the expectations and experiences of older people with regard to sex and sexual behaviour' (Smith et al. 2010: 41).

But embarrassment, amusement, denial and even disgust about older people's sex lives persist (maybe contributing to a new stereotype of 'sexy seniors'). Given an ageing population and increasing divorce among people over 50 who are dating and forming new relationships this issue is not going to go away; indeed it will eventually affect everyone reading this book.

With women now spending a third of their lives post-menopause, practitioners can no longer make assumptions about levels of sexual activity. Professionals' approaches to older people's sexual health can be seen as lying on a continuum. At one end of the spectrum sexual issues are ignored and/or avoided, for example, WHO (2009) reports that older people are less likely to be screened for sexually transmitted diseases and Smith et al. (2010) report anecdotally that at the other end of the spectrum professionals may be inappropriately direct.

The complexity and variety of older people's ideas about sex

As far as sexuality is concerned, there has been a revolution in Britain since the 1960s, and while this revolution in attitudes and behaviour is something most people under 35 might be dimly aware of, we cannot assume this for people twice that age. People now in their 80s were in their 30s when radical change began to take hold, and those now in their 60s were teenagers. In 1960 the new contraceptive pill was only available to married women; homosexuality was against the law; most women were virgins until they married (or had to claim to be), and once married it wasn't clear they could enjoy sex; most babies born out of wedlock 'had to be' adopted; and purchasable images of nakedness were confined to a magazine called *Health and Efficiency* with pubic hair airbrushed away.

Older people have lived through the changes, sometimes retaining the views held by their own parents, sometimes viewing personal change as just out of reach, sometimes changing with the times, or sometimes being key players in radical changes themselves. They are now exemplifying a further change, as the generation with a longer life expectancy than any previous one they have the opportunity to engage in sexual activity with relative good health, no fear of pregnancy, and no need to get up for work in the morning.

So, the generation now over retirement age contains many heterosexual couples who have only had each other as sexual partners and have never been concerned about the safer sex campaigns of the 1980s and 1990s. It includes those baby boomers that created the permissive society, with its more open and less secretive approach to sexuality, and doubtless some adults damaged by sexual abuse as children in an era when there was no one to tell. There are also those who still live with internalized shame and denial of being lesbian or gay, some men who went to prison for their sexual behaviour as late as the mid-1960s, some who have been openly gay or lesbian for decades and many heterosexuals who maintain the homophobic views that inflict stigma upon others.

Signs of the times

The timeline in Box 9.1 highlights some of the profound social changes that older people have lived through with regard to sexuality (the second column shows the age people aged 80 in 2010 would have been at each event).

Box 9.1		Social changes with regard to sexuality
1930s	0–10	Growing psychological work on sexuality, recognizing women had sexual feelings; Marie Stopes forms National Birth Control Council in 1930
1948	18	Kinsey's *Sexual Behaviour in the Human Male* published, reached top of bestseller lists
1949	19	Survey of British sexual behaviuor suppressed because of evidence of scale of adultery and men's use of prostitutes
1950s	20s	Children commonly warned that masturbation led to blindness, hairy hands or stunted growth
1953	23	Kinsey's *Sexual Behavior in the Human Female* revealed much of what would now be taken for granted; first edition of *Playboy*
1957	27	Wolfenden Committee recommends legalization of homosexual acts in private if over 21
1960	30	*Lady Chatterley's Lover* survives obscenity trial; barrister asks jury if it was the kind of book 'you would wish your wife or servants to read.' Contraceptive pill available, mostly restricted to married women
1966	36	Masters and Johnson's *Sexual Intercourse in the Normal Female*
1967	37	Sexual Offences Act partially legalizes homosexuality
1967	37	Abortion legalized in limited cases
1968	38	Pope reasserts prohibition of contraception
1968	38	End of government power to censor live theatre – large increase in sexual content
1970	40	Equal Pay Act: for equal work regardless of gender
		Pill available to unmarried women and widely used
1972	42	Explicit sex manual *The Joy of Sex* published
1973	43	*The Female Orgasm* contains study of 300 women of whom 61 per cent did not usually orgasm
1979	49	Rejected Home Office study suggests age of consent for gay/lesbian sex be lowered from 21 to 18
1980s	50	Growing awareness of hidden sexual abuse within families, and years of silence by children
1980	50	Scotland legalizes homosexuality

1982	52	Northern Ireland legalizes homosexuality
1983	53	First openly gay MP
1984	54	100th UK AIDS case
1986	56	First gay character on *Eastenders*
1988	58	Law to prevent local authorities 'promoting homosexuality' in schools
1990s	60	Revelations of years of sexual abuse in children's homes, and by priests, some victims from 1930s–1940s
1991	61	Marital rape illegal
1992	62	Homosexuality off World Health Organization 'diseases' list
1993	63	First lesbian kiss on *Brookside*
1994	64	Male rape made criminal offence
1997	67	First openly gay cabinet minister
2000	70	Age of consent 16 for gay and straight sex
		Homosexuality ban lifted in armed forces
2001	71	First openly gay high court judge, Metropolitan Police commander
2002	72	First openly gay Conservative MP
		First uniformed police in Gay Pride march
2003	73	Gay/lesbian people protected at work
		Homophobic assault recognized as hate crime
2004	74	First gay, non-celibate priest ordained as bishop in Episcopalian church
2005	75	Civil partnerships established

What is striking about these dates is how late they came for many older people. Those now in their 80s were in their 20s when women's sexual pleasure was becoming commonly recognized, and at the time of their birth many unmarried mothers were still sent to psychiatric hospitals as 'moral defectives'. If that tells us something of the moral climate surrounding heterosexuality, notice how much later any significant change occurred for gay and lesbian people.

These changes and the dates when they occurred have three legacies:

- Older people's ideas about sexuality cover a very wide spectrum.
- Older women have lived some of their lives in a culture which sexually repressed them.
- Gay and lesbian older people have lived most of their lives in a culture that stigmatized or criminalized them.

Minority ethnic older people

It's important not to exaggerate the rigidity of sexual codes in the 1940s and 1950s: the Second World War changed many things; people did have sex outside marriage and before it, but it was surrounded by secrecy and shame. Men were expected to marry pregnant girlfriends and they usually did: one study suggested that one in three pregnancies were conceived outside marriage and those who lived together unmarried were unusual. Nevertheless, older people have lived through the initial liberation brought about by the pill and the legalization of gay sex, later medical caution about side effects both of the pill and of several sexual partners and the icy wind of AIDS, and they now witness most of their grandchildren 'living in sin' as they might call it. However, all this applies to white British people and rather less to others.

Immigrants from Catholic Ireland were more likely to have been spectators or casualties of these sweeping changes than participants, and unmarried pregnant Irish women often had nowhere else to turn but punitive 'Magdalen asylums' back in Ireland.

For the most part, older people with roots in the Indian sub-continent have not witnessed these changes in their own or their families' lives and have looked with some disapproval – shared by many white British contemporaries – on Britain's changing sexual morality. There are exceptions, including a Peer who is both gay and a Muslim, but heterosexuality, pre-marital virginity (especially for girls) and monogamy are still part of the dominant moral expectation of British South Asians:

> For the older generations, especially the migrants from South Asia, they did not even think about the 'S' word. They were married young and did not have the chance or even a choice to explore this option. After marriage the next step was to produce children for which sex was the key purpose, and children came more or less straight away in the marriage. There usually was no real sex education so contraception and the role of sex in a relationship was never questioned.
>
> (Bains 2010: www.desiblitz.com)

Generalizations about African-Caribbean older people are harder to make. Part of the persisting legacy of fractured families under slavery meant that 'public' pregnancy out of wedlock was dramatically more common in 1950s Jamaica than it was in Britain (though British figures were disguised by illegal abortions and homes for 'fallen' women whose babies were then adopted). Caribbean women, on the other hand, tended to raise the child in an extended family, and there was much less outright condemnation of pre-marital sex and pregnancy. This coexisted, however, with higher levels of Christian religious observance among older Caribbean people (Modood et al. 1997), so the morality of heterosexual behaviour was contextual and more accepting of some kinds of 'sin'. Homosexual acts between men, on the other hand, are culturally taboo, and still carry ten year jail sentences in Jamaica.

These issues can combine in some people's lives:

> I have Black lesbian friends who have felt very vulnerable in case a 'carer' from 'their' community outed them, and who have stopped using services as a result. They have also experienced racism from 'carers' which is as traumatic as the homophobia that most of us have experienced at times.
>
> (cited by CSCI 2008: 13)

Lesbian, gay and bisexual (LGB) older people

Being in an environment in which their identity is visible and understood is likely to be important to older lesbians and gay men, whether care takes place in their own homes or elsewhere. Just like heterosexuals, they may have books and photos which reflect who they are; as one person told Fannin (2006: 32): 'My main concern would be that my carer would understand and respect my sexuality.'

Activity 9.1

Imagine you had felt compelled to keep your sexuality secret, but then needed to move into the communal setting of a care home, where other residents retain views of homosexuality as deviant behaviour. It is not surprising that many older lesbians and gay men would prefer to live in gay-specific care homes, while others disagreed: 'Although exclusively gay care sounds appealing, it is not a good thing in that it isolates older gay people from the community rather than integrating them into a society where homophobia is not tolerated' (Fannin 2006: 32).

What do you make of this dilemma about 'separatist' or 'integrated' care provision?

It's worth looking at the evaluation of the Open Doors Project for LGB people (Age Concern 2010).

If you're inclined against separate homes, should a note of residents' sexuality be kept (maybe to prevent jokes and comments assuming heterosexuality)?

The idea of monitoring sexual orientation raises strong feelings, though it is supported by the Equality and Human Rights Commission, and by the Commission for Inspection in Social Care, on the grounds that its purpose is to determine if treatment and provision is equitable (no one thinks it can be introduced quickly, without training, and reassurance that its uses will be benign). Research shows that 45 per cent of LGB people using social care services had faced discrimination while using services, while only nine per cent of sampled service providers had carried out any specific sexual orientation equality work (CSCI 2008).

Disabled older people

Older people who have had congenital or long term disabilities are likely to have experienced simultaneous discrimination, with limited opportunities to socialize and develop relationships and perhaps years in institutional single sex accommodation with limited interactions with the opposite sex, followed by community care in recent years. They may have had a lifetime of being considered asexual or requiring protection. Being discriminated against for being older, for being disabled and indeed for their sexual orientation, can make them particularly marginalized within each of these already marginalized groups. Especially when they were younger, society tended to approach them paternalistically seeking to protect them, while in practice limiting opportunities for them to socialize and develop relationships.

Sexuality and dementia

Dementia is a special case and should not be conflated with ageing and sexuality *per se*, but it highlights commonsense assumptions and presents particular challenges. The onset and development of dementia (as well as other forms of acquired brain injury-like strokes) can lead to changes in behaviour:

- more interest in sex;
- less interest, or no interest, in sex;
- more or less ability to perform sexually;
- changes in sexual 'manners' – for example, appearing less sensitive to the other person's needs or appearing sexually aggressive;
- changes in levels of inhibitions. (Alzheimer's Society 2010: http://alzheimers.org.uk)

Each of these changes may entail a social worker at least knowing what is happening and being able to discuss it with carers and potentially with the person with dementia – Alzheimer Scotland point out that people with dementia have lived with it for less time than they have lived with their sexuality. A key question to ask is whether they have an appropriate outlet for expressing their sexuality. The PLISSIT model (Annon 1974) is about practical steps in a measured and incremental approach, from providing information to arranging counselling. It is difficult to be too prescriptive, as actions should be individual and context specific, but the point of this approach is to go at the service user's pace – so if they don't want to discuss sexual matters they should not feel compelled to. An environment needs to be created where they feel safe to talk.

Where someone has cognitive difficulties due to dementia and engages in inappropriate sexual behaviour, attempts should be made to redirect the person towards more appropriate actions, like masturbating in their room rather than a care home lounge. In offering support social workers and nursing staff will encounter dilemmas between their wish to protect and to maintain people's dignity and their desire to meet sexual needs. In some cases interventions such as behaviour therapy and more rarely ('as a last resort' the Alzheimer's Society suggests) medical intervention may be appropriate.

> By changing the way a person feels, and reducing their inhibitions, dementia can expose their private thoughts, feelings and behaviours – including those relating to sex. Sometimes a person with dementia may appear to lose their inhibitions and make sexual advances to others or undress or touch themselves in public. Sometimes they might make sexual advances to someone who they mistake for their partner.
>
> These situations may be embarrassing for those close to the person, but they may also be very confusing, distressing or frustrating for the person themselves – especially if they cannot understand why their behaviour is considered inappropriate. It can help to be aware that such behaviour rarely involves sexual arousal, and to remember that dementia affects a person's understanding of social situations, so it may affect people's ability to behave within social norms.
>
> (Alzheimer's Society 2010: *ibid*)

Many websites offering advice on how carers can support those with dementia appreciate that what had been private between a couple may become public and many challenges are involved, including to attitudes and assumptions. Maintaining intimacy and a sexual relationship can be an important component of sustaining the relationship in which care occurs between partners. Nolan (2001) found that sustaining mutuality in relationships was a better indicator of care enduring than considering the burden of care, often focused on by professionals. While there tends to be an emphasis on social care, the provision of personal care can have a disastrous effect on a sexual relationship (Mantell 2010), for instance because of 'wanting to maintain the mystique'. Where carers provide all intimate care there is the risk, particularly where the partner has cognitive impairments, that they may infantilize them, removing sexual attraction and denying the person their sexuality. The carer may find they no longer want a sexual relationship because the partner's personality has changed from the person they loved. In cases where cognition has been affected, the issue of consent to sexual activity arises, though under the guiding principles of the Mental Capacity Act 2005 adults have the capacity to consent unless assessed otherwise. Capacity relates to a specific decision at a specific time; making a decision to have sex is different to entering into a long term relationship (see Letts 2011).

Person-centred practice and sexuality: some key issues

Recalling the PLISSIT model, staff have a responsibility to maintain the environment of permission within their agency, identifying what older people want as regards sexuality and its expression. 'Self-esteem is better among older people who have sex, body image is better, emotional wellbeing is greater and a feeling of togetherness exists which can be absent in others' (Gott, interviewed by *Observer*, 2001), and the recognition of this has to be communicated to older people even when recognizing restrictions, limited possibilities and frustration.

Many older people will find such discussion difficult because they were not used to it when they were younger. Shame may be felt by women freely expressing sexual feelings that in former times they found impossible. In particular, given the silence about such things in the past, a woman sexually abused in either adulthood or childhood needs to suppress the shame she will probably feel, requiring trust in social workers being 'unshockable' and sensitive, in the same way that we would not expect children to recount events in precise detail. This is not to confuse older people with children it is about adjusting communications skills to the person.

Activity 9.2

Imagine a sexual episode of your own that you remember as pleasurable and about which you feel no shame or sense of immorality.

Imagine describing what you did in detail to a stranger. How easy would that be?

Open-mindedness in staff, a willingness to talk, listen, answer questions, provide accurate information and make suggestions to resolve sexual problems have been found to be more effective in communicating with older clients about sexuality (Johnson 1997), though there's no point in denying that staff may find this sensitive and potentially embarrassing (Kessel 2001). Ward et al. (2005) point out that the sensitivity is gendered and that how professionals deal with their own feelings and interpret expressions of sexuality in older people depends upon how they see themselves. A training exercise suggested by Baker and Shears (2010) consists of being given an identity – such as a gay man living with his male partner – and responding to statements such as these:

- I would feel able to talk openly to friends about my partner.
- We can hold hands as we go down the street.
- There would be no problem telling my parents about my partner.
- We would be able to dance together at a party or function at work.
- My employer would be supportive of our relationship.
- I would be able to talk about my relationship openly in the company of my faith community.
- I could talk about my sex life to my doctor without being judged.
- If my relationship broke up my friends would mainly be supportive.
- There would be no problem sleeping with my partner if my parents came to stay.
- We could kiss in full public view without embarrassment.
- Most people would regard my sexuality as 'normal'.

Activity 9.3

You might score your own answers to these, with one point for every 'yes'. A low score indicates your perception of how hard it is to be an openly gay man.

How can social workers start the conversation about someone's sexual needs in a way that is not intrusive? One approach is to use questions that enable people to describe who is important to them, without pressuring people into giving answers, for example:

- Would you like to tell us the important people in your life?
- Do you need support to keep up contact with anyone in particular?
- How do you like to spend your leisure time?
- Do you need support to be involved with any groups or activities?
- Is there anything you would like to tell us about what is important in your life?

With single older people, whereas minimal expressions of affection for others may be accepted, there is a danger that anything more explicitly sexual is regarded as problematic, inappropriate, even disordered (Miles and Parker 1999); in men 'what is virility at

25 becomes lechery at 65' (Garner 2009: 7). It may be responded to by joking and banter, but this in itself conveys that it is not taken seriously. A good test for one's reaction is to consider whether the same response would be made to people in their 20s: laughing at their feelings or desire for someone else, acting as if they couldn't possibly be serious, ignoring what is said and changing the subject, taking away any material that might be considered stimulating, or treating the whole idea as distasteful.

Sexually transmitted infections are potentially an issue for older people, and while not as numerous as those among young people, a study in 2008 noted increases in older people's attendance at GUM clinics (Bodley-Tickell et al. 2008). Some emerging stereotypes need viewing with caution: despite evidence of greater sexual activity and enjoyment among older people than in the past, this does not mean it's a concern for everyone. Women maintain an interest longer than men (Beckman et al. 2008) though not necessarily in vaginal penetration, notwithstanding the publicity given to Viagra.

Good practice

An Israeli study showed that the complexities of individual variation, the emotional involvement of families, and staff experience and confidence, meant general prescriptive advice was of much less use than staff working through case studies to help them improve their skills (Ehrenfeld et al. 1997). We would suggest that practitioners need to:

- recognize the sensitivity of sexuality and sexual orientation and the variability of experiences and responses;
- consider and counter their own and colleagues' prejudices and assumptions, assuming neither heteronormativity nor asexuality;
- be willing to research and signpost supportive organizations and communities;
- be prepared to be proactive, positive and facilitative about the expression of sexuality;
- support and make use of relevant training.

In doing these we will be:

- *sensitive* – to people's needs;
- *open* – to hearing, learning and discussing issues;
- *aware* – of resources and how to locate them;
- *willing* – to raise the awareness of others to people's sexual needs;
- *professional* – clear about our boundaries, level of expertise and what is appropriate in a given situation.

Summary

This chapter has focused on four aspects of social work with regard to sexuality and older people: attitudes, knowledge, skills and comfort. We have noted the scale of change during older people's lives, as well as the diversity within the older population with regard to ethnicity, different kinds of disability, attitudes and values about sexuality, and sexual orientation.

Some useful definitions

Ageism: in the context of sexuality one should think of it in terms of cultural power. When the sexuality of older people is marginalized, trivialized, pathologized, or ignored, ageism is at work if the organization of care either ignores or colludes with this.

Bisexual women and men experience sexual and emotional feelings for both sexes.

Gay can be used in an insulting way but is also a self-description used by men who have an emotional and/or sexual orientation towards men; it's an adjective, like 'tall', so just as one wouldn't refer to someone as 'a tall' it makes sense to say 'a gay man' rather than 'a gay'. Beware of assuming everyone who is not heterosexual is in a 'community' and will think the same way.

Heterosexism: the beliefs, behaviours and associated practices that assume the inherent moral superiority of heterosexuality. It's not just that heterosexuality is assumed to be statistically 'normal', since normality in this context has overtones of right and wrong.

Heteronormativity: tends to be used in a similar way to heterosexism, referring to specifically sexual aspects of supposed normality and anything other than heterosexuality being regarded as deviant.

Homophobia: literally 'fear of the same' but it's taken to mean the phobia of anything to do with gay and lesbian people, expressed through avoidance, 'jokes', negative treatment and stigma.

Lesbian: signifying an emotional and/or sexual orientation towards women.

LGBT: the acronym used for lesbian, gay, bisexual and transgendered people.

Sexism: the assumption that one sex is superior to the other; in practice it is more often used in relation to male possession of greater economic, social and cultural power and to assumed male superiority. An aspect of sexism is male control and male definition of sexual pleasure.

Sexual health: 'a state of physical, mental and social well-being in relation to sexuality. It requires a positive and respectful approach to sexuality and sexual relationships as well as the possibility of having pleasurable and safe sexual experiences, free of coercion, discrimination and violence' (WHO 2010: 3).

Sexuality refers to the desire for sex and how people express themselves sexually.

Sexual orientation: the combination of emotional, romantic, sexual or affectionate attraction to another person; it involves the diversity of sexual acts and people's values and beliefs about them.

Transgendered refers to a person who feels their biological sex does not match their gender identity, for example, being a woman in a man's body. Transgendered does not denote a type of sexuality – the person may be heterosexual, gay, lesbian or bisexual.

Further reading

www.alzscot.org/pages/info/sexuality.htm
Knocker, S. (2006) *The Whole of Me*. London: Age Concern England.

References

Age Concern (2010) *Opening Doors Evaluation: The Story So Far* . . . London: Age Concern Camden, Hackney, Islington, Kensington and Chelsea, Westminster.

Alzheimer's Society (2010) http://alzheimers.org.uk/site/scripts/documents_info.php? documentID=129 (accessed 26 October 1010).

Annon, A. (1974) *Behavioral Treatment of Sexual Problems*. Honolulu, Hawaii: Enabling Systems.

Bains, S. (2010) *Sex Before Marriage?* www.desiblitz.com/ (accessed 14 November 2010).

Baker, M. and Shears, S. (2010) Sexuality training for health and social care professionals working with people with acquired brain injury, *Social Care and Neurodisability* 1(3): 4–12.

Beckman, N., Waern, M., Gustafson, D. and Skoog, I. (2008) Secular trends in self reported sexual activity and satisfaction in Swedish 70 year olds: cross sectional survey of four populations, 1971–2001, *British Medical Journal* 337: a279.

Bodley-Tickell, A., Olowokure, B., Bhaduri, S., White, D.J., Ward, D., Ross, J.D.C., Smith, G., Duggal, H.V. and Goold, P. (2008) Trends in sexually transmitted infections (other than HIV) in older people: analysis of data from an enhanced surveillance system, *Sexually Transmitted Infections* 84: 312–17.

CSCI (Commission for Social Care Inspection) (2008) *Putting People First: Equality and Diversity Matters 1: Providing Appropriate Services for Lesbian, Gay and Bisexual and Transgender People*. London: CSCI.

DH (Department of Health) (2000) *No Secrets: Guidance on Developing and Implementing Multi-agency Policies and Procedures to Protect Vulnerable Adults from Abuse*. London: Department of Health.

Ehrenfeld, M., Tabak, N., Bronner, G. and Bergman, R. (1997) Ethical dilemmas concerning sexuality of elderly patients suffering from dementia, *International Journal of Nursing Practice* 3: 255–9.

Fannin, A. (2006) Gay and grey: Lifting the lid on sexuality and ageing, *Working with Older People* 10(4): 31–4.

Gamer, J. (2009) Considerably better than the alternatives: positive aspects of getting older, *Quality in Aging* 10(1): 5–7.

Heath, H. (1999) Intimacy and sexuality, in H.M.B. Heath and I. Schofield (eds) *Healthy Ageing: Nursing Older People*. London: Mosby.

Johnson, B. (1997) Older adults' suggestions for health care providers regarding discussions of sex, *Geriatric Nursing* 18(2): 65–6.

Kessel, B. (2001) Sexuality in the older person, *Age and Ageing* 30(2): 121–4.

Letts, P. (2011) *Assessment of Mental Capacity – a Practical Guide for Doctors and Lawyers*, 3rd edn. London: Law Society.

Mantell, A. (2010) Under a cloud: carers' experiences of Huntington's Disease, *Social Care and Neurodisability* 1(2): 33–41.

Miles, S.H. and Parker, K. (1999) Sexuality in the nursing home: iatrogenic loneliness, *Generations* 23(1): 36–43.

Modood, T., Berthund, R., Lakey, J., Nazroo, J., Smith, P., Virdee, S., and Beishon, S. (1997) *Ethnic Minorities in Britain: Diversity and Disadvantage*. London: Policy Studies Institute.

Nolan, M. (2001) The positive aspects of caring, in S. Payne and C. Ellis-Hill (eds) *Chronic and Terminal Illness: New Perspectives on Caring and Carers*. Oxford: Oxford University Press.

Observer (2001) The older you are, the better your sex life (accessed 22 October 2010).

Saga (2010) http://home.saga.co.uk/health/healthyliving/bodymatters/frisky-50s-not-ready-to-retire-from-bedroom.asp (accessed 15 October 2010).

Smith, P., Cowell, J., McGarry, P. and Chandler, S. (2010) No sex please! We are over 50, *Working With Older People* 14(3): 40–3.

Ward, R., Vass, A., Aggarwal, N. and Cybyk, B. (2005) A kiss is still a kiss? The construction of sexuality in dementia care, *Dementia* 4(1): 49–72.

WHO (World Health Organization) (2009) *The Unexplored Story of HIV and Ageing*. Geneva: World Health Organization.

WHO (World Health Organization) (2010) *Measuring Sexual Health: Conceptual and Practical Considerations and Related Indicators*. http:dRwhqlibdoc.who.int/hq/2010/who_rhr_10.12_eng.pdf (accessed 1 November 2010).

www.nhs.uk/Livewell/Goodsex/Pages/Oldersex.aspx (accessed 20 October 2010).

10 Work with older people and spirituality

Graham Tooth and Andrea Linell

After reading this chapter you should be able to:

- describe the nature of the spiritual enterprise for older people and practitioners;
- identify and use provisional definitions of 'spirituality' and evaluate the relationship between spirituality and religion;
- understand ways in which the spiritual might be expressed and experienced in a diverse society;
- appreciate the importance for practice of getting alongside the older person's spiritual journey.

Introduction

By 2040 a quarter of the UK population will be over 85. The current focus of much care for older people emphasizes their biological, psychological and social needs. However, recent writings propose that spirituality is a neglected fourth dimension of being human and is the overarching and integrating experience that brings meaning to people's lives. This chapter explores how people's unfolding spiritual stories not exclusively aligned to religious beliefs might shape the experiences that older age heralds.

This chapter offers ideas to help practitioners engage in a therapeutic alliance with people by using everyday language and thinking as well as metaphor and imagery. It is an invitation for the practitioner to reflect on their own experiences of spirituality as well as joining with older people's spiritual enterprises in the knowledge that they are rarely complete or rounded. It is the enterprise, or as some would say, the struggle rather than the arriving, that is the hallmark of human spiritual experience.

Jewell (2004: 15) defines spirituality as 'that which lies at the core of each person's being, an essential dimension which brings meaning to life'. To make this broad statement more tangible we note that Richmond (2002), among others, points to four qualities of the spiritual that people explore throughout their lives:

- a search for meaning;
- living out shared values;

- having a purpose;
- what to do with this (my) life.

These are the very ordinary and fundamental questions and qualities that shape our relationships and attitudes to our bodies (survival, quality of life, physical frailty, illness), our thoughts and emotions, our social world and others (giving and receiving, hurting and winning), nature and the cosmos (oneness with all things, individuality, doubt).

There is a dynamic relationship between these spiritual qualities and the individual, cultural and generational perceptions and experiences that shape older age. At some points in older age the spiritual enterprise may relate to the coming of pain, isolation and restriction; at others, it may hold within it the continuation of lifelong joys and recently acquired freedoms as affirmations of life. Ultimately life ends with physical death and, for those wanting to, their spiritual journey may be to explore meaning in their life lived, the coming of its end and for some an after life.

Practitioners can offer older people the opportunity to explore the 'intangibles' of life; those spiritual aspects like love, hope, peace, 'wholeness', despair, doubt, integration, reconciliation and potentially transcendence. Like eddies in a stream these experiences appear and disappear, change speed, reshape and slip from our grasp but form the backcloth to people's lives. Each person's spirituality is going to be unique.

Case study 1

John, Jeff and Winston loved allotment gardening. None is any longer able to garden due to infirmity or dementia.

John was primarily occupied with the utility of growing his own vegetables and the challenge of controlling pests. He grew them as a supreme act of giving to his family and having a purpose.

Jeff used to spend hours sitting reflecting on his connection with the earth, the wonder of things growing from seed, being a part of the cosmic drama. He felt the loss of every plant but understood this is the true of face of life.

Winston enjoyed being out on a sunny day and often remarked at how amazing vegetables are when they grow. He would smile and carry on digging. He had a heart attack a year ago, since then he has struggled to live with anxiety.

Case study 2

Mary and Joan participated in a community drop-in for years. Both have lost mobility and are no longer able to get along and in their own words are 'frankly too tired to bother'.

For Mary it was a place to connect with the same friends, to share tea, conversation, have a laugh and experience a sense of solidarity.

Joan made it her life's work to be available for others attending the drop-in whatever their state of being or behaviour. She always took flowers. She made a point of not judging even when very challenged by others' behaviour. Her values of giving and generosity were foremost in giving expression to a sense of connectedness to all beings.

Activity 10.1

Using MacKinlay's definition and Richmond's spiritual qualities (as noted above) for the people in the case studies consider:

- What qualities might be present in each person's spirituality?
- How do you think these people might be affected by the loss of their ways of connecting with their spirituality and expressing their values, meaning and purpose in life?

Old age in Western society

Bearing in mind that each older person experiences a distinctive passage through life we can nonetheless identify along a spectrum the young older person, the middle older person and the old older person. Without holding these as watertight categories it is possible to see these groups as facing different tasks in relation to ageing and death. The younger older person may be facing retirement, grandparenthood and its demands and the transition into being the older generation as their parent's generation dies off. At the other end of the spectrum the older old person may be encountering isolation, physical frailty, memory loss and a much closer experience of encroaching death. At this stage in life, if not before, Erikson et al. (1986) suggest people often review their lives with increased interest and concern as the fact of mortality and physical decline become more evident.

'Successful ageing might mean that a person who has gained insight from earlier stages in life will be able to bring these into play in the later part of their lives' (Canda and Furman 2010: 255). In contrast, novelist Paul Auster (Open Book, Radio 4 24 October 2010) suggests that some older people become more vulnerable emotionally and spiritually because the mass of painful life experiences has undermined their resilience. Alternatively, Mowat (2004: 47) notes that older people interviewed in her research reported that 'old age was not, of itself, of interest . . . Their idea of success was linked to their whole life rather than their ageing process. The respondents revealed themselves as "unfolding stories"'. So, for some older people these streams or stories are shaped by positive beliefs and outgoing emotions and connections; for others, by adversity.

Adversity can be a source of growth, struggle and transformation. However, some adversity is so overwhelming that it inhibits a search for meaning. An accumulated loss of people, roles, physical health, mental wellness, memory and independence can adversely impact on the lives of older people. Additionally there is adversity through discrimination: for example, views that older people are societally redundant, no longer make a meaningful contribution and are a burden on society and their family. This is compounded by: a materialist tide in western society that is individualistic, goal and achievement orientated and prejudiced against people who are no longer economically productive; the use of a deficit perspective in care settings (what 'they' can't do) unbalanced by a strengths perspective (what older people can give); care giving characterized by infantilization, trivialization, medicalization, patronizing attitudes and institutionalization. The latter discriminations relate particularly to the care of people with dementia. Other discriminations may arise in response to a person's gender, sexuality, ethnicity or disability.

Apart from the practical effects of discriminations, the older person might internalize them as feelings of inferiority and a belief that, 'this is all that can be expected out of life'. Ameliorating or confronting such discriminations is the stuff of social work practice. It could be the act that supports a person's spiritual well-being. It is the spiritual experienced through everyday contact.

Spirituality – something new or a rediscovery?

Spirituality probably has a longer tradition than any other branch of human investigation. For some time it moved to the margins of care giving with medical, psychological and social sciences taking centre stage. Spirituality is currently regaining acceptance as an intrinsic part of well-being for a significant number of people receiving care. This development is rising out of a society with unprecedented access to new knowledge, ideas about the world and our place in it and social groupings. Out of this dynamism, diverse spiritual perspectives no longer shaped by established religions are emerging. They are diverse and fluid as groups evolve their spiritual stories.

While society is rediscovering and redefining spiritual experience practitioners in health and social care are challenging overly scientific biases in care giving. Extending Jenkins' (2004: 200) observations it seemed that in the rush to provide comprehensive, seamless, evidence based packages of quantifiable care to individuals, we had forgotten something in life about 'getting help and getting by'; about people (carers and helpers) connecting with the realities of life. That is, our relationship to one another, the fact of death, disappointment, pain, laughter, joy; our own, however flawed, efforts to be reasonable with ourselves and with others. Brandon (2000: 50) observes that 'this is the essential harmony of ordinary everyday living rather than devotion to self cherishing'.

The UK's diverse spiritual landscape

> Human spirituality is like an intricate tapestry of all aspects of human diversity woven together with spiritual experiences, values, beliefs and practices.
> (Canda and Furman 2010: 101)

Drawing on Buddhist teachings we might say 'Our sense of meaning is inextricably bound up with our beliefs and views, with our perspective on life' (Sarvananda 2009: 77). Cultures are rapidly diversifying in the UK today as people blend cultures in a search for new identities and meanings. The traditionally Judeo-Christian indigenous population is changing spiritual shape in the presence of emerging non-theistic beliefs. On the other hand significant numbers of people are committed to and part of theistic communities and traditions. The majority of older people in the UK at this time will be aligned to established Christian beliefs and if not practising then by virtue of the dominant Christian culture. The breadth of religious affiliations in the UK is outlined in Moss (2005: 28) and importantly includes ethnic minority communities with significant populations of older people including Muslim, Sikh and Jewish.

So, this makes for vibrant and contested times for the spiritual tapestry of the UK. People of all ages today are exploring spirituality through community, ecology, nature, cosmology, nutrition, sport, music, art, theology, systems of theistic and non-theistic thinking and practice, materialism and science. Ways of expressing the spiritual are equally diverse, for example, the annual pilgrimage of many festival goers, sitting in silence, seeing the greenest of green leaves in late spring, prayer or chanting. Sarvananda (2009: 108) expresses this drive for meaning forcefully: 'For although we are rational creatures who tend to literalize our experience, we're also mythical beings who are hungry for a prevailing story, who long for a more meaningful reality.' This could be said to be 'the human spirit' touched by something imaginal[1] and mythic.[2]

Case study 3

Mariah is a practising Christian. She believes that God offers forgiveness through Jesus Christ. She experiences guilt after doing wrong and believes in penance.

Eric is a practising Buddhist. He experiences all actions as arising on 'conditions'. He believes he can shape some 'conditions' through his practice. He feels shame when he acts unskilfully and transgresses Buddhist ethics. He resolves not to do it again by changing the 'conditions' in him that gave rise to those actions. He mentions 'the wheel of life'.

Activity 10.2

Responding to what Mariah and Eric have said, what questions would you begin to ask to get insights into their mythic or imaginal stories?

Notice from this activity that often we do not know or understand how others shape their worlds. The important task is to have the courage to keep an open mind, remain curious and ask questions.

Focusing on the spiritual in practice

We hope it is clear that person-centred care, dignity, respect, inclusion and empowerment only become truly meaningful when integrated with a person's unfolding story, the deeper and bigger reality emerging out of their spirituality. To paraphrase a Zen saying we might say that without this understanding 'practitioners risk spending too much time looking at the finger pointing to the moon and never seeing the moon'. We need to notice the everyday experiences and activities (the fingers) that give rise to extraordinarily ordinary spiritual experiences (the moon), which most people seek to rediscover throughout life.

Alternatively older people's lives could be likened to a process of forming and reforming eddies in a stream. In the initial stages of helping, the task for practitioners is to listen attentively.

The spiritual experience

Within the scope of the definition of spirituality so far, the search for spiritual experience is viewed as being as important as our daily preoccupations with survival, procreation and material development; it is just that we give more attention to the latter. The quality shared between these 'remarkable' everyday preoccupations and the spiritual is consciousness. If spirituality is so present in our lives it could be said to be 'nothing special'. And yet in the searching for and experiencing it is very special because it is the glue that binds our existence that helps to make sense of often fragmented internal and external joy, tedium and suffering.

We suggest that there are qualities universal to all spiritual endeavours and that spirituality is less an event and more akin to dynamically linked processes. Figure 10.1 expresses spiritual processes shared by all humans. The number in each oval shaded area in the diagram refers to each process as described below:

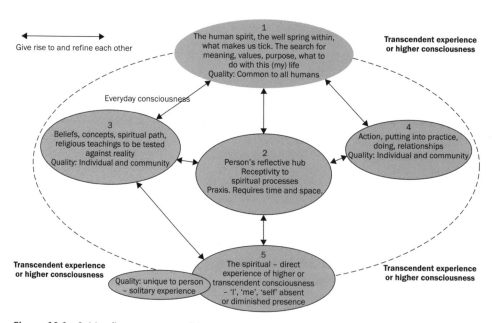

Figure 10.1 Spirituality common to all beings.

Process 1: 'The human spirit' These qualities, inherent in all people, are discussed in the introduction (Richmond 2002). They could be the starting point for a conversation that radically enhances the potential for helping older people.

Process 2: 'The reflective hub' To give life to process 1 there are qualities inherent in all people including a kind of consciousness that is capable of reflectivity and praxis and that is receptive to, shapes and is shaped through spiritual experience. Wherever people believe consciousness resides (and this is contested) it is what gives meaning to life. It is what people draw on in times of well-being and of crisis. It is often overlooked in people perceived as vulnerable. For some the spiritual is an accessible source of hope, courage and forbearance or a spur to action. For others it may need nurturing to develop. For example, Holloway and Moss (2010: 54) cite research to show that suicide among older people is disproportionately high and that 'spiritual despair' was a contributory factor.

Process 3: 'Beliefs' All humans construct their own or take on other's imaginal and mythic belief systems, philosophies and values to shape their spiritual stories and, for some, to realize the sacred or transcendent. The spiritual, therefore, involves some effort to conceptualize a desired state of being and a way to get there. Spirituality is very practical in the same way that we generally have no problems imagining desired work situations, relationships or societies and how to make them reality.

Process 4: 'Actions' In one way it is necessary to engage with activities or practices, to develop and give expression to beliefs and values, to test them out in the world, to bring about a sense of relationship and to discover whether our spiritual experience has meaning. Put another way it is through 'doing' (whether mental, physical or emotional) that we experience 'being' (spiritual experience). However, the model also describes spirituality as reflexive and beliefs may arise through a direct connection with or experience of the sacred or cosmic. This is an area for exploration with people being helped.

Brandon, Richmond and others note that the spiritual is routinely experienced and can be found in people's everyday activities and environments. It may mean ensuring older people access activities that mean something to them. A person may not be able to do that activity any more but the practitioner could find ways to bring the experience to them. For example, in Winston's case it may mean bringing him seed packets, pots of seeds, pictures of sunflowers, earth, a spade, flowers to smell. The possibilities are endless and emphasize the importance of talking with the person and others who know them, observing, and having the courage to be creative.

Practitioners need to think about how to provide people with opportunities:

- to engage with their creative capabilities;
- to explore their values and beliefs;
- to encourage positive emotions;
- to give space to reflect on how 'it' is all coming together or falling apart.

Activity 10.4

Imagine you are an older person glued to a seat on the edge of an arid lounge, 'like an ante-room to death', deprived of the chance to engage with the opportunities noted above. In what ways might this impact on your spiritual well-being?

Process 5: 'The spiritual' This is a particular quality of spiritual experience. It is a state of transcendent or higher consciousness which contains little or no sense of 'I', 'me' or 'self'. It may contain experiences of unity, oneness, expansiveness, harmony and integration. Most people have had some, albeit fleeting, experience of this. This experience of being often develops through consistent practice within established belief systems and practices but it may also arise spontaneously. Figure 10.2 includes the spiritual enterprise that may be more present in older age.

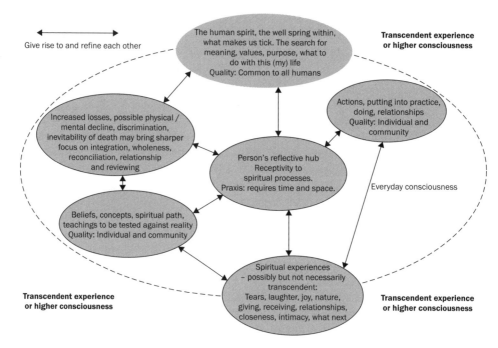

Figure 10.2   Additional factors shaping spirituality in older age.

Qualities of the spiritual are as follows:

1   The spiritual lives and breathes; it is subject to expansion and contraction, experimentation, revision, doubt and certainty. At times when things get rocky, intention, effort and the support of others may be the only anchors.

2   The spiritual is not 'fluffy' (Brandon 2000), monochrome or linear. Spiritual challenges define people's lives and the communities or people through which they find strength and give expression. The spiritual ground on which we stand can be as diverse as fighting for rights, refusing medication, having a picnic with friends, facing death with equanimity, painting, taking risks or worshipping.

3   Independence and interdependence are fundamental to human experience. Spirituality holds within it the effort to live in harmony with the paradox and tension between shaping and being shaped.

4   It may transcend our usual intense experience of 'me', 'I' or 'self'. It points to the human ability to experience a quality of consciousness beyond our familiar limited physical and mental senses.

5   How we express the spiritual is as much embedded in our history and culture as shaped by our present intentions. However, the experiencing may transcend all cultures. For example, Christianity, Buddhism and maybe ecology are universal rather than ethnic.

6   Practitioners cannot determine spiritual experience. However, they can support the conditions that make spiritual experiences possible.

The relationship between the religious and the spiritual

There is not space here to explore this relationship in depth. For the purposes of this chapter it is sufficient to understand that spirituality can be experienced and practised both within and outside formal structured practices. It seems inappropriate to talk of spirituality as either secular or religious. At one level the spiritual is just what it is but developed and expressed through different stories and practices. Non-theistic and theistic religions both provide a training within which to discover and give expression to the spiritual. For a further wide ranging exploration of this relationship read Holloway and Moss (2010).

Activity 10.5

Which, if any, of Jeff, Winston and Eric's stories of spirituality are you drawn towards or away from?

How would you appreciate the spiritual in their stories if you experience personal reservations about them?

Spirituality and dementia

About a quarter of people in the UK over the age of 80 are likely to have dementia. Kitwood (1997) noted that with a loss of or reduction in cognitive powers people with dementia were no longer seen as being fully human and that dominant methods of care depersonalized and ignored their true nature. They were often ignored, interrupted, disparaged and mocked for unusual behaviour. However, Kitwood discovered that people with dementia can retain or even develop spiritual lives.

Some have suggested that with the loss of cognitive powers a stronger sensory, emotional and spiritual aspect to a person's life could emerge. They may be able to demonstrate what it means to be truly human without the encumbrances of a logical/rational mind. 'The presence of dementia does not remove our essential humanity; the greatest threat to our dignity with such illnesses lies in the misrepresentations of others' insensitivities in the care system and stereotyping of illnesses' (O'Neill 2009). Moments of great simplicity and true appreciation of what happens between the person with dementia and another, or of the beauty of their immediate environment may light up their world and that of their carer.

Practitioners need to develop openness to the potentials within people with dementia and to learn communication skills to draw them closer. This can be easier if the person's spiritual history is available. There may well be symbols, rituals or music that resonate for the person and bring comfort and peace. For the person with no obvious spiritual life before the onset of dementia there still could be ways to build a relationship by experimenting with activities and seeing what enables the person to move from agitation, anxiety and possible aggression towards acceptance and contentment. It is possible that people with dementia can benefit from finding meaning and value in life. (See also Chapter 5.)

Orientating social work practice towards spirituality

Thompson (cited in Holloway and Moss 2010) and Gilbert (2010) note that spirituality is intimately connected to the passion for and commitment to values and the sense of community and justice that lie at the core of social work practice. The desire to offer empathy, to give space, to bring fun, to relieve distress, to pursue advocacy, to protect, to challenge services, to provide effective care and to support taking positive risks as an affirmation of identity cannot be understood in rational terms alone. Below are some ideas for connecting spirituality to practice.

First, how we live with the spiritual in ourselves will affect our practice.

- Do you have an experience of spirituality and what is your attitude towards that?
- Do you have a view about spirituality and social work?
- Do you believe spirituality is not always attached to religion?
- Do you believe a person can develop spirituality?
- How is it expressed, if at all, in your practice?
- If you don't 'do' the spiritual what strategies will you develop to support the people who do?

Gottberg (2003), Zohar and Marshall (2001) and De Mello (1997) are sources for exploring spirituality in yourself. Poetry, singing, TV programmes about life on earth or the solar system are others.

Second, think of your social work practice as bringing core skills to the person's spiritual experience.

- Curiosity – ask questions in an open and tentative way and be prepared to experiment to find a way to connect with the person's experience and to overcome what Gilbert et al. (2010: 29) call the 'fear of spiritual language'.
- Receptivity – connecting with the person's life as it is now rather than just the assessment tools; seeing who is in front of you. Bear in mind that the nature and intensity of people's spiritual experiences will vary across their lives.
- Courage – to be present, to give space and to ask. It is better to ask and miss the mark.
- Observation – use tools (including Figures 10.1 and 10.2) and disinterested observation in a way that helps people to articulate their spiritual needs. Brandon (2000) emphasizes the need to apply tools with a light touch. 'Many of us (tutors, trainers, policy makers) give students a series of diagrams and carefully organised strategies from handbooks that look more like car repair manuals.' This chapter and the reference section offer well-travelled tools. The Spirituality and Mental Health online leaflet (The Spirituality and Psychiatry Special Interest Group of the Royal College of Psychiatry 2010) offers more ideas for practice.

Reshaping the earlier Zen saying: 'If necessary, first observe the finger well using manuals, diagrams, tools and then, remember to look to the person's moon.'

Third, orientate social work practice around the reflexive nature of spirituality. 'Being' arises out of 'doing' as much as 'doing' arises out of 'being'. For example, here is a person talking about spirituality: 'I often think about how my Gran brought up her children, how she lived her life, and she had a deep spiritual being, not necessarily formatted to a fixed religion . . . she was very wise, very funny and her zest for life, I don't know, that sort of spiritual inner self, that deeper sort of thing, I think it is important' (Mental Health Foundation 2002).

Activity 10.6

In what ways do you see yourself or other people in this description?

What human actions lift your spirits or touch your heart?

Fourth, while there may be spiritual challenges specific to ageing, an older person is their unfolding story. Think of yourself as being alongside that story, to witness, to listen, to help clarify, offer guidance and get things done.

Lastly, discover the resources people bring to their situations that help to express or develop their spiritual journey – poetry, music, pictures, ritual, prayer, special objects, a daily chat, memories of spirited relatives or heroes (real or fictional), nature, looking after others, non-theistic and theistic spiritual communities important to the person, and cloud appreciation.

Activity 10.7

What resources do you think the people in the case studies might access?

Dilemmas in practice

It is worth saying more about asking. In physical, psychological and social assessment it is professionally and culturally acceptable to ask probing questions in initial assessments. Being with the spiritual may require adjusting the pace of our usual practice of enquiry. There can be a temptation to press too quickly to find answers and reach conclusions. People will often not know what they are experiencing because it is so much a part of their patterned life and tied up in their story. With spirituality, social workers need to be sensitive to this issue by engaging their verbal, observational and networking skills to 'grow' a picture of a person's spiritual expressions and experiences. It may take time.

Practitioner boundaries may need to be more fluid in relation to spirituality. Sometimes we need to be prepared to be part of the person's journey. Experienced social workers will be familiar with the experience of boundaries between helped and helper temporarily blurring – a sharing of the self. It is as if the expression of human solidarity and connection is the important part of helping. This should not be confused with over-involvement, abuse of power or imposing our beliefs on others.

Spirituality is not always a smooth experience of progress and contentment. As Rumi poetically writes, life can also 'violently sweep your house empty of furniture' (Helminski 1998). It can shake the very foundations of your spiritual certainties or beliefs. The violence or intensity of a person's spiritual crisis may leave the practitioner adrift, deskilled and concerned. It can help to remember that for most people spirituality at its core is about connection, solidarity, relationship and integration. Spiritual crisis typically throws these into doubt but the search continues.

If a crisis does arise for the person we could check who makes up the community of people who might offer us or the person support. Sources of support might include: a spiritual community the person has an affinity with; someone the person is asking to be with or someone with a depth of knowledge of a particular belief system; or general pastoral/spiritual support may be available through denominational pastors or through colleagues with relevant experience. You may find it helpful to refer to Holloway and Moss's (2010: 114) 'fellow traveller' model which describes the four stages of intervention as: joining, listening, understanding and interpreting. Involving others comes with the caveat that you have weighed up issues relating to oppression, discrimination and power when deciding who to connect a vulnerable person with. Not all spiritual communities or individuals are supportive or concerned for the person's welfare.

However, it is important not to underestimate the impact your presence and support may have, particularly where your relationship with the person feels supportive. If you are sincere in your curiosity and receptivity this connection could be what sustains that person spiritually. How often do you hear service users or carers say the important thing is that they felt listened to and valued? Nothing practical may have changed but 'being' a living connection was paramount.

Activity 10.8

If either Mariah or Eric reveals that they had an extramarital affair when younger and this is now troubling them greatly, what questions with a spiritual focus would you want to ask either person based on what you know about their beliefs and using ideas from Figures 10.1 and 10.2?

In our relationship with spiritual care we need to be serious but not too earnest. Gilbert (2010: 23) describes an absence of earnestness as 'an openness to an interior spirituality'. Spirituality is often a source of great compassion, humour, perseverance, patience, creativity and adaptation to changing life circumstances; we could say 'a celebration of life'. If you have the sense of getting bogged down, stuck or lifeless when engaging with a person's spiritual life you have probably succumbed to an earnest stereotype of the spiritual or are lost in the person's experience. Alternatively there may be something amiss with a person's spiritual community or understanding.

All spiritual/religious communities have the capacity to be oppressive or abusive. Deciding if there is oppression can be very complex because of the inherent interde-pendence between the individual and the spiritual community and all other commu-nities in life (work, social club, political party). The individual expresses or develops individuality through community; the community is defined by the actions of its indi-viduals. Suzuki (1999) encapsulates this experience neatly: 'we are neither one nor two but both one and two'. So, how might we decide how freely someone entered into any spiritual community or identify subtle but powerful forms of coercion? Aside from any objective evidence related to safeguarding adults at risk a starting point might be that the spiritual community supports a search for growth and liberation, an enhancement of true individuality, a free joining with community and a sense that the person can contribute to that community in their own right.

Evaluating spiritual relevance in person-centred care

All older people might not perceive spirituality as relevant. For others spirituality plays a big part in their lives but is not perceived by them as relevant to the needs which services might support. Sadly, too many services still think they decide whether things spiritual are relevant to the way these are provided. Table 10.1 and Figure 10.3 are tools to evaluate spiritual relevance with the proviso that service users and carers have been meaningfully consulted.

Where on this continuum would you place some of the characters from the case studies?

Table 10.1 Evaluating spiritual significance

Spiritual experiences	No engagement with things spiritual	Recognizes and enjoys experiences as they arise – not cultivated. e.g. Winston	Cultivates the spiritual actively. e.g. Jeff, Mariah, Eric, Joan	Cultivates within formal practice. e.g. Mariah, Eric
No experience acknowledged				
Occasional experience acknowledged				
Regular experience acknowledged				
Immersed				

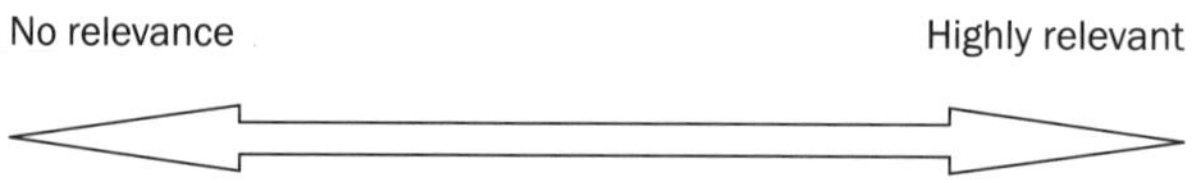

No relevance   Highly relevant

Figure 10.3   Relevance of spirituality to assessment and care outcomes.

Summary

The variety of ways in which people experience and develop spirituality can be seen as both daunting and encouraging; daunting, as it means we cannot pigeon hole people's spirituality (even those attached to a religious community) and have to be prepared to be surprised, humbled, angered, confused and generous. The heart of effective practice is working honestly, courageously and creatively with diversity. It is also encouraging, as it indicates that people are resourceful and given time and support will usually find spiritual sustenance even in adversity.

This chapter suggested that spirituality as defined is the fourth dimension of human experience. We considered that older people's spiritual journeys, however imperfect, are what bring meaning and integration to life and includes those with a diagnosis of dementia. We considered the crucial role that social workers can play in supporting older people's spiritual lives by acquiring the skills and attitudes necessary to assess and plan for spiritual needs and through challenging discriminations experienced by older people.

Notes

1 To paraphrase Sangharakshita (2002: 233), imaginal is the stirring into life of a visionary faculty, which is the reaction of the whole being when confronted by its ideals whether embodied in human form or in writings and teachings. In the case studies Jeff and Joan are people who are stirring their 'visionary faculty' into life.

2 '[B]y myth I do not mean something untrue but something that has universal significance and touches everyone of us . . . a kind of inspiration . . . sustained by deep archetypes' (Moksananda 2004: 38). This quest could show in a search for peace, caring for the planet, love, spiritual knowledge and so on. For example, Jeff may be living out the archetypes of creator, bringer of life. For Joan it may be that of compassion, the helper, the warrior. John might be the archetypal hero and protector.

Further reading

Eggar, S. (2001) *Love in the Time of Old Age.* Royal College of Psychiatry, available at http://www.rcpsych.ac.uk/ (accessed 24 September 2010).
De Mello, A. (1997) *The Heart of the Enlightened.* St Ives: Fount Paperbacks.
Matthews, I. (2009) *Social Work and Spirituality.* Exeter: Learning Matters.
Owen, H. (2000) *The Power of Spirit.* San Francisco, CA: Berrett Kohler.

Some helpful websites

A Guide to the Assessment of Spiritual Concerns in Mental Healthcare (2009) http://www.rcpsych.ac.uk/college/specialinterestgroups/spirituality.aspx
The Centre for Spirituality and Health has been established to (a) encourage and support those who find a spiritual dimension in health and social care. https:/www.staffs.ac.uk/faculties/health/research/spirituality.jsp
Culliford, L. and Johnson, S. (2003) *Healing from Within: A Guide for Assessing the Religious and Spiritual Aspects of People's Lives,* http://www.rcpsych.ac.uk/pdf/CullifordJohnsonHealing.pdf (accessed 24 September 2010).
Spirituality special interest group the Royal College of Psychiatry, http://rcpsych.ac.uk
The Cloud Appreciation Society, http://cloudappreciationsociety.org/ (accessed 24 September 2010).
http://mhspirituality.org.uk/resources.html

References

Brandon, D. (2000) *Tao of Survival, Spirituality in Social Care and Counselling.* Birmingham: Venture Press.
Canda, E. and Furman, L. (2010) *Spiritual Diversity in Social Work Practice.* Oxford: Oxford University Press.
Erikson, E.H., Erikson, J.H. and Kivnick, H.Q. (1986) *Vital Involvement in Old Age.* New York: W.W. Norton.
Gilbert, P. (2010) Integrating a spirited dimension into health and social care, *British Journal of Wellbeing* 1(3): 20–4.
Gilbert, P., Kaur, N. and Parkes, M. (2010) Let's get spiritual, *Mental Health Today,* October, pp. 29–33.

Gottberg, K. (2003) *The Findhorn Book of Practical Spirituality*. Scotland: Findhorn Press.

Helminski, K. (1998) *The Rumi Collection*. Boston and London: Shambhala.

Holloway, M. and Moss, B. (2010) *Spirituality and Social Work*. Palgrave Macmillan.

Jenkins, D. (2004) Geriatric burden or elderly blessing?, in A. Jewell (ed.) *Ageing, Spirituality and Well-being*. London: Jessica Kingsley.

Jewell, A. (2004) Nourishing the inner being: a spiritual model, in A. Jewell (ed.) *Ageing, Spirituality and Well-being*. London: Jessica Kingsley.

Kitwood, T. (1997) *Dementia Reconsidered: The Person Comes First*. Buckingham: Open University Press.

Mental Health Foundation (2002) *Taken Seriously: The Somerset Spirituality Project*. London: Mental Health Foundation.

Moksananda (2004) *Ordination*. Birmingham: Windhorse Publications.

Moss, B. (2005) *Religion and Spirituality*. Lyme Regis: Russell House Publishing.

Mowat, H. (2004) Successful ageing and the spiritual journey, in A. Jewell (ed.) *Ageing, Spirituality and Well-being*. London: Jessica Kingsley.

O'Neill, D. (2009) Letter in the *Guardian*, 13 May.

Richmond, P. (2002) *Notes from an Unsourced Article on Spirituality and Mental Health*. East Kent Chaplaincy.

Sangharakshita (2002) *Know Your Mind: The Psychological Dimension of Ethics in Buddhism*. Birmingham: Windhorse Publications.

Sarvananda (2009) *Meaning in Life: A Buddhist View*. Birmingham: Windhorse Publications.

Suzuki, S. (1999) *Zen Mind, Beginner's Mind*. New York: Weatherhill Inc.

The Spirituality and Psychiatry Special Interest Group of the Royal College of Psychiatry (2010) *Spirituality and Mental Health*. http://www.rcpsych.ac.uk/mentalhealthinformation/therapies/spiritualityandmentalhealth.aspx (accessed 24 September 2010).

Zohar, D. and Marshall, I. (2001) *Spiritual Intelligence: The Ultimate Intelligence*. London: Bloomsbury.

PART 3

Enhancing the well-being of older people and safeguarding issues

11 Skills in working with risk

Chris Smethurst, Vivienne Killner,
Deborah Smallbones and Christine Wright

After reading this chapter you should be able to:

- discuss how risk is constructed and understood by older people, governments and practitioners;
- critically evaluate and apply models of risk assessment and intervention;
- identify the emotional impact of risk on older people and practitioners.

Introduction

This chapter will explore person-centred approaches to working with risk and older people. An understanding of risk and how it is constructed, defined and addressed, is integral to an informed analysis of the policy and practice of social care. However, there is a danger of assuming a shared, universal understanding of risk, one that does not fully reflect the different meanings and interpretations attached to an apparently simple word. Alewszewski (1998) provides a metaphor for the manner in which the word 'risk' carries with it a range of distinct, but interrelated meanings. Alewzewski invites us to conceive of risk as being like the tip of an iceberg, beneath which lurk a number of different, and potentially threatening, concepts: harm, blame, hazard and accountability.

The concepts of harm and blame are frequently linked, to the extent that harm is often assumed to be 'someone's fault' (Douglas 2003). Within this context risk becomes an emotive concept, involving risk for the practitioner. A practitioner, fearful of error, may believe that defensive, procedural ways of working offer a degree of certainty, an antidote to the anxieties and uncertainties of practice. Of course this may also reduce the complexity of individual lives to a narrow menu of categories, labels and processes (Webb 2006).

This chapter raises an obvious question: what knowledge and skills are required of practitioners to enable them to work with risk in a person-centred way? This chapter will seek to unravel the complexity of risk by exploring how risk is understood by older people and practitioners. Suggestions for person-centred risk assessment will be made and the chapter will conclude with an exploration of the emotional impact of working with risk.

What is risk?

Carson defines risk as: 'A course of action or inaction, taken under conditions of uncertainty, which exposes one (or more people) to possible loss in order to reach a desired outcome' (Carson 1995: 75). It is significant that this definition retains a focus on potentially beneficial outcomes. However, in social work, risk is often viewed as being synonymous with the concept of danger (O'Sullivan 2002) or as, 'risk-of-bads, and specifically extreme bads' (Macdonald and Macdonald 2010: 1174).

Research suggests that social workers view risk in primarily negative terms: concepts of harm, abuse and danger being dominant concerns (Stanford 2007, 2008). Practitioners may also struggle when dealing with multi-faceted and fluid 'risk identities': clients may be defined as being 'at risk' or 'vulnerable', but also as a risk to others (Stanford 2010). Navigating these ambiguous and complex identities poses a challenge: how should practitioners intervene, if at all?

Ethical questions of service user autonomy and independence add to the uncertainty highlighted by Stanford (2010). Embedded within the apparently neutral concepts of 'risk assessment' and 'risk management' lie questions of control and power. If risk is something practitioners are required to predict and manage, what degree of influence should practitioners exert over the choices and behaviour of others? The *Codes of Practice for Social Care Workers* provide potentially contradictory imperatives:

> Social care workers must:
> 'Promote the independence of service users while protecting them as far as possible from danger or harm'.
> and
> 'Respect the rights whilst seeking to ensure that their behaviour does not harm themselves or other people'.
>
> (GSCC 2004: 12)

Balancing these potentially conflicting demands is perhaps complicated by the presence of fear and anxiety in many social workers' conceptualization of risk (Stanford 2010). Definitions of risk, and in particular an understanding of what constitutes acceptable and unacceptable risk, are influenced by personal attitudes. These in turn are shaped by the individual's emotional response to risk (Joffe 1999). The spectre of error and blame haunts many practitioners (Smith 2005). This can lead to a fatalistic attitude: that risk and harm are random and beyond control or influence (Shaw and Shaw 2001).

Parton (1998) called for the need to recognize that uncertainty is an inevitable feature of practice. However, this is perhaps out of step with societal expectation that every contingency should be planned for and that every accident is blameworthy

(Douglas 2003; Munro 2011). This inevitably encourages defensive, 'safety-first' approaches to risk (Furedi 2002; Munro 2011).

Activity 11.1

Consider this extract from Douglas (1992): 'The (system) we are in now is almost ready to treat every death as chargeable to someone's account, every accident as caused by someone's criminal negligence, every sickness a threatened prosecution. Whose fault is the first question.' (Douglas 1992: 15–16)

Do you think this is a fair reflection of societal attitudes to risk? If so, why do you think this is?

Blame and risk

The close correlation of risk with blame is an interesting phenomenon, and one that deserves further explanation. Social psychologists provide some interesting hypotheses. First, attributing events to the failure of others reduces our sense of insecurity and vulnerability; it reinforces our belief that the world is predictable and controllable, that we are not all hostage to the fickle hand of fate (Burger 1981). Secondly, human beings have a tendency to focus on the human actor in a situation while diminishing the influence of other factors. Therefore, misfortune is more frequently attributed to human behaviour or error than to the complex interplay of situational factors (Ross 1977).

If risk is assumed to be subject to human control, logically it follows that it should be possible for risk to be identified and measured. Essentially, risk prediction and prevention become the subject of calculation: what are the possible outcomes of a situation, or course of action, and how likely are they to occur? Yet the prediction, assessment and management of risk by scientific means are deeply problematic.

The problem of calculating risk

Alberg et al. (1996: 9) provide the following definition of risk: 'the possibility of beneficial and harmful outcomes and the likelihood of their occurrence in a stated time-scale'. Estimating the likelihood of particular outcomes occurring introduces probability into the assessment of risk: the possibility that something may occur does not make it probable that it will do so. Furthermore, that possibility may increase or decrease over time and so it is important to consider time scale when assessing probability. Arguably, this is particularly important if judgements concerning risk are based on snapshots of a situation, or one-off assessments.

Managing risk through the calculation of probabilities is attractive to policy makers and practitioners: it offers the promise of introducing predictability into the uncertain world of practice (Webb 2006; Kemshall 2010). However, risk remains an elusive subject for scientific management. Factors that may have an effect on a particular event or chain of events may be subject to change in ways that are difficult to predict. These changing factors constitute 'variables', which may themselves interact in a 'cat's cradle' of cause and effect. Reason (1995) wrote of the 'accident sequence', where one (often apparently insignificant) event triggers another. This can create a domino effect that can result in a harmful outcome of far greater impact than the initial trigger would have indicated.

Reason's study of industrial accidents analysed the catastrophic breakdown of mechanical systems following minor infractions or errors by humans. That the most technical and rational processes, with 'fail safe' systems, can be upset by the vagaries of human action should perhaps be noted in health and social care, where human behaviour is not merely a cog in a mechanical system. Szmukler (2000: 6) cautions against viewing individuals as 'automatons', progressing along tramlines of predictable behaviour. This fallacy legitimizes assumptions made with the benefit of hindsight, where:

> an outcome begins to look inevitable; a plausible chain of causes can easily be traced backwards through time. One loses an awareness of the multitude of possibilities presenting themselves at any moment in 'real', forward-moving time, and the immense range of possibilities consequent upon this range of choices'.
>
> (Szmuckler 2000: 6)

Hindsight frequently conflates with blame and complex situations become reduced to simplistic equations: 'if x had done y, or not done z, this need not have happened' (Szmuckler 2000: 6).

The conclusions drawn by Szmuckler (2000) and Reason (1995) can perhaps be compared with those of Douglas (2003) and the discussion of psychological bias given above. A pattern appears to emerge, where risk is often conceived of in simplistic terms: as a linear relationship of cause and effect; predictable, manageable, and thus 'blameable'. In reality, risk is often multi-faceted and complex, a nexus of interwoven situational and human variables. Decision making can involve the balancing of conflicting demands, where there are several potential courses of action and no one obvious solution (Titterton 2005). An illustration of these complexities is provided in the following case study.

Case study

Mrs Carter is 85 years old and lives alone. She has failing eyesight and low blood pressure and has had a number of falls in the last year. Although she struggles financially, Mrs Carter refuses any assistance from her family. Consequently, she saves money by cutting back on heating and food, and only turns on lights when it is impossible to see. Despite her independence, she has increasingly relied on emergency assistance from her son. He has often been summoned from home or work following a fall or other mishap. He is very worried about the falls, but also by the general sense that his mother is 'not coping'. The son's anxiety is increased by the suspicion that his mother is concealing the true extent of her difficulties. This is a source of some stress and, increasingly, anger between them. Mrs Carter's daughter-in-law is concerned about the negative impact all this is having on her husband, and on their family life. She has suggested to Mrs Carter that she should move into residential care. This has prompted a family row.

What are the risks in this situation, and to whom?

Comment

The case study illustrates the extent to which risks are multi-layered and interconnected. Focusing on Mrs Carter in isolation, the risk of falling could be influenced by a range of variables. Oliver and Healey (2009) argue that these variables are often extremely difficult to predict and control, even in the relatively structured environment of a hospital. However, in the case study the issue of falls could be the 'tip of the iceberg': a focal point for other, less obvious, anxieties. These could include general concerns about 'not coping' and other submerged family tensions. The mirror image of an individual being deemed 'at risk' or 'vulnerable' are the risks and vulnerabilities experienced by those who are close to them. Of course, the case study also illustrates the potential hazards of ill-judged, reactive intervention. A practitioner may be tempted to quickly intervene, only to make matters worse when issues that they had not considered later become apparent (O'Hagan 1986). In summary, it is perhaps important to consider that risk is frequently subjective: a matter of interpretation, differing perspectives and potential conflict (Parton 1998). Within this context risk can be an emotive concept, subject to the distortions of perception, 'commonsense' knowledge and popular prejudice.

The social construction of risk

Defining risk within an objective, scientific framework of probability may provide a limited perspective on how it is actually understood. Risk can be *socially constructed* to the extent that an individual's or society's perception of hazard risk may be at variance with objective reality (Douglas 1992; Furedi 1997). What was missing from Mrs Carter's case study was any detail about how she may have perceived the risk of falling, or how she may have managed that risk. Research by Martin (1999) provides an interesting summary of how falls may be perceived by older people:

- Falls cannot be predicted and therefore cannot be prevented.
- Falls are things that happen to other people.
- 'Fall' carries with it negative connotations of vulnerability; 'trips' are accidents that can happen to anyone.
- Consequently, older people will often conceal falls from others.
- Under 75s don't conceive of themselves as being 'old' (because of the negative association with vulnerability).
- There is a reluctance to acknowledge risks associated with older people and a disinclination to engage with services that imply vulnerability.

(Martin 1999)

Individuals selectively interpret information to construct their own narrative about actual risk to themselves. This can involve the avoidance or reinterpretation of factual information to justify existing behaviour (Thirlaway and Hegg 2005). Policy makers often assume that, when supplied with factual information, individuals will make rational, objective decisions about risk. However, this assumption is frequently at odds with the way individuals actually respond (Kemshall 2010).

Individual risk narratives occur within a societal context, where safety and security are dominant concerns (Beck 2003). Although enjoying unparalleled levels of physical security, it has been noted that Western societies are characterized by perceptions of insecurity, where threats and hazards can potentially emerge at random (Beck 2003; Giddens 2003). Exposure to mass media perhaps creates an awareness of potential threats of which earlier generations would have remained ignorant. These can be distorted by the influence of moral panics, where concerns about, among others, particular foods, diseases and types of crime can be inflamed to apocalyptic proportions; then quickly forgotten within weeks (Cohen 2002).

This overload of information poses particular challenges for the citizen attempting to navigate an uncertain world. It is perhaps unsurprising if the individual adopts a 'pick and mix' approach to the menu of potential hazards and defensive actions presented to them by the media, government and professionals. As Wynne (1996) illustrates, rational decision making is complicated by scepticism towards expert or official advice. Subjective fears, anxieties and commonsense understandings of risk can assume the status of 'cultural facts', directly challenging objective evidence (Garland 2001). For example, people 'know' that crime is getting worse where they live even though, statistically, the opposite may be true. For older people, fear of crime correlates with an enhanced sense of personal vulnerability; this can impact upon other areas of their lives (Taylor and Donnelly 2006).

The subjective, personal or cultural construction of risk is underpinned by uncertainty. Individuals are unsure of the severity of threats presented to them and of the best course of action to ensure their security (Furedi 2007). Consequently, it is argued that modern life is characterized by general feelings of anxiety or unease, where even the humdrum existence of everyday life may be littered with hazard (Hubbard 2003). The only way to ensure one's safety is to assume and prepare for the worst case scenario, or adopt a fatalistic attitude towards the multitude of potential threats (Furedi 2007).

Vulnerability

Within a societal context of uncertainty and anxiety, vulnerability to specific threats is supplanted by an ambient sense of vulnerability: in an unpredictable world of random harm we are all potentially 'vulnerable' (Furedi 1997). However, by virtue of age older people are deemed by policy makers to be specifically vulnerable. The extent to which this is a legitimate construction will be explored in the following sections.

Activity 11.2

Are older people intrinsically vulnerable, or are there specific features of the person and their life that create vulnerability?

> From your own experience are there any features of a person's circumstances or attitude that can guard against them being or becoming vulnerable?
>
> Compare your own understanding with the research findings below.

Vulnerability exists as a label but also as a felt reality; arguably the two are not always identical. Schroder-Butterfill and Marianti (2006) maintain that vulnerability consists of an individual's *exposure* to a threat and their ability to *cope* with it. This suggests an individualized construction of vulnerability, not an overarching categorization based on age. Hazards do not affect everyone in the same way; an individual's *coping capacity* is contingent upon their internal resources and external support.

Schroder-Butterfill and Marianti's conclusions about vulnerability parallel those of crisis intervention theory, to the extent that ability to cope is a product of the perception of the severity of the crisis event, and external and internal coping resources (Caplan 1961). Similarly, vulnerability links to notions of resilience: the ability to withstand and recover from harmful events (Luthar and Cicchetti 2000). Tanner (2007: 20) revealed that resilience in older people is linked to the maintenance of psychological well-being and personal control through action-oriented responses to problems; through 'keeping going' and navigating the 'slippery slope' of threats posed by illness, disability and crises. The risk of giving up or giving in following a crisis is therefore a function of 'the perceptions and feelings of the individual at the centre of it and the degree of risk they sense in trying to cope' (O'Hagan 1986: 14–15).

The interconnectedness of vulnerability, crisis and resilience is helpful in understanding how older people may respond to risks, and how these risks may be perceived by others. Taylor and Donnelly (2006) noted a correlation between anxiety, the perception of risk and the likelihood of admission to institutional care following a fall. Some people manage the anxiety and 'live with falls'; others have strategies for getting around which makes home safer than an institutional setting. The individual's and others' anxiety and perceptions of risk would appear to be key. Falls tend to be dramatic events, which trigger crises and heighten anxiety levels in a way that gradually escalating difficulties do not.

O'Hagan (1986) notes that crises often create demands for the removal, perhaps into institutional care, of the person deemed to be the cause (O'Hagan 1986). These 'plea for removal' crises often originate in unacknowledged tensions and anxieties that become crystallized around a specific event. This 'final straw' triggers demands for urgent, often drastic, action. However, these demands are frequently driven by the concerns of others, not the person who is the focus of the crisis. Therefore practitioners need to be aware that perceptions of risk and vulnerability may be amplified in times of crisis and may distort any intervention. It is perhaps easy to become embroiled in situations where it is assumed that there is only one course of action, and that the practitioner is the only person capable of resolving the crisis (O'Hagan 1986).

Vulnerability appears to be located in the specific circumstances, characteristics and attitudes of the individual; it may be issue specific. However, this distinction is lost when the term 'vulnerable adult' is used to categorize populations by age or disability. Vulnerability becomes a fixed characteristic of the individual, implying 'at risk' status, passivity and dependency (Furedi 2007). Paradoxically, research indicates that older people are resilient, resourceful and active in managing the risks they encounter (Godfrey et al. 2004; Tanner 2007; Bornat and Bytheway 2010).

Arguably, the blanket categorization implied by the term 'vulnerable adult' reflects underlying ageist assumptions of dependency. Stevenson (2008) argues that ageist assumptions portray older people as an economic and emotional burden, a drain on the resources of the younger population and a reminder to them of a potentially unpleasant future. Social care practitioners are in danger of internalizing these views of old age, as their involvement primarily occurs in times of crisis, or in times of declining health (Richards et al. 2007; Bornat and Bytheway 2010). A construction of older people as intrinsically vulnerable can legitimize over-protective approaches to risk (Ray et al. 2009). Perversely, these can increase risk; by undermining their personal autonomy and psychological well-being, the resilience of older people to hazards and setbacks may be compromised (Tanner 2007).

Risk and the principles of person-centred practice

Risk assessments are an integral part of social care practice. In the experience of the authors these are often issue specific, initiated at the behest of others, and potentially driven by their concerns when a problem is identified and defined. However, it is evident that risk is often multilayered, with apparently single issues being the focus of an interconnected network of people, their perceptions and anxieties about safety and well-being. According to O'Sullivan (2002), practitioners should satisfy themselves of the answers to four main questions: What is meant by 'risk' in a situation? What is the social context of any decision making: who is involved? How are the risks to be assessed? What will be the best approach to risk management?

These questions need to be considered with the awareness that many practitioner interventions with older people are brief. This limits the opportunities to develop the reciprocal, trusting relationships that are the cornerstone of inclusive practice (Manthorpe et al. 2008). Consequently, practitioners need to be aware that their impressions of a situation, and its attendant risks, may merely be a snapshot of the present. This creates a bias towards the significance of immediate risks, which may overlook the role of past events in shaping the current problem, or upon the interconnectedness of risk with other areas in older people's lives (Bornat and Bytheway 2010).

Biographical approaches, which rely on the older person's narrative construction of the significance of hazards within the wider context of their lives, have been shown to be more effective than snapshot assessments (Victor et al. 2005; Bornat and Bytheway 2010). Consequently, 'close attention to people's framing of risk can often show them as expert risk managers' (Kemshall 2010: 1250). It follows that risk assessments may need to be an ongoing process rather than a one-off event. The case study illustrates how a presenting risk overshadowed other potential problems. These emerged after the initial problem had apparently been addressed.

Case study

Mrs Carr fell at home and was admitted to hospital. Despite intensive input from the physio-therapist and occupational therapist her mobility remained severely impaired. Health professionals concluded that Mrs Carr would continue to be at high risk of falling. They strongly recommended that Mrs Carr should be discharged to residential care. Mrs Carr was very anxious about the risk of further falls and dreaded the prospect of returning home. She was very enthusiastic about the prospect of residential care, where she felt she would feel safe. However, within a short time of being discharged from hospital she spoke of how depressed she felt at being in an unfamiliar environment. During the six weeks Mrs Carr was in the care home she did not fall and was able to move about her room and manage tasks. Once the anxiety and drama of the immediate risk of falling had abated new risks emerged: feelings of being disorientated; of being isolated and lonely; of feeling a loss of identity (Pritchard 1996). Eventually Mrs Carr returned to her home with support, to the daily life where she felt secure.

Comment

In the case study the professionals initially focused on the narrow issues of falling and physical harm. Mrs Carr shared these concerns, although it is possible that her own fears were amplified by the concerns of those around her. However, the primary risks to Mrs Carr eventually emerged as the less tangible, less dramatic, but equally important threats to her independence and identity.

Immediate risks can sometimes conflate with a sense of 'pressure or emergency' to result in admission to institutional care (Ray et al. 2009: 49). This is characteristic of plea for removal crises, but can be particularly problematic in hospital discharge situations. Individuals may be asked to make life changing decisions, under pressure and in an unfamiliar environment (CSCI 2004, 2005). Away from the security of home, individuals may have an enhanced sense of their own vulnerability. Consequently, the risk of inappropriate admission to institutional care may be increased (CSCI 2004, 2005). It may not fit with the organizational or professional demands for brief intervention but, as the case of Mrs Carr illustrates, once immediate hazards have been addressed, effective risk assessment and management may need to take a longer term view. The role of the practitioner may need to be that, 'People are encouraged to find their own way in their own time' (Trevithick 2005: 271).

Risk and multidisciplinary working

The case study was an example of multidisciplinary risk assessment and management. To be effective it is essential that those involved understand their own and others' roles, responsibilities and organizational policies (Biggs 1997). However, the nature of multidisciplinary working can be more complex and nuanced. Collaborative relationships between individual practitioners are often stronger than formal partnerships at organizational level (Hudson 2005). Similarly, a focus on structures and procedures may obscure the influence of differences in professional cultures, status and values (Hudson 2002; Littlechild 2008; Morris 2008).

The difference between the medical and social work models of practice is typically revealed in the way problems and priorities for intervention are defined. However, the differences between professional groups are not absolute and tensions may well be the result of perception as much as action. Health practitioners, schooled in a task oriented professional culture, may perceive social workers as being slow to commit to action. Conversely, social workers may conclude that their health colleagues reduce complexity to simple diagnoses and hurried intervention (Kharicha et al. 2005). Practitioners from either professional culture may be committed to collaborative working; but believe that this would be more effective if only the other profession would change (Kharicha et al. 2005). However, multidisciplinary working can be successful and genuinely collaborative. This was witnessed in the Admission Avoidance Project created by NHS West Sussex and West Sussex County Council (2010). The primary aim of the multidisciplinary team was to provide rapid assessment and intervention with older people in crisis situations, and at risk of admission to institutional care. The effectiveness of the project relied upon a shared understanding of risk and its assessment and management. Within a year the project had prevented 509 people from being admitted to hospital, their identified needs being met by community health and social care services.

Risk, rationing and resources

The Admission Avoidance Project illustrates the value of preventative work in addressing risks before they reach a critical stage. A focus on preventative services for older people has been the goal of recent national policy (Tanner 2007). However this aspiration is undermined by the inadequate resource base for social care and the consequent rationing of support for older people (Lymbery 2010). Publicly-funded social care has increasingly become a residual service of last resort, available only to those in greatest need. Within this context 'risk' has supplanted 'need' as the primary determinant of service eligibility (Kemshall 2002). Assessment of risk has become a gate keeping activity, providing a perverse incentive to define older people as being 'at risk' in order to gain access to resources (Ray et al. 2009).

Risk assessment has become co-opted into the bureaucratic requirements of resource allocation. This promotes reductionist 'tick-box' assessment, where complex lives are pared down into narrow categories and standardized responses (Webb 2006; Crisp et al. 2007). These processes discourage a person-centred understanding of risk: the subtleties of the older person's perspective can be subordinate to the process of categorization. Similarly, skills in assessment and decision making can be undermined by the twin constraints of limited autonomy and limited time (Postle 2002). This obviously has implications for the effectiveness of any intervention and returns us to the question posed in the Introduction to this chapter: What knowledge and skills are required to work with risk in a person-centred way?

Working with risk

Research suggests that many practitioners adopt a procedural understanding of older people's lives. This may be modified or reinforced by the practice wisdom of personal experience, but may not necessarily incorporate any application of relevant theoretical knowledge (Taylor 2006; Richards et al. 2007). The bureaucratization of social care practice is well documented (Postle 2002; Gorman and Postle 2003). However, Kemshall (2010) suggests that even the most bureaucratic and mechanistic processes are mitigated by the values and attitudes of the worker. Within the environment of an older person's front room, a hospital ward or residential care home the skills, knowledge and personal qualities of the practitioner still count, and are valued by older people (Manthorpe et al. 2008).

Checklist-based assessment tools typically do not address the older person's experience of risk as an element of the wider context of their life (Bornat and Bytheway 2010). Assessments that provide a snapshot in time produce only a partial account of the perceived realities of risk and how these may change over time. Mrs Carr's case study was an example of how risk evolves. Effective risk assessment needs to address these complexities. However, attempts to capture the intricate realities of social care practice have resulted in the development of ever more complex models and theories. These can seem at odds with the need to be flexible, creative and responsive to the fluid dynamics of practice situations (Payne 2007). Person-centred risk assessment models need to:

- accurately reflect the older person's understanding of risk, what it means to them in the present, but also within the context of their past experience and future aspirations;
- ensure that the older person's views and wishes are not overshadowed by the competing perspectives of others;
- reflect the way in which risk is accommodated by many older people – 'keeping going' and avoiding the 'slippery slope' may mean that difficulties may not be immediately apparent;
- acknowledge that risk may be multi-faceted; that there may be no one best solution and that any one course of action or solution may involve further risks for the older person or others;
- be simple and flexible enough to survive the rigours of application in practice.

Activity 11.3

Consider the assessment models and tools that you use in practice. To what extent do they meet the above criteria?

Have you or your colleagues adapted or modified them to apply them in practice?

If so, how have you adapted them and why?

Many agencies will have their preferred assessment models and tools. Many are service or issue specific, so it is beyond the scope of this chapter to provide an overview. However, the following three approaches meet most, if not all, of the above criteria and have the added benefit of being easy to remember!

Approach 1: working with crises

The first approach, from Wright (1993), is drawn from the theories of crisis intervention. Working in a hospital setting Wright was required to respond rapidly and flexibly to any number of situations where people had experienced loss, trauma and shock. Wright's approach involved the gradual exploration of three, key factors:

1   the person's perception of the event;
2   their external resources;
3   their inner resources.

Establishing the individual's perception of the event requires the practitioner to support the person to tell their story: What has happened? What has been lost? How significant is the loss for the individual? Does the crisis event create other risks for the individual or other people? This is not an exhaustive list of questions, and skilled practitioners will know that the discussion with the individual will rely on an intuitive sense of 'the right questions to ask', 'the right things to say'. Compassionate, skilful intervention does not rely on a menu card of fixed questions, but is an 'improvised performance', drawing upon the practitioner's theoretical knowledge and practice wisdom (Payne 2007). The key here is not to leap to conclusions or start seeking solutions, but to explore the problem at the person's own pace, using their language not professional jargon. Theories of crisis intervention stress the importance of the person's perception of the event in determining the severity of the crisis (Caplan 1961). This obviously links to what is understood about vulnerability and the coping abilities of older people.

The second component of Wright's approach involves the identification of coping mechanisms and external support. The exploration of 'external resources' focuses on the practical and material support that the individual can draw upon and any needs they may have. Social care assessment often focuses on these needs to the exclusion of emotional and psychological needs (Richards 2000). Therefore, practitioners must avoid any temptation to rush into task focused intervention, without first establishing what the problem is.

The third component requires the practitioner to explore the person's 'inner resources'. These resources link to notions of resilience and vulnerability and Wright (1993) emphasizes the importance of identifying how crises have been managed in the past as a means of understanding how the person may cope now.

Approach 2: values and principles in action

This approach was devised by Lawson (1996). It should be compatible with any number of risk assessment tools as the primary focus is to make explicit the principles that should inform assessment and intervention. Lawson recognizes the potential for the voice of the older person to become lost, particularly in situations of conflict. In addition, the values and principles that health and social care professionals take to be self evident may not be apparent to all (Carson 1996). Ensuring that these principles are an integral part of any recording of decision making may help to justify and defend contentious courses of action.

Lawson (1996) suggests that the following principles should underpin risk assessments with older people:

- User focus. What does the person want and why? What anxieties do they have? Lawson suggests that service users and carers and other 'stakeholders' may have differing views; these may be recorded separately.
- Encouraging independence. In addition to being congruent with social work values, this principle is enshrined in policy and legislation.
- Self determination. All service users are presumed to have the capacity to exercise informed choice unless determined otherwise. Again, these principles have a legal basis.
- Confidentiality. The principles, and limits, of confidentiality should be explored and made explicit.

Approach 3: exploring alternative courses of action

Titterton (2005) recognizes that there may be no one best way to address a problem, but that there may be a variety of options. Therefore the role of the worker is to help identify the options and support the process of decision making. Each option may have advantages and drawbacks and carry attendant risks. The advantages and disadvantages for each option may be different from the perspective of each of the individuals involved. Therefore these should be separately recorded.

This approach has the benefit of being able to incorporate the differing perspectives of those who may have a stake in the decision-making process. However, equally important is the fact that this model allows the consideration of complexity and is not limited to the consideration of one or two risks in isolation.

Titterton's (2005: 57) approach is characterized by two questions:

1   What are the choices available in this situation?
2   What are the dangers and advantages of each choice for each of the parties involved?

Titterton (2005: 59) emphasizes the importance of exploring each option in detail, weighing up the pros and cons of potential courses of action to support the making of informed choices. It is clear that choosing options may require individuals to accommodate certain risks: risk may not be entirely eliminated and the choice may be to determine what risks can be 'lived with'. This process may not always be an easy one; it may involve conflict and high levels of anxiety. The skill of the practitioner may be required in the process of negotiation, to enable compromise to be achieved (Titterton

2005). Of course, this process may not be an emotionally neutral one for the practitioner: dealing with conflict, the emotions of others and the anxieties created by 'making the best of a bad job' can all have an impact on the worker.

Working with risk: the emotional impact

The emotional aspects of working with risk will vary from worker to worker, but most practitioners will at some point, and sometimes often, find themselves worrying about the decisions they, or others, have made. Each risk decision is not isolated; working with risk is an integral part of the practitioner's role, therefore pressures and anxieties can have a cumulative effect on the worker. In addition, person-centred practice arguably requires the practitioner to empathize with the individuals with whom they work. It follows that this requires practitioners to empathize with individuals who are experiencing loss, trauma, anxiety and pain. Similarly, working in situations of conflict, anxiety and pressure will require 'emotional labour': the ability to manage the worker's own emotions and deal with the emotions of others (Hochschild 1983).

Empathy and the long term effects on social workers

Devore and Schlesinger (1996: 25) question the degree to which practitioners can empathically identify with clients whose life experiences may be 'vastly different' to their own. However, to become a skilled practitioner it is important to make the attempt to imagine the experiences of others (Endicott 2006). In recent years, research in the field of social cognitive neuroscience has emerged that identifies the biophysical components that mediate empathy in the brain (Decety and Moriguchi 2007; Gerdes and Segal 2009).

Gerdes and Segal note that brain imaging equipment confirms: 'that when we see another person's actions (for example pain, laughing or crying), our bodies respond as if we feel a degree of that action too' (2009: 117). Neuroscience has revealed that the human brain is wired to mimic other people; this mimicry involves involuntary, physiological responses which are largely unconscious and automatic. Consequently, when we witness others expressing their emotions, our own brains react, making us feel the emotion we are witnessing. It is perhaps no wonder that prolonged, continuous exposure to the emotions and traumatic life experiences of others can have a direct effect on the health and well-being of practitioners.

Emotional burnout

The term 'burnout 'was coined by Herbert Freudenberger in 1981 and was initially defined as:

> a debilitating psychological condition brought about by unrelieved work stress, resulting in: depleted energy and emotional exhaustion, lower resistance to illness, increased depersonalisation in interpersonal relationships,

increased dissatisfaction and pessimism, and increased absenteeism and work inefficiency.

(Freudenberger and Richelson, 1981: 4)

Some evidence suggests that social workers display higher levels of burnout than those in comparable occupations (Bride et al. 2007). Although there is the potential for making simplistic links of cause and effect, it is alarming that a study revealed that 74 per cent of social workers experience borderline or pathological levels of anxiety (Lloyd et al. 2002). Baruch-Feldman et al. (2002) linked feelings of anxiety, anger and depression to excessive workload. This creates a working environment where there is insufficient time for processing stressful situations and for effective decision making. These are prerequisites of effective risk intervention (Munro 2011).

The development of burnout 'spreads gradually and continuously over time, putting people into a downward spiral from which it is hard to recover' (Maslach and Leiter 1997: 17). Consequently, the onset of burnout may not be immediately obvious. To guard against this Butler (2007) suggests developing emotional self-awareness. Similarly, Collins (2008) identifies a correlation between reflective ability and emotional resilience. These approaches are in marked contrast to the findings of research by Fineman (1985) where the internalization of difficulties was the dominant coping style of social workers: they hoped that anxiety would simply go away.

Maintaining motivation and effectiveness

Despite all the pressures in social care work there is clear evidence that social care workers get satisfaction from their work, despite the fact that this work may be demanding and stressful (Cameron 2003; Huxley et al. 2005). Jones (2001) indicates that statutory social workers generally get satisfaction from their actual work with users and that stress is primarily generated by policy, procedure and other practices within the organization. It would seem that social workers have a high commitment to their work, are well motivated by contact with service users and feel they can make a real difference to people's lives (McLean and Andrew 2000; Eborall and Garmeson 2001; Huxley et al. 2005).

When working with risk, fear of failure and the negative reactions of colleagues were a major source of practitioner anxiety (Smith 2005; Stanford 2010). Therefore it is unsurprising that support from colleagues is an important buffer against stress and anxiety (Smith 2005). This is significant if organizations devote insufficient attention to the development of team cohesion and mutual support.

Although the Laming Report (2009) emphasized the necessity of social workers needing to develop resilience, there seemed to be an implied message that this was an individual responsibility. Arguably, insufficient attention has been devoted by social care agencies to the situational and organizational supports that promote resilience. Nevertheless, there is evidence that individual differences between social workers can influence motivation and resilience (Collins 2007: 255). Two of the strategies employed by workers are particularly interesting. The first involves 'goal directed' or 'problem focused' work (Collins 2008).

Completing tasks, problem solving and working towards particular objectives can give the worker a sense of purpose and achievement. Arguably, this is particularly important if the worker experiences organizational structures and processes as a barrier to good practice (Cameron 2003; Huxley et al. 2005). Of course, the challenge for workers who pursue a goal directed or problem-focused approach is that they do not adopt a fragmented and reductionist view of the client's circumstances or problems. It is tempting to find meaning through concentration on short-term achievable tasks, but this can be at the expense of depersonalizing the client and distancing oneself from their problems and emotions (Collins 2008). Therefore, Collins reports that social work staff can develop resilience through finding meaning in their work. This can be difficult, as alienation appears to be a feature of the experience of many practitioners (Postle 2002; Ferguson and Lavalette 2004).

The lesson perhaps, is that protective distancing does not, in fact, protect the worker; it merely heightens anxiety, alienation and the risk of burnout. The authors' experience is that the search for meaning in the work is precisely that: it involves an active process of search and recognition. It is not a passive process of 'waiting for success stories'. Viktor Frankl (1963) believed that the human condition is characterized by the search for meaning in life, and that despair and decline were the inevitable consequences of giving up that search. Perhaps there is a lesson here for social care practice?

Summary

This chapter has explored definitions of risk and blame and how these can be the consequence of societal constructions of risk and attitudes towards older people. The issue of vulnerability is examined and its relation to ageism and the risks that internalization of vulnerability can legitimize overprotection which undermines the independence of older people. Working with risk explores how practitioners can adopt a person-centred approach to risk assessment that recognizes the complexity of a service user's situation and avoids a narrow interpretation of risk. Finally the chapter summarizes the effect on practitioners of working with uncertainty, anxiety and conflict.

Further reading

Ray, M., Bernard, M. and Phillips, J. (2008) *Critical Issues in Social Work with Older People (Re-shaping Social Work)*. Basingstoke: Palgrave Macmillan.
Titterton, M. (2005) *Risk and Risk Taking in Health and Social Welfare*. London: Jessica Kingsley.

References

Alberg, C., Hatfield, B. and Huxley, P. (eds) (1996) *Learning Materials on Mental Health: Risk Assessment*. Manchester: University of Manchester Department of Health.

Alewzewski, A. (1998) Risk in modern society, in A. Alewzewski, L. Harrison and J. Manthorpe (eds) *Risk, Health and Welfare.* Buckingham: Open University Press.

Baruch-Feldman, C., Brondolo, E., Ben-Dayan, D. and Schwartz, J. (2002) Sources of social support and burnout, job satisfaction and productivity, *Journal of Occupational Health Psychology* 7(1): 84–93.

Beck, U. (2003) *World Risk Society.* Cambridge: Polity Press.

Biggs, S. (1997). Interprofessional collaboration: problems and prospects, in J. Ovreteit, P. Mathias and T. Thompson (eds) *Interprofessional Working for Health and Social Care.* Basingstoke: Macmillan.

Bornat, J. and Bytheway, B. (2010) Perceptions and presentations of living with everyday risk in later life, *British Journal of Social Work* 40(4): 1118–34.

Bride, B.E., Radey, M. and Figley, C.R. (2007) Measuring compassion fatigue, *Clinical Social Work Journal* 35(3): 155–63.

Burger, J.M. (1981) Motivational biases in the attribution of responsibility for an accident: a meta-analysis of the defensive-attribution hypothesis, *Psychological Bulletin* 90: 496–512.

Butler, G. (2007) Reflecting on emotion in social work, in C. Knott and T. Scragg (eds) *Reflective Practice in Social Work.* Exeter: Learning Matters.

Cameron, C. (2003) Care work and care workers, in *Social Care Workforce Research: Needs and Priorities.* London: King's College.

Caplan, G. (1961) *Prevention of Mental Disorders in Children.* New York: Basic Books.

Carson, D. (1995) From risk to risk management, in J. Braggins and C. Martin (eds) *Managing Risk: Achieving the Impossible.* London: Institute for the Study and Treatment of Delinquency.

Carson, D. (1996) Rising legal repercussions, in H. Kemshall and J. Pritchard (eds) *Good Practice in Risk Assessment and Risk Management 1.* London: Jessica Kingsley.

Cohen, S. (2002) *Folk Devils and Moral Panics,* 3rd edn. Routledge: London.

Collins, S. (2007) Social workers, resilience, positive emotions and optimism, *Practice* 19(4): 255–69.

Collins, S. (2008) Statutory social workers: stress, job satisfaction, coping, social support and individual differences, *British Journal of Social Work* 38: 1173–93.

Crisp, B.R., Anderson, M.A., Orme, J. and Lister, P.G. (2007) Assessment frameworks: a critical reflection, *British Journal of Social Work* 37(6): 1059–77.

CSCI (Commission for Social Care Inspection) (2004) *Leaving Hospital: The Price of Delays.* London: CSCI.

CSCI (Commission for Social Care Inspection) (2005) *Leaving Hospital: Revisited.* London: CSCI.

Decety, J. and Moriguchi, Y. (2007) The empathic brain and its dysfunction in psychiatric populations: implications for intervention across different clinical conditions, *BioPsychosocial Medicine* 1: 22–43.

Devore, W. and Schlesinger, E.G. (1996) *Ethnic-sensitive Social Work Practice.* Boston, MA: Allyn and Bacon.

Douglas, M. (1992) *Risk and Blame: Essays in Cultural Theory.* London: Routledge.

Douglas, M. (2003) *Risk and Blame: Essays in Cultural Theory* (reprint). London: Routledge.

Eborall, C. and Garmeson, K. (2001) *Desk Research on Recruitment and Retention in Social Care and Social Work.* London: Business and Industrial Market of Research.

Endicott, L. (2006) *Self-care of the Professional: Managing Compassion Fatigue and Burnout in One's Practice*. http://www.nacsw.org/Publications/Proceedings2006/CFEndicottBOSE. pdf (accessed 4 June 2010).

Ferguson, I. and Lavalette, M. (2004) Beyond power discourse: alienation and social work, *British Journal of Social Work* 34(3): 297–312.

Fineman, S. (1985) *Social Work Stress and Intervention*. London: Ashgate Publishing.

Frankl, V. (1963) *Man's Search for Meaning: An Introduction to Logotherapy*. New York: Simon and Schuster.

Freudenberger, H. and Richelson, G. (1981) *Burnout: The High Cost of High Achievement*. New York: Doubleday.

Furedi, F. (1997) *Culture of Fear: Risk Taking and the Morality of Low Expectation*. London/New York: Cassell.

Furedi, F. (2002) *Culture of Fear: Risk Taking and the Morality of Low Expectations*, 2nd edn. London: Continuum Press.

Furedi, F. (2007) The only thing we have to fear is the 'culture of fear' itself, *Spiked*, April 4. http://www.spiked-online.com/index.php?/site/article/3053/ (accessed 5 June 2011).

Garland, D. (2001) *The Culture of Control: Crime and Social Order in Contemporary Society*. Oxford: Oxford University Press.

Gerdes, K.E. and Segal, E.A. (2009) A social work model of empathy, *Advances in Social Work* 10(2): 115–27.

Giddens, A. (2003) *The Consequences of Modernity*. Stanford, CA: Stanford University Press.

Godfrey, M., Townsend, J. and Denby, T. (2004) *Building a Good Life for Older People in Local Communities*. York: Joseph Rowntree Foundation.

Gorman, H. and Postle, K. (2003) *Transforming Community Care: A Distorted Vision?* Birmingham: Venture Press.

GSCC (General Social Care Council) (2004) *Code of Practice for Social Care Workers and Code of Practice for Employers of Social Care Workers*. London: General Social Care Council.

Hochschild, A. (1983) *The Managed Heart: Commercialization of Human Feeling*. Berkeley, CA: University of California Press.

Hubbard, P. (2003) Fear and loathing at the multi-plex: everyday anxiety in the post-industrial city, *Capital and Class*, 80: 51–76.

Hudson, B. (2002) Interprofessionality in health and social care: the Achilles heel of partnerships?, *Journal of Interprofessional Care*, 16: 199–210.

Hudson, B. (2005) Grounds for optimism, *Community Care*, 1 December.

Huxley, P., Evans, S., Gately, C., Webber, M., Mears, A., Pajak, S., Kendall, T., Medina, J. and Katona, C. (2005) Stress and pressure in mental health social work: the worker speaks, *British Journal of Social work*, 35(7): 1063–79.

Joffe, H. (1999) *Risk and the Other*. Cambridge: Cambridge University Press.

Jones, C. (2001) Voices from the front line: social workers and New Labour, *British Journal of Social Work* 31(4): 547–63.

Kemshall, H. (2002) *Risk, Social Policy and Welfare*. Buckingham: Open University Press.

Kemshall, H. (2010) Risk rationalities in contemporary social work policy and practice, *British Journal of Social Work* 40(4): 1247–62.

Kharicha, K., Iliffe, S., Levin, E., Davey, B. and Fleming, C. (2005) Tearing down the Berlin Wall: social workers' perspectives on joint working with general practice, *Family Practice*, 22(4): 399–405

Laming, H. (2009) *The Protection of Children in England: A Progress Report*. London: The Stationery Office.

Lawson, J. (1996) A framework of risk assessment and management for older people, in H. Kemshall and J. Pritchard (eds) *Good Practice in Risk Assessment and Risk Management 1*. London: Jessica Kingsley.

Littlechild, R. (2008) Social work practice with older people, in K. Morris (ed.) *Social Work and Multi-agency Working*. Bristol: Policy Press.

Lloyd, C., King, R. and Chenoweth, L. (2002) Social work, stress and burnout: a review, *Journal of Mental Health* 11(3): 255–66.

Luthar, S.S. and Cicchetti, D. (2000) The construct of resilience: implications for interventions and social policies, *Development and Psychopathology* 12: 857–85.

Lymbery, M. (2010) Continuities and change in the care of older people, *Critical Social Policy* 30(1): 5–26.

Macdonald, K. and Macdonald, G. (2010) Safeguarding: a case for intelligent risk management, *British Journal of Social Work* 40(4): 1174–91.

McLean, J. and Andrew, T. (2000) Commitment, satisfaction, stress and control among social services managers and social workers in the UK, *Administration in Social Work* 23(3/4): 93–117.

Manthorpe, J., Moriarty, J., Rapaport, J., Clough, R., Cornes, M., Bright, L., Iliffe, S. and OPSRI (2008) There are wonderful social workers, but it's a lottery: older people's views about social workers, *British Journal of Social Work* 38: 1132–50.

Martin, M. (1999) *The Construction of the Risks of Falling in Older People: Lay and Professional Perspectives Final Report*. Edinburgh: Scottish Health Feedback.

Maslach, C. and Leiter, M.P. (1997) *The Truth About Burnout: How Organizations Cause Personal Stress and What to Do About it*. San Francisco, CA: Jossey-Bass.

Morris, K. (2008) *Social Work and Multi-Agency Working*. Bristol: Policy Press.

Munro, E. (2011) *The Munro Review of Child Protection: Final Report. A Child-centred System*. London: The Stationery Office.

NHS West Sussex and West Sussex County Council (2010) *Admission Avoidance Project*. Chichester: West Sussex County Council.

O'Hagan, K. (1986) *Crisis Intervention in Social Services*. London: Macmillan.

Oliver, D. and Healey, F. (2009) Falls risk prediction tools for hospital inpatients: do they work?, *Nursing Times* 105(7): 18–21.

O'Sullivan, T. (2002) Managing risk and decision making, in R. Adams, L. Dominelli and M. Payne (eds) *Critical Practice in Social Work*. Basingstoke: Palgrave.

Parton, N. (1998) Risk, advanced liberalism and child welfare: the need to rediscover uncertainty and ambiguity, *British Journal of Social Work* 28(1): 5–27.

Payne, M. (2007) Performing as a 'wise person' in social work practice, *Practice: Social Work in Action* 19(2): 85–96.

Postle, K. (2002) Working 'between the idea and the reality': ambiguities and tensions in care managers' work, *British Journal of Social Work* 32(3): 335–51.

Pritchard, J. (1996) Risk and older people, in H. Kemshall and J. Pritchard (eds) *Good Practice in Risk Assessment and Risk Management*. London: Jessica Kingsley.

Ray, M., Bernard, M. and Phillips, J. (2009) *Critical Issues in Social Work with Older People*. Basingstoke: Palgrave Macmillan.

Reason, J. (1995) A systems approach to organizational error, *Ergonomics* 38(8): 1708–21.

Richard, S., Donovan, S., Victor, C. and Ross, F. (2007) Standing secure amidst a falling world? Practitioner understandings of old age in responses to a case vignette, *Journal of Interprofessional Care* 21(3): 335–49.

Richards, S. (2000) Bridging the divide: elders and the assessment process, *British Journal of Social Work* 30(1): 37–49.

Ross, L. (1977) The intuitive psychologist and his shortcomings: distortions in the attribution process, in L. Berkowitz (ed.) *Advances in Experimental Social Psychology* (vol. 10: 173–220). New York: Academic Press.

Schroder-Butterfill, E. and Marianti, R. (2006) A framework for understanding old-age vulnerabilities, *Ageing and Society* 26(1): 9–35.

Shaw, A. and Shaw, I. (2001) Risk research in a risk society, *Research Policy and Planning* 19(1): 3–6.

Smith, M. (2005) *Surviving Fears in Health and Social Care: The Terrors of Night and the Arrows of Day*. London: Jessica Kingsley.

Stanford, S. (2007) The operations of risk: the meaning, emotion and morality of risk identities in social work practice. Unpublished PhD thesis.

Stanford, S.N. (2008) Taking a stand or playing it safe? Resisting the moral conservatism of risk in social work practice, *European Journal of Social Work* 11(3): 209–20.

Stanford, S.N. (2010) 'Speaking back' to fear: responding to the moral dilemmas of risk in social work practice, *British Journal of Social Work* 40(4): 1065–80.

Stevenson, O. (2008) Neglect as an aspect of the mistreatment of elderly people: reflections on the issues, *Journal of Adult Protection* 10(1): 24–35.

Szmukler, G. (2000) Homicide inquiries: What sense do they make?, *The Psychiatrist* 24: 6–10.

Tanner, D. (2007) Starting with lives: supporting older people's strategies and ways of coping, *Journal of Social Work* 7(1): 7–30.

Taylor, B. (2006) Risk management paradigms in health and social services for professional decision making on the long-term care of older people, *British Journal of Social Work* 36(4): 1411–29.

Taylor, B.J. and Donnelly, M. (2006) Professional perspectives on decision making about the long-term care of older people, *British Journal of Social Work* 36(5): 807–26.

Thirlaway, K.J. and Hegg, D.A. (2005) Interpreting risk messages: women's responses to a health story, *Health, Risk and Society* 7: 107–21.

Titterton, M. (2005) *Risk and Risk Taking in Health and Social Welfare*. London: Jessica Kingsley.

Trevithick, P. (2005) *Social Work Skills: A Practice Handbook*, 2nd edn. Maidenhead: Open University Press.

Victor, C.R., Scambler, S.J., Bowling, A. and Bond, J. (2005) The prevalence of, and risk factors for, loneliness in later life: a survey of older people in Great Britain, *Ageing and Society* 25(3): 357–75.

Webb, S.A. (2006) *Social Work in a Risk Society: Social and Political Perspectives*. Basingstoke: Macmillan.

Wright, B. (1993) *Caring in Crisis: A Handbook of Intervention Skills.* Edinburgh: Churchill Livingstone.

Wynne, B. (1996) May the sheep safely graze?: a reflexive view of the expert–lay knowledge divide, in S. Lash, B. Szerszynski and B. Wynne (eds) *Risk, Environment and Modernity: Towards a New Ecology.* Sage: London.

12 Skills in safeguarding and supporting older people

John Gisby and Gill Butler

After reading this chapter you should be able to:

- identify key concepts in adult safeguarding and protection, how these are framed within current legislation and policy guidance and why debate continues over the need for a stronger legislative framework and changes in terminology;
- comment on the prevalence of abuse, including domestic violence, and the particular issues faced by older people experiencing abuse;
- understand why the promotion of empowerment, interdependence and autonomy rather than control might reduce the likelihood of abuse, and increase the potential for more positive outcomes;
- discuss the practices and skills which may enhance the practitioner's approach to safeguarding, and support the empowerment of older people at risk of abuse.

Introduction

While awareness of abuse of older people has increased, its occurrence remains widespread with acknowledgement that recognition of society's response to the problem lags behind that for child abuse. Abuse of the elderly is not a new phenomenon as it forms part of a spectrum of interpersonal violence, often in close intimate relationships and sometimes across generations. The stigma associated with the perceived failure to sustain positive relationships or to be worthy of respect ensures that such abuse is often hidden within society and considered a taboo subject. Research suggests the prevalence of abuse against individuals aged 66 or over within private household settings could be 4 per cent of that population (O'Keefe et al. 2007). If we also accept that homicide figures provide some measure of the extreme end of violent and abusive relationships, it is clear that the impact on women is more severe. The British Crime Survey figures for 2008–9 identify a homicide rate of 10 per million for women over 70, contrasted with 5 per million for men (Home Office 2011).

In approaching good safeguarding practice it is necessary to understand what constitutes abuse and why certain individuals or groups, including women, are more vulnerable. To effectively address abuse requires an awareness of the risk of it, to know what forms abuse may take, who might abuse, why abuse takes place and the impact abuse can have on the individual. Practitioners should be receptive to subtle changes in behaviour, which could indicate abuse, and need to be conscious that their actions and words can be contentious and emotive, sometimes shaping the effectiveness of the response.

Consideration therefore needs to be given to the social worker's role in existing processes and legislative structures, to ensure the older person's self-determination is not lost to the expediency of systems we work within. This chapter will consider the continuing evolution of adult protection policy, contrasting its fragmented legislative framework with child protection and new adult safeguarding legislation in Scotland, and will consider how the response to adult abuse has shifted from protection to safeguarding.

Responses to concerns about abuse should be proportionate and holistic in nature, fully involving the person experiencing abuse to ensure they remain central to any plan of support. The importance of adopting approaches which recognize rights as well as vulnerability are emphasized. Older people experiencing abuse often require information, options and support to make informed choices about how they might live their lives as safely as possible, even if risk is involved. What may seem self-evident may be less easy to achieve because many individuals experiencing abuse feel the safeguarding system fails them (CSCI 2008a; DH 2009). We will reflect on lessons learnt from supporting women experiencing domestic violence to illustrate good person-centred practice, and consider how we can address the need for someone 'who will listen to me AND understands what I am saying', 'who knows and can evaluate my situation', 'who is there for me, can prevent crises and think laterally' and 'who is objective and non-judgemental' (Barnes 2002).

Case study

George is a 72-year-old widower and ex-policeman. After several falls at home and declining physical status, George's son, a serving policeman, suggested his father moved into a residential care home. George settled in well but following falls while getting out of bed agreed to bed rails being fitted. Shortly after however, an incident resulted in George falling from his bed again which cut his leg. Supported by other night staff, the principal carer responded to the incident. An ambulance was called and the care home manager and George's son were notified. George told staff he had used the bed rail to pull himself up but it collapsed beneath him. George's son believed his father had been physically abused. He demanded the Police were called and a safeguarding alert made. The carer was suspended while a Police investigation was undertaken, which confirmed a faulty locking mechanism on the bed rails as the cause. The son continued to insist his father was abused and 'someone has to pay'. A safeguarding investigation was initiated in which the home's management, care staff and the son were interviewed. The investigation found the allegation of abuse unsubstantiated. Unable to accept the finding the son forcefully insisted his father was moved to another residential home.

Comment

Although George's explanation of the incident is given initially, it is ignored. When Police and Adult Service investigations are initiated statements are taken from others, but not from George. His voice appears to be silenced by his son's protestations.

Activity 12.1

Consider why an older person's views often fail to be considered.

Those receiving care are often denied a voice, with primacy of views given to carers, family and professionals. Shakespeare (2000), in exploring disability and dependency, discusses stereotyping of older people as incapable and physically dependent. This perceived dependency can lead to an infantilization of adults who, like children, need 'protection', with increasing age being equated to a lack of capacity to make choices. In George's situation, his son believes he knows what is best for his father.

How would you support George to express his wishes? Consider:

- ensuring his consent is obtained for the safeguarding process to occur, and how much involvement he wishes to have in it;
- providing him with a safe environment to be interviewed; where the process is explained and confidentiality boundaries defined;
- developing empathy with George, listening actively and being open-minded and non-judgemental; inspiring confidence through your abilities and knowledge to support him in the ways he might need to make informed choices.

What defines abuse?

With no overarching legislative framework for adult abuse, the guidance provided by the document *No Secrets* (DH and Home Office 2000) frames multi-agency working addressing abuse of vulnerable adults in England. *No Secrets* places an explicit expectation on social service departments to take the lead in the process, and is viewed as statutory guidance being established under Section 7 of the Local Authority Social Services Act 1970, where substantial deviation from it may be unlawful. However, in strict legal terms safeguarding vulnerable adults is not undertaken solely through statutory powers or duties, rather within an assessment and care planning framework.

No Secrets defines abuse as 'A violation of an individual's human and civil rights by any other person or persons'. As such, abuse may consist of a single act or repeated acts, and may take the following forms: physical, sexual, psychological, financial or material, discriminatory or neglect and acts of omission.

It is also useful to consider the definition used by the UK charity Action on Elder Abuse: 'A single or repeated act or lack of appropriate action, occurring within any relationship where there is an expectation of trust, which causes harm or distress to an older person'. This definition links abuse with breach of trust and was adopted for The Toronto Declaration on the Global Prevention of Elder Abuse in 2002, and is used by the International Network for the Prevention of Elder Abuse. Interestingly, there is no reference to gender as a significant dimension of abuse, although a similar definition has evolved to frame domestic violence.

Thus the UK Government defines domestic violence as:

> Any incident of threatening behaviour, violence or abuse (psychological, physical, sexual, financial or emotional) between adults who are or have been intimate partners or family members, regardless of gender or sexuality. This includes issues of concern to black and minority ethnic (BME) communities such as so called honour killings.
>
> (National Archive 2010)

The definition reflects parallels between domestic violence and other abuses of vulnerable adults. These abuses, although widespread, were slow to be recognized and accepted, with disagreements over definitions and concepts used (Penhale and Parker 1999). Both are associated with unequal power relationships and social structures, often involving the maintenance of silence and control of the victim by the perpetrator (Butler 2008). Like elder abuse, there is no single criminal offence of 'domestic violence' although many forms are crimes (e.g. harassment, assault, rape and false imprisonment).

In defining the concept of a 'vulnerable adult', *No Secrets* used the Lord Chancellor's Department's 1997 consultation paper 'Who Decides'. To be deemed 'vulnerable' the adult was:

> a person aged 18 years or over who is or may be in need of community care services by reason of mental or other disability, age or illness; and who is or may be unable to take care of him or herself; or unable to protect him or herself against significant harm or serious exploitation.

The term, however, is a contentious one.

Activity 12.2

Why might the term 'vulnerable adult' be seen by some as inappropriate?

In what circumstances would you feel it could (one day) be appropriate for you to be labelled in this way?

List ways in which this would be helpful/unhelpful.

The health/social care model used in adult safeguarding assumes all individuals who need care provision are 'vulnerable' and focuses on deficits rather than strengths. Rather than focusing on the individual's risk of abuse, the model locates cause with the individual, for example, because of age or disability, rather than placing responsibility with actions or omissions of others (ADSS 2005), or looking at the structural and cultural factors providing the context for abuse. Terms like 'vulnerable', 'the elderly' and 'the dying' may label people as if an homogenous group, not individuals with widely differing experiences and outlooks (Penhale and Parker 2008). This may also stigmatize and insufficiently reflect the oppression experienced by them (Martin 2007). Moreover, the possible significance of gender is not highlighted within this language. The case study below helps us to consider the significance of gender and question the appropriateness of labels focusing on vulnerability.

Case study

Violet is 68 years old and has been married to John, aged 74, for 46 years. John has Parkinson's disease and finds everyday activities increasingly difficult. He insists Violet gives up her part time cleaning job to look after him. Early in their marriage John was often physically violent and when she was pregnant he targeted her abdomen. Over the years she found ways of avoiding upsetting him. She gave up nearly all contact with family and friends and always made sure everything was just as he liked it. Her contact with their children was limited to monthly visits and phone calls which he monitored. Now she does not go out to work she has no escape from his constant criticism and verbal abuse. His moods are unpredictable and she feels trapped and terrified.

In the last year she has taken two overdoses. On each occasion John called the emergency services. In the A&E department Violet was asked what triggered this and simply says she is finding it hard to cope. She is prescribed antidepressants by her GP. However at A&E she is also given a local Women's Aid Outreach Support Worker card with a helpline number in case she wants to talk to someone.

Violet contacts the Outreach worker and arranges to meet in a nearby shopping centre for coffee when she does her weekly shop. Violet finds relief in having someone to talk to, listen and understand. The contact continues for several months, giving Violet the confidence to talk to her GP without feeling a failure and to gradually access a range of support services for John. This enables her to join a support group, while he is at day-care. Listening to other women's experiences, Violet begins to understand the abusive nature of her marriage. She enjoys making the tea for the group, most of whom are much younger than her, and feels she is valued. After twelve months' contact with the Outreach worker, and with her assistance, Violet gains a place in a housing scheme for older people. She starts to babysit regularly for her grandchildren, enjoying closer contact with them as well as finding another part time cleaning job which gives her independence.

Comment

The outreach worker's supportive person-centred approach empowers Violet, but this takes time. In the interim, Violet remains in a situation where she is exposed to risk. The worker accepts Violet has found her own way of living with this over the years and is not ready to change this immediately.

Ninety per cent of respondents to a *No Secrets* review consultation felt the term 'vulnerable' should be changed (DH 2009). Labelling Violet or John in this way masks the complexity of their lives and does not encourage a focus on their strengths and skills. Similar discussion continues over terms such as 'abuse' or 'perpetrator' and, in domestic violence, over the appropriateness of the terms 'domestic', which may trivialize the issue, and 'violence', which is seen as too narrow a term for abuse.

Scotland does not use the term 'vulnerable adult'. Instead it uses 'adult at risk of abuse' within legislation and guidance. To be identified as an 'adult at risk' the individual must be aged 16 years or older, and meet all of the following criteria:

- unable to safeguard their own well-being, property, rights or other interests;
- at risk of harm; and
- because they are affected by disability, mental disorder, illness or physical or mental infirmity, are more vulnerable to being harmed than adults who are not so affected.

For Scotland the presence of a particular condition does not automatically mean the individual is 'at risk', rather it is the entirety of individual circumstances which combine to make an individual more vulnerable to harm than others. As well as providing national definitions, the Adult Support and Protection (Scotland) Act 2007 places clear requirements on agencies to establish multi-agency adult protection committees, investigate where harm is suspected, intervene in an adult's affairs where necessary and apply to the courts for statutory powers to perform these duties. Whether such legislation is the way forward across the rest of the UK is too early to say, but to be a success it needs all concerned to work with and listen to adults at risk (Fennell 2011).

The need for change in safeguarding terminology is recommended in The Law Commission report on Adult Social Care in England (Law Commission 2011). It suggests replacing the term 'vulnerable adult' with 'adults at risk of abuse'. Some local authorities, for example Sussex, have already implemented this change.

The view of vulnerability was also broadened by the Safeguarding Vulnerable Groups Act 2006. 'Vulnerability' here encompasses any person aged 18 years or over in receipt of care within residential, domiciliary or sheltered housing accommodation; or who is receiving any form of health care; or is detained in lawful custody. The Act acknowledges that those who require assistance to conduct their own affairs because of diminishing mental capacity are particularly vulnerable. Additional protection is provided through the provisions of the Mental Capacity Act 2005. Recognition is also made of the increase in self-directed care which provides greater choice, control and independence.

Prevalence of abuse against older people

Campaigns like World Elder Abuse Awareness Day (annually 15 June) have increased awareness and reporting of incidents of abuse against older people. However, this greater sensitivity to abuse against adults, particularly older adults, still lags behind that for child abuse (Baeza 2008). In 2007, Care Minister Ivan Lewis reflected 'we need to have a fresh look at the whole adult protection regime in this country. I want to see a situation where people are as outraged by the abuse of older people as they are by the abuse of a child. Sadly we are nowhere near that as a society, but that culture has to change' (Thompson 2007).

In a systematic review of prevalence reported in 49 studies up to 2006, Cooper et al. (2008) calculated that in general population studies 6 per cent of older people reported significant abuse, with 5.6 per cent of couples reporting physical violence in their relationship. The study concluded one in four older adults could be at risk of abuse, with only a small proportion of this abuse currently being detected.

In 2007 a UK study quantifying abuse experienced by older people (O'Keefe et al.) set out to explore the life experiences and well-being of older people living in their homes and in sheltered housing. Of the 2100 adults aged 66 and over who were interviewed, 2.6 per cent had experienced mistreatment involving a family member, friend or care worker in the previous 12 months. Extrapolated to the entire older population this equates to 227,000 people, or one in 40 people. Prevalence increased to 4 per cent when incidents involved neighbours and acquaintances. In terms of all individuals aged 65 or older this suggested over a third of a million individuals are subject to some form of abuse.

Like most studies, O'Keefe's data were constrained by the parameters used, with the study excluding many groups who could be perceived as being particularly vulnerable, including those with a mental incapacity, those residing in hospitals or care homes, or self-excluding individuals fearful of repercussions. The real rate therefore could be higher, possibly 7 per cent (Action on Elder Abuse 2011).

Abuse involving older people in domestic settings can fall between two social issues – domestic violence and elder abuse. Prevalence figures last recorded for this age group suggest abuse could account for up to 2 per cent of all domestic violence (Home Office 1993). Unfortunately the British Crime Survey self-completion questionnaire which enables people to reveal domestic abuse is not now given to people over 59. This perhaps reflects an assumption that people 'age out' of domestic abuse. However, such evidence as there is (homicide figures cited previously) would tend to suggest this is not the case.

Activity 12.3

Consider why society often has a different level of reaction to the abuse of an older person compared to abuse of children.

The abuse of a child tends to elicit a more empathic response, perhaps because of an innate need to protect smaller, weaker individuals who have less control over what happens to them, and are *de facto* more 'vulnerable'. Moreover we have all been children, so perhaps find it easier to identify with their vulnerability. Adults with capacity in contrast are mostly viewed as having more control over their lives, and therefore as less vulnerable. The view of older people in society has changed, with increasing ageism and devaluation of the elderly. The reasons are likely to be complex, perhaps involving our own fear of ageing, a bias towards youth, or a negative perception of economic worth (Macnicol 2010). The casual disregard sometimes shown to some older people is illustrated in ten NHS case studies of poor care highlighted by the Health Service Ombudsman (Parliamentary and Health Service Ombudsman 2011).

How have current adult protection safeguards evolved?

It is generally accepted elder abuse began to creep into public consciousness in the mid-1970s when the term 'Granny-Battering' was used (Baker 1975; Burston 1975). Fitzgerald (2008) suggests local authority guidelines emerged in the 1980s against a backdrop of statutory agencies struggling with child abuse scandals during the preceding decade. This probably helped agencies to be more receptive to the possibility of abuse within other vulnerable groups. Professional terminology and processes used for elder abuse reflected those developed through the experience of protecting children. However while there are similarities, there are also critical differences in how the response to adult abuse is undertaken, particularly in capacity to make informed choices.

Policy and legislative development for child and adult safeguarding are driven by past inquiries and scandals. Looking at the lessons safeguarding adults takes from child protection, Baeza (2008) identified how the abuse and murder of Maria Colwell and Susan Auckland influenced the drafting of legislation. Child safeguarding policy continues to reflect outcomes of more recent inquiries, for example, Victoria Climbié in 2001 and Baby Peter in 2007 (Laming 2003, 2009).

Adult protection policy and practice has similarly been informed by the findings of inquiries and serious case reviews (SCRs). Revelations about the mistreatment of older people in Beech House in the mid-1990s shocked the public who learnt mentally ill adults were subjected to slapping, cold baths, intimidation and illegal restraint. The inquiry highlighted ignorance, poor management, low morale and inadequate training as key issues (Tonks and Bennett 1999), unfortunately repeatedly identified in subsequent inquiries, for example, the Mid-Staffordshire NHS Foundation Trust inquiry (Francis 2010). Inquiries and SCRs influence practice and policy, but are not necessarily reflected in legislative (Gaylard 2011) or organizational (Scragg 2011) change.

In the 1990s the Department of Health began to provide guidance on elder abuse of individuals in their own homes, and consideration was given to a draft Bill based on 1995 Law Commission consultation recommendations suggesting social workers be given powers to intervene where adult harm or exploitation was feared. However these recommendations were not implemented.

Instead policy guidance was provided by the Department of Health document *No Secrets* (DH and Home Office 2000). Its aim was:

> to create a framework for action within which all responsible agencies work together to ensure a coherent policy for the protection of vulnerable adults at risk of abuse and a consistent and effective response to any circumstances giving ground for concern or formal complaints or expressions of anxiety. The agencies' primary aim should be to prevent abuse where possible, but if the preventative strategy fails, agencies should ensure that robust procedures are in place for dealing with incidents of abuse.
>
> (p.6)

In doing so *No Secrets*:

- defines who is at risk and in what way;
- suggests how multi-agency working processes can be established and who should be involved;
- defines how multi-agency policy should be developed, and what the guiding principles should be (empowerment, promotion of well-being, the right to self-determination and choice, the acceptance of risk);
- states that policy and procedures are to be implemented via a strategy which acknowledges how roles, responsibilities and accountability reflect the requirements of specific investigations;
- identifies the need for specialist services such as refuges and counselling;
- identifies the need for training;
- identifies the need for properly coordinated investigations and multi-agency processes which lead to the achievement of the goals recommended by the Longcare Inquiry.

No Secrets together with *Safeguarding Adults* (Association of Directors of Social Service ADSS 2005) provides a national framework for standards of good practice and forms the core of current adult safeguarding policy and practice in England. *Safeguarding Adults* reinforced key elements introduced by *No Secrets*, strengthening the need for an effective multi-agency approach to intervention where abuse is suspected, and robust local procedures providing good coordination between agencies. It highlights the need for better staff training and greater awareness of adult abuse among professionals and in the community. The establishment of adult protection committees to oversee local implementation was also recommended. Scottish legislation requires such committees to be established. English law will also do so if recommendations from the 2011 Law Commission report are enacted.

While these two documents provide the framework for adult protection policy and procedures in England, a raft of additional legislation underpins implementation, intervention and sanctions including the following:

The NHS & Community Care Act 1990 places a duty on local authorities to assess (s. 47) and provide services to those with an eligible need and, in doing so, consider risks to the individual's well-being.

The Human Rights Act 1998 defines the expected respect for rights of individuals and encourages high standards of practice by public bodies. Its articles include the right to:

- life (article 2);
- freedom from torture, inhuman or degrading treatment or punishment (article 3);
- respect for a person's home, private and personal life (article 8);
- not suffer discrimination (article 14).

The Care Standards Act 2000 and Regulations created a regulated framework setting out minimum standards for social care, including requirements for providers to have adult protection procedures and to include in recruitment processes a check against the Protection of Vulnerable Adults (PoVA) list. The 2000 Act was superseded by the Health and Social Care Act 2008 (Regulated Activities) Regulations 2010 and the Care Quality Commission (CQC) (Registration) Regulations 2009. These established the CQC as regulator of all health and social care services and requires health and care providers to comply with Section 20 regulations and meet 28 outcomes in Essential Standards of Quality and Safety (Care Quality Commission 2010) including those for safeguarding adults (Outcome 7).

The Safeguarding Vulnerable Groups Act 2006 widened the definition of 'vulnerability' and introduced a Vetting and Barring Scheme incorporating the PoVA list into a new list containing names of those barred from working with vulnerable children and adults. The scheme was radically redefined in 2010/11 and its functions may be underpinned by legislation in a Protection of Freedoms Bill.

The Mental Capacity Act 2005 is a key piece of legislation providing a statutory framework which empowers and protects adults who lack capacity to make their own decisions. The Act should be applied before any health, care or welfare decision is made for someone who lacks capacity. At its core are five principles:

1. A person must be assumed to have capacity unless established it is lacking.
2. A person must not be treated as unable to make a decision until all practical steps to help them have been taken without success.
3. A person must not be treated as unable to make a decision purely because they make an unwise decision.
4. Acts and decisions should be made in the individual's best interest once lack of capacity is established.
5. Before an act or decision is made, consideration should be given to whether its purpose can effectively be achieved in ways less restrictive to the person's rights and freedoms of action.

The 2005 Act was amended in 2009 with the introduction of the Deprivation of Liberty Safeguards providing additional protection for individuals lacking capacity.

The Domestic Violence Crimes and Victim's Act 2004 created an offence of causing or allowing the death of a child or vulnerable adult where they died by an unlawful act. It also criminalizes breaches of non-molestation orders under the Family Law Act 1996.

Debate continues over the need for new primary law, or for current laws to be 'tidied up' to be more effective. Those suggesting new safeguarding legislation point to Scotland for clearer definitions and more intrusive powers. Others caution against this because of ethical dilemmas about personal freedom and human rights raised by the Scottish laws (DH 2009; Mackay 2009). The need for a new statute is made in the 2011 Law Commission report.

Categories of abuse

No Secrets defines abuse as the violation of an individual's human and civil rights by any other person or persons. Abuse may consist of single or repeated acts taking the forms of the following:

Physical abuse

This includes hitting, pinching, slapping, misuse of medication, restraint or inappropriate sanctions. Indicators include injuries inconsistent with life style or not fully explained by the causes given. Parley (2010) found practitioners were more aware of the potential for physical and sexual abuse than other forms.

Sexual abuse

This includes rape, sexual assault or sexual acts to which the person has not consented, could not consent or is pressurized into. It may include being forced to watch pornography or talked to or touched in a sexual way. Indicators might include social withdrawal, or the abused person using explicit or untypical sexual language or behaviour. There may be physical evidence, e.g. torn, stained or bloody clothing, trauma to the rectum or genitals, or presence of unexplained sexually transmitted diseases.

Psychological or emotional abuse

This includes threats of harm or abandonment, intimidation, coercion, verbal abuse, isolation/withdrawal from services or support networks. It is a likely component of other abuses and has a corrosive impact on the individual who may become emotionally withdrawn, depressed and exhibit behavioural changes, e.g. unexplained fear, defensiveness or ambivalence. Psychological abuse recently received greater recognition in a Supreme Court judgment confirming violence in 'domestic violence' situations is not limited to physical abuse but includes acts of psychological abuse (Yemshaw vs. London Borough of Hounslow 2011). It is also important not to make assumptions about who may be the abuser, as identified in the case studies above.

Neglect and acts of omission

These may include ignoring medical or physical care needs and failure to provide access to appropriate services. Examples of poor care practice include withholding medication, inadequate nutrition or heating. Neglect can be deliberate or unintentional, and the Mental Capacity Act 2005 now makes wilful neglect of a person lacking capacity a criminal act. Deterioration of health and functioning in later life increases frailty and vulnerability to abuse and neglect. Effective care becomes critical as frailty and medical conditions increase with neglect often triggering a 'domino effect' impacting on the older person's physical, psychological and spiritual health resulting in harm (Heath and Phair 2009).

Financial abuse

This can be complex and diverse in nature; it is often perpetrated by individuals considered trustworthy by virtue of position, for example family or carers. Financial abuse includes theft, fraud, exploitation, undue pressure over wills, property, inheritance or financial transactions; or the misuse or misappropriation of property, possessions or benefits. As people live longer, ownership of assets such as property and benefits increase potential for financial abuse, particularly as mental capacity diminishes. Most financial abuse occurs in the home, the abuser is often a family member and abuse is attributed to societal attitudes to inheritance (Crosby et al. 2008).

Discriminatory abuse

This includes forms of harassment, slurs, inappropriate language or threats focused on the victim's sex, race, age, religion, sexuality or disability and leads to individuals receiving unequal treatment in, or being excluded from, opportunities such as health care, justice and protection from others. As factors like decreased mobility, loss of family/friends, or physical and mental health problems occur, this increases the potential for discrimination by restricting access to health, community life and other services (Smeaton and Vegeris 2009).

Institutional abuse

Poor or inadequate care practice can affect whole care settings, e.g. hospitals, residential or nursing homes, and impacts on multiple individuals. Individual needs and wishes are often ignored or placed secondary to organizational requirements and are exemplified by rigid and inflexible regimes for activities such as mealtimes, toileting and bed times.

Reasons for and effects of abuse

The reasons for, and effects of, abuse are as multifaceted as the forms of abuse. Individuals may be traumatized by the experience, seem quietly accepting of it or not even recognize abuse has occurred. The mental and physical health of individuals can be markedly affected by abuse. In domestic violence situations abused individuals are more likely to suffer depression, anxiety and psychosomatic symptoms, as well as physical harm (WHO 2000). The cost of treatment runs into millions of pounds each year (Walby 2004). An American study has linked increased mortality rates for older people affected by self-neglect or abuse. Across matched groups, abused individuals had a higher risk of dying within the first year of the incident, particularly where the individual had lower physical and cognitive functions (Dong et al. 2009). Therefore where any abuse is acknowledged by the individual or others, it is important that action is taken so the abuse does not go unchallenged and individuals are supported appropriately.

Who abuses and why

Abuse against older adults needs to be understood within a structural context of patriarchy, ageism and sexism, whereby it is recognized that cultural norms give tacit acceptance to notions suggesting some people within society are of less value than others. Economic productivity and youth are prized, which is reflected within cultural norms. On an individual level abuse is committed by a wide range of people and for many reasons. Abusers may be family or friends, paid or volunteer carers, professional staff, other users of services or complete strangers. Although there is no specific type of person who abuses, patterns of behaviour are identified in *No Secrets*.

Activity 12.5

What is your understanding of terms such as serial, opportunistic, situational or long term abuse?

These terms are usually used in the following ways:

Serial abuse: behaviour often associated with sexual, financial and emotional abuse. Abusers may actively target, befriend and 'groom' individuals at risk.

Opportunistic abuse: e.g. where money or other valuables left lying around is stolen.

Situational abuse: sometimes associated with alcohol or substance misuse, or carer stress resulting from dealing with difficult or challenging behaviour, e.g. abuse of older people with dementia by family carers is reportedly common (Cooper 2009).

Carer abuse: has also been associated with factors other than stress, for instance pre-illness relationships between carer and recipient, duration of care, or issues such as the caregiver's financial situation (Wolf 1998; Nerenberg 2002). Informal/family carers by virtue of their caring are themselves seen as at risk of abuse, which may be addressed through safeguarding policies.

Long term abuse: may be seen in the context of family relationships, for example domestic abuse between partners or generations within families.

Domestic violence against older women can sometimes be a continuation of long-standing abuse into old age, 'elder abuse is often spouse abuse grown old' (Walsh et al. 2007), or may result from a worsening of earlier strained relations or emotional abuse as the partners age (Women's Aid Report 2007a). These findings are reflected in the work of Band-Winterstein and Eisokovits (2009) in a study of twenty couples in Israel aged 60 to 84 who had lived in violent relationships for most of their lives. They identified four clusters of living in violence:

- continuing violence with no change over time;
- a constant atmosphere of fear, as the history of conflict continues to impact on daily interactions;
- the nature of the abuse changes, but is at a similar level of intensity;
- violence perpetrated in the context of illness, continuing to the end of life.

Long term abuse within domestic settings is viewed by some as a cycle of violence, explained through models where violence is continued across generations, the abused becoming the abuser; or the abuse is followed by remorse then more abuse as the cycle repeats. Neither model has universal acceptance as responsibility is distanced from the perpetrator.

In contrast, the 'Power and Control Wheel' model developed by the Duluth Domestic Violence Project is seen as a more helpful model, viewing violence and abuse as the means of controlling the abused partner and forming a consistent pattern of behaviour rather than isolated incidents of abuse (Women's Aid Report 2007b).

Older people at risk of abuse: empowerment, safeguarding or protection?

From the early 2000s there has been a move from an interventionist approach of protecting vulnerable adults to a position seeking prevention through the realistic management of risk. This shift reflects recognition that adults with capacity should make decisions about their own welfare and safety, supported where necessary, even when risk is present. Where an individual has impaired mental capacity others may need to make decisions in the individual's best interest.

The emphasis on prevention is likely to continue as it reflects the current government's view of 'Big Society' and its vision for adult social care (DH 2010b) where localism is underpinned by individual and community empowerment, protection and choice. For safeguarding older people at risk of abuse the need for continuing awareness-raising is required if each member of society is to play a greater part in prevention.

Risk by definition involves uncertainty of outcome, whether as a negative threat or positive opportunity. Focusing on what can potentially go wrong limits opportunities for empowerment which can deliver positive benefits to an individual. The tensions between protection and safeguarding are exemplified in concerns expressed about the move to greater personalization of services. Here, individuals receive their own budgets and purchase the support they need from services which may not be commissioned by councils or overseen by regulators. For some this raises the fear of greater abuse because the person seen as vulnerable 'holds the money' and statutory oversight is less. For practitioners working with the assessment and management of risk this can generate tension, particularly when society looks to apportion blame if things go wrong. This can produce a defensive attitude to risk, serving to disempower those in receipt of services.

Smethurst (2008) reflects on the social construction of risk, suggesting our view of vulnerability is influenced by cultural norms and attitudes. This places greater emphasis on some risks than others, for example impact of excessive alcohol usage appears to elicit less concern than statistically smaller problems caused by illicit drugs, and can put pressure on practitioners when working to safeguard adults because practitioners' actions are frequently based on incomplete or inadequate information. Practice is also influenced by competing demands, time frames and pressures of work, producing anxiety about potential criticism of decisions made and consequences that follow. The lack of a specific legal framework underpinning adult safeguarding can leave parties involved feeling confused and powerless, and highlights the challenges of seeking to ensure the individual's autonomy while recognizing the limitations of professional responsibility (Jones and Spreadbury 2008).

If it is accepted it is better for people to be fully involved in any decisions regarding their safety, then effective safeguarding measures begin with provision of quality information on which individuals base their choices to determine what support they need. Working collaboratively with the individual the practitioner should conduct an assessment which allows the person to reflect on risks and their ability to stay safe from harm, recognizing the individual as an 'expert in their own life'. Mullender (1996) suggests we should reject negative labels attributed to the abused person (e.g. nagging, impossible) and focus on their rights, strengths and survival strategies instead.

Where a person's capacity to make decisions is reduced or absent, decisions need to be made in their best interest using an advocate when appropriate, and Mental Capacity Act guidance. Support plans developed with the individual concerned provide the opportunity to reflect on what measures can be adopted to minimize risk of harm while achieving the outcomes they want for their life. The use of risk or decision-making tools and matrices may assist this process, with plans reviewed regularly with the individual to ensure they continue to meet their needs (Pritchard 2009; DH 2010a).

Where prevention fails and abuse occurs, the need for person-centred approaches to support the individual remain critical. Unfortunately reports show abused individuals often feel disempowered by processes which focus more on the interests of the care system (CSCI 2008b; DH 2009). When recognized as active participants in safeguarding processes, older people will often voice their need for supportive discussion of their experiences, practical advice and information, a place of safety and ongoing support (Pritchard 2000, 2002). Straka (2006) suggests collaborative approaches to service provision are needed which take account of age, and where relevant, gender dimensions of the problem.

Effective practice

In seeking effective outcomes for older individuals experiencing abuse, lessons can be drawn from support provided to those affected by domestic violence. However, one of the first hurdles practitioners often need to confront is their own feelings about the abuse, which may result in conflicting emotions.

Activity 12.6

Understanding emotional reactions to domestic violence and elder abuse
(adapted from http//familyvio.csw.fsu.edu/rural/elderly)

How do you react to knowing a service user has lived with an abusive partner for many decades and has previously received good advice and support which would have enabled them to leave their partner?

Use Table 12.1 to help you to reflect on some of the possible feelings which may impact on the ability to work effectively and collaboratively.

Table 12.1   Possible feelings and reactions to abuse

Possible emotional reactions	Worker	Service user	Abuser
Fear	of getting involved.	What will he do to me today?	Will I be found out?
Anger	Why doesn't she leave/do something about this? How can he do this?	Why do I put up with this? Why doesn't anyone realize what is happening?	Why does she put me in this situation?
Anxiety	Possible serious harm. Could I be criticized if I don't take action to protect?	Discussing/acknowledging the abuse.	Will she tell someone? What might happen to me?
Overwhelmed	It is too complicated to change. I feel powerless.	I can do nothing about this.	I don't know how to stop this.
Ambivalence	Who should I believe? Who is responsible?	It's probably my fault.	It's her fault.
Depression	It is hopeless.	It will never end.	Nothing will change.

Practitioners can sometimes be left feeling powerless and angry, particularly where the inability (perhaps seen as a refusal) to leave a violent partner results in serious harm and lasting damage to family relationships. It is important to recognize the complex feelings involved in such situations, and identify where they come from in order to recognize transference and work effectively with all involved.

In discussing practical implications for supporting individuals in violent situations, Butler (2008) introduces the 'Equality Wheel' model developed by the Wisconsin Coalition against Domestic Violence. It identifies some of the characteristics crucial for establishing equality and interdependence within relationships. The characteristics described in relation to domestic abuse equally relate to good practice for supporting people affected by other forms of abuse as they promote the following:

Dignity, respect and use of positive communication

Listening non-judgementally is important when working with both the abused person and the abuser, as is valuing and respecting opinions expressed. The way we communicate with individuals in terms of attitude and language will influence the success of that dialogue, which can be improved by being emotionally affirming and understanding.

Non-threatening behaviour

To support positive communication, the way we talk and behave can ensure the person feels safe in expressing themselves. Older people often feel deeply uncomfortable talking about abuse because of the stigma and shame attached to it, particularly with abused individuals within BME communities concerned about family honour.

Honesty and accountability

In identifying what has led to the abuse and what needs to occur to prevent its recurrence, all parties need to communicate openly and truthfully, admitting where things may have gone wrong and accepting responsibility.

Trust, support and shared responsibility

In supporting the abused person's life goals in terms of safety and support needed to achieve these, the practitioner needs to respect the individual's right to their own feelings, opinions, friends and activities. Through negotiation and compromise, the practitioner can seek to support the older person to make decisions which safeguard them without restricting unduly their freedom to live the way they want. Success in the choices made can be enhanced by encouraging and supporting the individual to build a network of relationships and contacts with others such as family, friends, carers, community groups and professionals so as to minimize the isolation older people often experience.

These characteristics emphasize the need to empower individuals to allow them to guide practitioners to facilitate outcomes which can enrich their lives while making them safer.

Summary

This chapter has considered the importance of empowerment strategies which minimize risk of abuse to older people, so ensuring their rights, strengths and autonomy remain central to any support offered. Consideration was given to the evolution of current legislation and guidance which frame how safeguarding practice should be conducted, contrasting it with child protection, and adult safeguarding in Scotland. Reflecting on practice development, links are made between elder and domestic abuse, suggesting practitioners be aware that safeguarding issues may have long roots which precede old age, and recognition of structural issues which may be key in developing effective support, rather than concentrating on individual pathology. In addressing aspirations of older people for safer but not necessarily risk-free lives, more appropriate education and awareness-raising is needed with regard to safeguarding, together with shared responsibility in identifying and minimizing risk. Practitioner reflection on the importance of positive communication, observation, narrative approaches and taking time with the individual can provide better understanding of the impact of the present situation.

Further reading

Mantel, A. and Scragg, T. (eds) (2011) *Safeguarding Adults in Social Work*, 2nd edn. Exeter: Learning Matters.

References

Action on Elder Abuse (2011) *Striking the Balance: The Case for a Common Sense Approach to the Vetting and Barring Process*. http://www.elderabuse.org.uk/documents/Striking%20 the%20Balance%20Report.pdf (accessed 10 February 2011).

ADSS (Association of Directors of Adult Social Services) (2005) *Adult Safeguarding: A National Framework of Standards for Good Practice and Outcomes in Adult Protection Work*. London: ADSS.

Baeza, S. (2008) Learning from safeguarding children, in A. Mantell and T. Scragg (eds) *Safeguarding Adults in Social Work*, 2nd edn. Exeter: Learning Matters.

Baker, A.A. (1975) Granny battering, *Modern Geriatrics* 5(8): 20–4.

Band-Winterstein, T. and Eisokovits, Z. (2009) 'Ageing Out' of violence: the multiple faces of intimate violence over the life span, *Journal of Qualitative Health Research* 19: 164.

Barnes, J. (2002) *Reform of Social Work Education and Training: Focus on the Future – Key Messages from Focus Groups About the Future of Social Work Training*. http://www.dh.gov. uk/prod_consum_dh/groups/dh_digitalassets/@dh/@en/documents/digitalasset/ dh_4082378.pdf (accessed 26 April 2010).

Burston, G.R. (1975) Granny battering, *British Medical Journal* (3): 592.

Butler, G. (2008) Domestic violence: understanding the connections, in A. Mantell and T. Scragg (eds) *Safeguarding Adults in Social Work*, 2nd edn. Exeter: Learning Matters.

Care Quality Commission (2010) *Guidelines About Compliance. Essential Standards of Quality and Safety*. London: CQC.

Cooper, C., Selwood, A. and Livingston, G. (2008) The prevalence of elder abuse and neglect: a systematic review, *Age and Ageing* 37: 151–60.

Cooper, C. (2009) Abuse of people with dementia by family carers: representative cross sectional survey, *British Medical Journal* 338: b155.

Crosby, G., Clark, A., Hayes, R., Jones, K. and Lievesley, N. (2008) *The Financial Abuse of Older People: A Review from the Literature*. Centre for Policy on Aging on behalf of Help the Aged. London: Help the Aged.

CSCI (Commission for Social Care Inspection) (2008a) *Safeguarding: A Study of the Effectiveness of Arrangement to Safeguard Vulnerable Adults*. Newcastle: CSCI.

CSCI (Commission for Social Care Inspection) (2008b) *Raising Voices: Views on Safeguarding Adults*. Newcastle: CSCI.

DH (Department of Health) (2009) *Safeguarding Adults: Report on the Consultation on the Review of 'No Secrets'*. London: Department of Health.

DH (Department of Health) (2010a) *Practical Approaches to Safeguarding and Personalisation*. London: Department of Health.

DH (Department of Health) (2010b) *A Vision for Adult Social Care: Capable Communities and Active Citizens*. London: Department of Health.

DH (Department of Health) and Home Office (2000) *'No Secrets': Guidance on Developing and Implementing Multi-agency Policy and Procedures to Protect Vulnerable Adults from Abuse*. London: Department of Health.

Dong, X., Simon, M., Mendes de Leon, C., Fulmer, T., Beck, T., Hebert, L., Dyer, C., Paveza, G. and Evans, D. (2009) Elder self-neglect and abuse and mortality rate in a community-dwelling population, *Journal of the American Medical Association* 302(5): 517–26.

Fennell, K. (2011) Adult protection: the Scottish legislative framework, in A. Mantell and T. Scragg (eds) *Safeguarding Adults in Social Work*, 2nd edn. Exeter: Learning Matters.

Fitzgerald, G. (2008) No secrets, safeguarding adults and adult protection, in J. Pritchard (ed.) *Good Practice in Safeguarding Adults. Working Effectively in Adult Protection*. London: Jessica Kingsley.

Francis, R. (2010) *Independent Inquiry into Care at the Mid Staffordshire NHS Foundation Trust Jan 2005 – March 2009*. Chaired by Robert Francis QC (Feb 2010). London: The Stationery Office.

Gaylard, D. (2011) Policy into practice, in A. Mantell and T. Scragg (eds) *Safeguarding Adults in Social Work*, 2nd edn. Exeter: Learning Matters.

Heath, H. and Phair, L. (2009) The concept of frailty and its significance in the consequences of care or neglect for older people: an analysis, *International Journal of Older People Nursing* 4: 120–31.

Home Office (1993) *The 1992 British Crime Survey*. London: HMSO.

Home Office (2011) *Home Office Statistical Bulletin*. Available at http://www.homeoffice.gov.uk/rds/pdf (accessed 6 February 2011).

Jones, K. and Spreadbury, K. (2008) Best practice in adult protection: safety, choice and inclusion, in. K. Jones, B. Cooper and H. Ferguson (eds) *Best Practice in Social Work: Critical Perspectives*. Basingstoke: Palgrave Macmillan.

Laming, Lord (2003) *The Victoria Climbié Inquiry*. London: The Stationery Office.

Laming, Lord (2009) *The Protection of Children in England: A Progress Report*. London: The Stationery Office.

Law Commission (2011) *Adult Social Care* (Law Com no. 326). HC 941. London: The Stationery Office.

Mackay, K. (2009) Scottish legislative framework for supporting and protecting adults, in J. Pritchard (ed.) *Good Practice in the Law and Safeguarding Adults: Criminal Justice and Adult Protection*. London: Jessica Kingsley.

Macnicol, J. (2010) *Ageism and Age Discrimination: Some Analytical Issues*. An ILC-UK think piece. http://www.ilcuk.org.uk/files/pdf_pdf_139.pdf (accessed 19 August 2010).

Martin, J. (2007) Adults in a victimising society, in N. Thompson (ed.) *Safeguarding Adults: Theory into Practice*. Lyme Regis: Russell House Publishing.

Mullender, A. (1996) *Rethinking Domestic Violence*. London: Routledge.

National Archive (2010) *Domestic Violence Definition*. Crown Copyright. http://webarchive.nationalarchives.gov.uk/20110220105210/http://rds.homeoffice.gov.uk/rds (accessed 21 July 2011).

Nerenberg, L. (2002) *Preventing Elder Abuse by Family Caregivers: Caregiver Stress and Elder Abuse*. Washington, DC: National Center on Elder Abuse.

O'Keeffe, M., Hills, A., Doyle, M., McCreadie, C., Scholes, S., Constantine, R., Tinker, A., Manthorpe, J., Biggs, S. and Erens, B. (2007) *UK Study of Elder Abuse and Neglect of Older People: Prevalence Survey Report*. London: National Centre for Social Research.

Parley, F. (2010) The understanding that care staff bring to abuse: a research paper, *Journal of Adult Protection* 12(1):13–26.

Parliamentary and Health Service Ombudsman (2011) *Care and Compassion: Report of the Health Service Ombudsman on Ten Investigations into NHS Care of Older People*. London: The Stationery Office.

Penhale, B. and Parker, J. (1999) *Elder abuse and older men: towards an understanding*. Seminar Proceedings: Men and Violence Against Women. Strasbourg, 7–8 October.

Penhale, B. and Parker, J. (2008) Understanding social work today, in *Working with Vulnerable Adults*. London: Routledge.

Pritchard, J. (2000) *The Needs of Older Women: Services for Victims of Elder Abuse and Other Abuse*. Findings. May 2000. York: Joseph Rowntree Trust.

Pritchard, J. (2002) *Male Victims of Elder Abuse: Their Experiences and Needs*. Findings. York: Joseph Rowntree Trust.

Pritchard, J. (2009) Doing risk assessment properly in adult protection work, in J. Pritchard (ed.) *Good Practice in the Law and Safeguarding Adults: Criminal Justice and Adult Protection*. London: Jessica Kingsley.

Scragg, T. (2011) Organizational cultures and the management of change, in A. Mantell and T. Scragg (eds) *Safeguarding Adults in Social Work*, 2nd edn. Exeter: Learning Matters.

Shakespeare, T. (2000) Helpless, in *Help*. Birmingham: Venture Press.

Smeaton, D. and Vegeris, S. (2009) *Older People in and Outside the Labour Market: A Review. Research Report: 22*. Manchester: Equality and Human Rights Commission.

Smethurst, C. (2008) Working with risk, in A. Mantell and T. Scragg (eds) *Safeguarding Adults in Social Work*, 2nd edn. Exeter: Learning Matters.

Thompson, M. (2007) 700,000 elderly 'abused at home or in care', in *The Telegraph* (online) http://www.telegraph.co.uk/news/uknews/1554190/700000-elderly-abused-at-home-or-in-care.html (accessed 19 August 2010).

Tonks, A. and Bennett, G. (1999) Elder abuse: doctors must acknowledge it, look for it and learn how to prevent it, *British Medical Journal* 318(7179): 278.

Walby, S. (2004) *The Cost of Domestic Violence*. London: Women and Equality Unit.

Walsh, C.A., Ploeg, J., Lohfeld, L., Horne, J., MacMillan, H. and Lai, D. (2007) Violence across the lifespan: interconnections among forms of abuse as described by marginalized Canadian elders and their caregivers, *British Journal of Social Work* 37: 491–514.

WHO (World Health Organization) (2000) *Violence Against Women*. Factsheet No. 239. Geneva: WHO.

Wolf, R.S. (1998) Caregiver stress, Alzheimer's disease and elder abuse, *American Journal of Alzheimer's Disease* 13(2): 81–3.

Women's Aid Report (2007a) *Older Women and Domestic Violence: An Overview*. http://www.womensaid.org.uk/downloads/Olderwomenanddvreport(1).pdf (accessed 3 June 2010).

Women's Aid Report (2007b) *Cycles of Violence*. http://www.womensaid.org.uk/domesticviolencearticles.asp?section=00010001002200390001&itemid=1279 (accessed 10 June 2010).

Yemshaw vs. London Borough of Hounslow (2011) Supreme Court judgment. 26 January 2011. UKSC3.

Index

fairness 32
falls
  risk of 183
  risk of for those with long term conditions
    124
families
  needs of 2
family
  support from 41
family carers
  older people with learning disabilities 107–8
family crises
  carers 107
family structure
  black and ethnic minorities 61–3
family support
  older people with long term conditions 120
  South Asians 62
fatigue
  response to grief 139
fear
  as indicator of ill-being 94
  reaction to abuse of older people 215
'fellow traveller' model
  spirituality 172
Female Orgasm, The
  publication of 150
financial abuse
  scope of 211
financial circumstances 19
fulfilment
  working with older people 1
funding
  complexity of for care 18
  services for older people with long term
    conditions 128
funding levels
  test case on 121–2
furniture raisers
  to assist older people with long term
    conditions 126

gay
  definition 158
Gay Pride march 151
gender 17
  black and ethnic minorities 59–60, 63–4
  religious aspects of 65
generalization
  problems of 58
government guidance 39
grab handles
  to assist older people with long term
    conditions 126

'Granny-Battering'
  recognition of in 1970s 207
grief
  applying models of to practice with older
    people 137
  factors relating to social work with 142–3
  intensified by other factors 133
  models of 2, 134–6
  persistent 139
  possible responses to 139
  practitioner issues relating to 142–3
  risk factors in 136
  support through various stages of 138–9
  supporting 133
  tasks of 134
  understanding 133–6
  Western perception of 139
Growing Older 41
guilt
  response to grief 139

hanging as method of suicide 80
harm
  concept of 179
  risks of 19
hate crime
  homophobic assault recognized as 151
health
  relationship with psychological well-being
    43–4
Health Act (2009) 120
health care
  delivery of 38
Health and Efficiency 149
health inequality 17
health need
  distinction between social need and 39
health problems 2
Health and Social Care Act 2008 (Regulated
    Activities) Regulations (2010)
  provisions related to safeguarding older
    people 209
Health and Social Care Bill (2011) 23
healthy lifestyles
  older people with learning disabilities 109
Hearing Voices Networks 82
heart failure 122
heightened toilet seats
  to assist older people with long term
    conditions 126
helpfulness
  as indicator of well-being 94
helplessness
  response to grief 139

Local Housing Allowance 46
London Friend helpline 144
loneliness 75–6
  mental health and 73
  response to grief 139
  trigger for depression 77
long term abuse 213
long term condition model 117–18
long term conditions 2
  common among older people 122–4
  definition 116–7
  distinctions between 117
  factors affecting services for 128–9
  informal carers and 124–6
  key issues in services for older people with
    128–9
  management of 117–18
  numbers affected by 117
  older people with 116–29
long-stay hospitals
  closure of 102
longevity
  consequences of increasing 103
loss 2
  engaging with 137
  future of social work with older people
    experiencing 143
  multiple 133
  range of responses to 135
  understanding 133–6
  working with older people in 132–44
low incomes
  black and ethnic minorities 69
low status
  social work with older people perceived as 1

MacPherson Report (1999) 68–9
Magdalen asylums 152
male rape
  made criminal offence 151
Malignant Social Psychology (MSP) 92
managerial power 25
managerialism 25
marginalization 36–7
  disability 36
  older people 32
marital rape 151
marketing
  influence on ageing 35
masturbation
  attitude towards 1950s 150
materialism
  western society 163
Mead, George Herbert [1863–1931] 13

meaning-making support
  factor relevant to care in grieving 143
medical interventions 34
medical needs 19
medicalization
  characteristic of care giving 164
medication
  alcohol and 83
  misuse of 85
memory books 97
Mencap Report (2007) 104
Mental Capacity Act (2005) 89, 94, 128, 211, 214
  main provisions of 209–10
mental health 2
  assessment 78
  defining good 73
  effect of age discrimination on 74
  factors affecting 72
  key standard of National Service Framework for
    Older People 74
  needs of older people 72–85
Mental Health Foundation 76
mental health problems
  grief and 133
mental health services
  'cut off' point 74–5
mental heath
  recovery 81
mental illness
  people with learning disabilities 105
mental maps 9–10
Mental Protection Act (2005) 205
metabolic disorders
  dementia in 90
metabolic system
  long term conditions affecting 123–4
Michaels Report (2008) 104
Mid-Staffordshire NHS Foundation Trust inquiry
  207
mixed dementia 90
mobility problems 104
Modernising Social Services 22
money worries
  trigger for depression 77
monitoring
  clinical 127
  lack of in people with learning disabilities 104
mood disorders
  as risk factor for suicide 79
'moral defectives'
  unmarried mothers sent to psychiatric
    hospitals as 151
motivation
  maintaining 193–4

respiratory system
 long term conditions affecting 122
Retail Price Index (RPI) pension increases related
  to 46
retirement
 transition into 12
retirement age
 increase in 36
riots
 1980s 68
risk 2, 214
 associated with grief 136
 biographical approaches 186–7
 blame and 181
 checklist-based assessment tools 189
 conflicting demands 180
 decision making 182
 definition 180–1
 distinguishing between short term and long
  term in respect of suicide 77–8
 emotional impact of working with 192–3
 identifying those at risk of suicide 79
 information to assess 183–4
 multidisciplinary working 187–8
 negative view of 180
 person-centred approach to working with
  179–94
 person-centred assessment models 189–90
 person-centred practice and 186–7
 policy making 183–4
 problems associated with calculating 181–3
 rationing and resources 188
 social construction of 183–4
 variables 182
 vulnerability and 184–6
 working with 189–93
risk assessment 180–3, 188
 abuse 204
 principles with older people 191
risk assessor
 key role in social work 21
risk management 180–3
ritual 171
rituals
 spirituality 170
Roads to Recovery survey 81
Rogerian psychotherapy 91
'rolling back the state' 40
Royal College of General Practitioners
 checklist of factors indicating suicide risk
  79

sadness
 response to grief 139

safeguarding 2, 200–17
 evolution of adult protection 207–10
 health/social care model of adult 204
 lack of legal framework safeguarding 214
Safeguarding Adults 208
Safeguarding Vulnerable Groups Act (2006)
  205
 provisions related to safeguarding older
  people 209
Samaritans 144
schizophrenia
 recovery from 82
Scotland
 adults at risk 205
 legalization of homosexuality in (1980) 150
screening
 sexually transmitted diseases 149
Seebohm Report (1968) 22–3, 25
segregation
 people with learning disabilities 102
 residential 62, 68
self
 definition 13
self determination 45, 191
self-care
 capacity for 19
self-esteem
 lowering 74
 sexuality and 155
self-expression
 as indicator of well-being 94
 maintaining skills for 109
self-identity 13
self-management
 long term conditions 128
self-poisoning
 as method of suicide 80
self-reflection 9
self-reproach
 response to grief 139
self-respect
 as indicator of well-being 94
'selfhood'
 perspective of 12–13
Selfs 1–3 framework 13
sensitivity
 sexuality 157
sensitivity to others' needs
 as indicator of well-being 94
separation 75
serial abuse 212
serious case reviews (SCRs) 207
service provision
 long term conditions 119–20

**AN INTRODUCTION TO
APPLYING SOCIAL WORK
THEORIES AND METHODS**

Barbra Teater

9780335237784 (Paperback)
2010

eBook also available

This practical book provides a basic introduction to the most commonly used theories and methods in social work practice. The book explores the concept of a theory and a method, the difference between the two and the ways in which they are connected. Teater also discusses the social worker-client relationship and offers a handy overview of anti-oppressive practice.

Key features:

- Assuming little to no prior knowledge, each chapter explores a single theory or method in depth.
- A variety of interactive tools to encourage you to explore your own thoughts and beliefs.
- Step-by-step illustrations show how to apply the theory/method to a social work case example

www.openup.co.uk

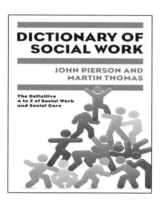

DICTIONARY OF SOCIAL WORK
The Definitive A to Z of Social
Work and Social Care

John Pierson and Martin Thomas

9780335238811 (Paperback)
2010

eBook also available

With over 1500 entries, this popular dictionary provides concise and
up to date explanations of the theories, approaches and terminology
that define front-line social work and social care. These entries
explain, in jargon-free language, how key concepts can be used to
improve practice. Clear explanations outline significant developments
such as Every Child Matters and the personalization of adult services.

Key features:

- Entries are helpfully cross referenced and are evidence based.
- Entries are explained in jargon-free language.
- Written by specialists in the field, with a specific focus on the
  most recent legislation and policy guidance from government.

www.openup.co.uk

OPEN UNIVERSITY PRESS
McGraw - Hill Education